Genius Under House Arrest

The Cancelation of James Watson

Edward Dutton

.

Genius Under House Arrest
The Cancelation of James Watson

Edward Dutton

Academica Press
Washington

Library of Congress Cataloging-in-Publication Data
Names: Dutton, Edward (author)
Title: Genius under house arrest : the cancelation of james watson | Dutton, Edward.
Description: Washington : Academica Press, 2025.
Identifiers: LCCN 2025944454 | ISBN 9781680535839 (hardcover) | ISBN 9781680536003 (paperback) | ISBN 9781680535846 (ebook)

"Jim Watson is well known for being provocative and politically incorrect. But it would be a sad world if such a distinguished scientist was silenced because of his more unpalatable views."

Prof. Sir Colin Blakemore (1944-2022),
Professor of Neuroscience at Oxford University in 2007.

Contents

Acknowledgements

I would like to thank Dr Bruce Charlton for reading earlier versions of this manuscript and providing useful feedback. This book has benefited from stimulating conversations with Prof. Gregory Feist, Dr Raj Persaud and Dr Hannah Spier. Thank you to Cathy Soref for a great deal of helpful information and to Prof. Bruce Stillman for corresponding with me. Finally, I would like to thank Jim for inspiring the whole project. I dedicate this book to him.

Edward Dutton
21 June 2025
Oulu, Finland

About the Author

Edward Dutton is a researcher based in Oulu in northern Finland. Born in London in 1980, he read Theology at Durham University and did a PhD in Religious Studies at Aberdeen University, during which he was a guest researcher at Leiden University in the Netherlands. He is titular Professor of the Evolutionary Psychology of Business at Asbiro University in Poland, Honorary Professor in the Institute of Psychology at the Russian Academy of Sciences and Research Associate in Scientific Research at Tabuk University in Saudi Arabia. Dutton is best known for his channel *The Jolly Heretic*. He is the author of over 20 books including, most recently, *The Naked Classroom: The Evolutionary Psychology of Your Time at School* (Jolly Heretic Publications, 2023), *Breeding the Human Herd: Eugenics, Dysgenics and the Future of the Species* (Imperium Press, 2023) and (with J.O.A. Rayner-Hilles) *Woke Eugenics: How Social Justice is a Mask for Social Darwinism* (Imperium Press, 2024). Dutton has penned four previous biographies: *The Ruler of Cheshire: Sir Piers Dutton, Tudor Gangland and the Violent Politics of the Palatine* (Leonié Press, 2015); *J. Philippe Rushton: A Life History Perspective* (Thomas Edward Press, 2018), *Churchill's Headmaster: The 'Sadist' Who Nearly Saved the British Empire* (Manticore Press, 2019) and *Shaman of the Radical Right: The Life and Mind of Jonathan Bowden* (Imperium Press, 2025).

Chapter One

The Cancellation of One
of the Only Living Geniuses

A Galileo Situation

As I write this, Western Civilization has a "Galileo Situation" on its hands. In this book, we will see that reaching this perilous point, one that should be abhorrent to all those who believe in the pursuit of truth and in making sense of the world, was highly predictable. Civilization, and universities themselves, go through cycles; so it would be unusual if we had not reached a Galileo Situation, and we have.

Galileo (1564-1642) changed our understanding of the world; yet, for offending against the dogmas of the Church, he died under house arrest. On 21st December 1633, six months into his sentence, Galileo wrote to his friend, the mathematician Benedetto Casteli (1578-1643): "I am still being closely watched. I live under the supervision of the Holy Office, where I am forbidden from speaking or writing about certain subjects that have brought me into trouble. My health continues to suffer, and I feel the weight of this situation heavy upon me, yet my spirit remains dedicated to science."[1]

In July 1639, Galileo wrote of similar feelings to his illegitimate daughter, a nun called Sister Maria Celeste (1600-1634)[2]: "The burden of my confinement and the pain in my failing eyesight weigh heavily upon

---

[1] G. Galilei, "Letter to Benedetto Castelli" in S. Drake, (Ed.), *Discoveries and Opinions of Galileo* (New York: Doubleday Anchor Books, 1957).

[2] In the sixteenth century, having illegitimate offspring by mistresses was common among the upper classes and there were many cases of the daughters being sent to convents. For more detail see, E. Dutton, *The Ruler of Cheshire: Sir Piers Dutton, Tudor Gangland and the Violent Politics of the Palatine* (Northwich: Leonie Press, 2015).

me, but I find some solace in the work I continue to do, though it is restricted by the conditions of my sentence. I often think of the joys of science that we once shared, and it grieves me that I may never return to my full liberty. Pray for me, dear daughter, as I do for you every day."[3] In his very last letter, to a former pupil, on 2nd December 1641, the semi-blind scientist's enthusiasm for making sense of the world remained undimmed: "I still have a great desire to learn about your latest studies on the motion of fluids and projectiles. I am certain that you will make discoveries that will benefit the field of science for many years to come."[4] Imagine the frustration of knowing that you risked everything if you expressed certain empirically accurate views that were unacceptable to the Inquisition.

Yet we have reached this situation again. A scientific genius of our times is living under, and will likely die under, *de facto* house arrest. He cannot attend conferences nor give interviews, despite remaining as sharp and cuttingly intelligent as ever, lest the very psychological type which brought about his breakthrough also causes him to offend against the dogmas of the new system of thought control. For if he does this again, he knows that he may cause a media storm, embarrass his family and friends and end up even further ostracised, having already been thoroughly cancelled. He knows he may say something empirically accurate but highly "offensive." It is as though Watson has truth-Tourettes, he just can't help himself. As we will see, he may even fear that any such lapse will have extremely serious personal consequences.

"Sexual Intercourse Began . . ."

Some years go down in history as clear turning points. The year 1963 is probably one of the best examples. The English poet Philip Larkin (1922-1985) wrote that, "Sexual intercourse began/ In nineteen sixty three . . . / Between the end of the *Chatterley* ban/ And the Beatles' first LP." These lines succinctly summarise just what a watershed 1963 was, especially in the UK and in the US.

---

[3] G. Galilei, "Letter to Sister Maria Celeste" in S. Sobel, *Galileo's Daughter: Letters and Dialogues* (New York: Walker and Company, 1999).
[4] G. Galilei, "Letter to Evangelista Torricelli" in M. Allan-Olney, (Ed.), *The Letters of Galileo* (London: Longmanns, Green and Co., 1864).

The novel *Lady Chatterley's Lover* by English writer D.H. Lawrence (1885-1930) – privately printed in 1928 and banned in Britain for being obscene – had been published in the UK in 1960, resulting in an obscenity trial in which a Church of England bishop had argued in its favour.[5] In 1963, this same prelate – John A.T. Robinson (1919-1983), Bishop of Woolwich - published a book, *Honest to God,* in which he seemed to deny almost every Christian doctrine, including the literal existence of the Almighty.[6] How different it was from the conservative England of the 1950s, in which homosexuals were persecuted and thousands of young women collapsed in religious fervour at Billy Graham rallies.[7] In 1963, aristocratic rule was falling apart. The Conservative government, most of whom were educated at the public school (in British English: prestigious private boarding school)[8] Eton, was rocked to its foundations by revelations that the Minister for War, John Profumo (1915-2006), had been having an adulterous affair with a 19-year old model called Christine Keeler (1942-2017). Keeler had also been having a sexual relationship with Yevgeny Ivanov (1926-1994) who was the naval attaché at London's Soviet Embassy and who was also a spy. This was an appalling security risk. Profumo lied to the House of Commons, denying the affair, and he was forced to resign when a police investigation proved that the affair had occurred. The traditional Establishment had colluded to cover-up what had happened and were left looking dishonest, out of touch and foolish.[9] A left-wing government was elected the following year. By the end of the 1960s, male homosexuality was legal in England, abortion had been decriminalized, there were growing campaigns for the rights of women

---

[5] C. Rembar, *The End of Obscenity: The Trials of Lady Chatterley, Tropic of Cancer and Fanny Hill* (London: Harper & Row, 1986).

[6] J.A.T. Robinson, *Honest to God* (London: SCM Press, 1963).

[7] C. Brown, *The Death of Christian Britain: Understanding Secularisation, 1800-2000* (London: Routledge, 2001).

[8] There is no clear definition of a public school. For further discussion see, E. Dutton, *Churchill's Headmaster: The 'Sadist' Who Nearly Saved the British Empire* (Melbourne: Manticore Press, 2019).

[9] V. Holburn, *The Profumo Affair* (Barnsley: Pen and Sword, 2024).

and for the rights of ethnic minorities and the music of *The Beatles* and the "teenage" culture surrounding it was no longer shocking.[10]

In the US, president, John F. Kennedy (1917-1963), was assassinated in November 1963 in Dallas, having given a speech on civil rights earlier in the year. The Civil Rights Bill was signed by his successor in July 1964, meaning that the southern states were compelled to end racial segregation and to allow blacks equal rights, including voting rights. This was an absolutely fundamental change.[11] In many ways, 1963 was the point at which the UK and the US, and then other Western societies, fundamentally shifted from being conservative, and thus concerned with traditional religion, in-group loyalty, traditional sexual propriety and obedience to traditional authority, to being liberal and, therefore, far more concerned with equality and the avoidance of harm to individuals, including to their feelings, as we will explore in greater depth anon.[12] "Oh, what a night!/ Late December back in '63/ What a very special time for me . . ." later sang Frankie Valli and The Four Seasons. This was the year in which it was clear that something had changed, and, for young people at least, the future seemed exciting: An old world was passing away and a new world was replacing it.

The Rise of Wokeness

If 1963 heralded the change to a liberal world-order - to an "old liberalism" which emphasized ideas such as treating people equally no matter their race or sex and permitting equal opportunities regardless of sex, race or social class - the year 2007 witnessed a very different turning point. It marked the ascent to power not of the liberalism of the 1960s and not even of the leftism of the 1960s, which fought for the rights of workers, but rather of the Cultural Marxism of the 1960s as manifested in the widespread youth protests of 1968; what has more recently been called

---

[10] D. Goodhart, *The Road to Somewhere: The New Tribes Shaping British Politics* (London: Penguin, 2017).
[11] See, C. Murray, *Coming Apart: The State of White America, 1960-2010* (New York: Forum Books, 2013).
[12] For further discussion of this division see, J. Haidt, *The Righteous Mind: Why Good People Are Divided by Politics and Religion* (London: Vintage, 2013).

"Wokeness." We didn't know it at the time, but one particular "cancellation" proved beyond reasonable doubt this this was the case.

What is Wokeness?

By "Wokeness" I refer, in essence, to a philosophy which aims to achieve not socioeconomic equality but equality for various identity-based groups whom its proponents consider to be in some way marginalized; hence it used to be referred to as "Cultural Marxism" or "Political Correctness," this being a shorthand for what Marxists termed "Revolutionary Consciousness." With both Marxism and Cultural Marxism, it might be argued that, though its proponents may speak of "equality," what they are actually talking about is "revolution": the emancipation of the oppressed group from the oppressor; the overthrow of the oppressor by the oppressed; the oppressed being duly empowered. In that they are focused on empowerment above all else, we would not expect their worldview to be consistent in its finer details and we will see examples of this later. The oppressor - the male, the white person and so on - is morally bad and must be overthrown by the morally good (oppressed) woman or non-white.[13]

It might be averred that this process, which has culminated in the excesses of Wokeness, began with equality for females before moving onto different races, religions, sexual orientations, gender identifications, certain disabilities, and so on. Slavonic-studies expert Frank Ellis has traced in depth the history of Political Correctness. Ellis observes that the term "Political Correctness" was used by the Soviet Communist Party to mean "the party line." Ellis traces modern Political Correctness back to the Frankfurt School, founded in the 1920s and of which Hungarian philosopher George Lukacs (1885–1971) and German philosopher Herbert Marcuse (1898–1979) were leading members. This school was heavily influenced by the writings of Italian revolutionary Antonio Gramsci (1891–1937) who argued that Marxist revolutionaries must focus not on simply controlling the means of production and distribution but on controlling how people think, through controlling the ideological state apparatus.

---

[13] M. Spencer, "Multiculturalism, 'Political Correctness,' and the Politics of Identity," *Sociological Forum,* 9 (1994): 547–567.

Controlling the words people feel able to use - as Political Correctness does by continuously tabooing old terms, used prior to the revolution, as immoral - is an important part of this, because it means that debate is only conducted on the revolutionaries' terms and their power and superior morality (and even intellect or degree of civility) is inherently conceded. The moment you use the term "cis-male," for example, you are arguing on their terms and ceding authority to them. Altering language also creates a fundamental break with the (uncivilized) past. The Frankfurt School moved the Marxist focus away from economic groups and towards cultural groups. Ellis argues, therefore, that Political Correctness is a "Neo-Marxist" ideology - "Cultural Marxism" - which promotes the supposedly disempowered but focuses on "ethnic minorities" and other identity-groups rather than "the worker." Many analyses of Political Correctness concur with Ellis.[14] For example, economist Anthony Browne observes that Political Correctness is "Marxism converted from economic into cultural terms."[15]

By the 2010s, the fashionable term for advocates of this worldview was "Social Justice Warriors," shortened to "SJWs." "Woke," which derived from African-American parlance about being "Woke" to injustice, has simply replaced these earlier terms.[16] In a sense, it involves an endless revolution; a constant struggle for "equality" and, indeed, empowerment, as well as various assumptions, such as that all human psychological differences are environmentally-mediated or even that "race" and "gender" are "social constructs," implying that even these are a matter of environment. However, in some contexts Wokeness *does* seem to accept the existence of races, such as in advancing the narrative of good/oppressed race versus bad/oppressor race or if there is a shortage of black organ donors. When that happens then race appears to become a biological construct, though only implicitly; they will not entirely admit

---

[14] F. Ellis, *Political Correctness and the Theoretical Struggle: From Lenin and Mao to Marcus and Foucault* (Auckland: Maxim Institute, 2004).

[15] A. Browne, *The Retreat of Reason: Political Correctness and the Corruption of Public Debate in Modern Britain* (London: Civitas, 2006), 3.

[16] For a more detailed discussion of the origins of Wokeness, see, E. Dutton and J.O.A. Rayner-Hilles, *Woke Eugenics: How Social Justice is a Mask for Social Darwinism* (Perth: Imperium Press, 2024).

this. This inconsistency would seem to reflect the way in which Wokeness is focused on power, not reason. The Party states that race is biological today and a social construct tomorrow: You, Winston, must accept what the Party says. In many respects Wokeness reflects aspects of traditional Christianity or forms of it, in particular dogmas, fervour and the inability to brook dissent, with any dissenters becoming heretics or infidels who are to be anathematized.[17]

"In Two Thousand and Seven . . ."

The new turning point, marking the ascent of this form of liberalism, came in the year 2007. Interestingly, since the year 2007 there has been an enormous rise in the use of "feelings" words in representative samples of texts and a collapse in the use of "analytic" words. Between the 1850s and the 1980s, words were increasingly analytic. This went into reverse in the 1980s with a huge acceleration from about the year 2007 onwards.[18] Something in the culture shifted in that year.

In 2007, James D. Watson, who, in 1962, had won the Nobel Prize for Physiology or Medicine for co-discovering the structure of DNA, was "cancelled." Due to unquestionably empirically accurate, if discomforting for some, comments he made about race differences in intelligence, this elderly man, whose discovery had fundamentally changed the world, was subject to a worldwide character assassination as well as, thereafter, being excluded from public life. In October 2007, Watson was promoting his memoir *Avoid Boring People: Lessons from a Life in Science*[19] in the UK, when an interview he had given to *The Sunday Times Magazine* came out. Watson had met English science writer Charlotte Hunt-Grubbe (b. 1978) in about 1996 and brought her to his Cold Spring Harbor Laboratory as part of his desire to seek out talented women in science. She had lived with Watson and his wife and worked as a post-doctoral laboratory assistant.[20]

---

[17] J. Williams, *How Woke Won: The Elitist Movement That Threatens Democracy, Tolerance and Reason* (London: John Wilkes Publishing, 2022).

[18] M. Scheffer, I. van de Leemput, E. Weinans and J. Bollen, "The rise and fall of rationality in language," *PNAS,* 118 (2021) e2107848118.

[19] J.D. Watson, *Avoid Boring People: Lessons from a Life in Science* (Oxford: Oxford University Press, 2007).

[20] D. McCormick, "King Lear and Dr Watson," *BioTechniques* (16th May 2018).

It came to the attention of the editor of *The Sunday Times Magazine* (for which she was working by 2007) that Hunt-Grubbe was close to Watson. The editor asked if she might interview him for the newspaper. Watson, a keen tennis player, was stepping off the court at the Piping Rock Club, his country club on Long Island, when Hunt-Grubbe asked Watson about black people.

Watson told her that he was "inherently gloomy about the prospect of Africa" because "all our social policies are based on the fact that their intelligence is the same as ours — whereas all the testing says not really."[21] However, he later emphasised that he did not think sub-Saharan Africans were genetically inferior.[22] Watson added that people aver that all races are equal but that "people who have to deal with black employees find this is not true." Hunt-Grubbe further wrote that:

> "He says that you should not discriminate on the basis of colour, because "there are many people of colour who are very talented, but don't promote them when they haven't succeeded at the lower level." He writes that "there is no firm reason to anticipate that the intellectual capacities of peoples geographically separated in their evolution should prove to have evolved identically. Our wanting to reserve equal powers of reason as some universal heritage of humanity will not be enough to make it so."[23]

According to philanthropist Cathy Soref, a long-time friend of Watson's and Emeritus Director of the Cold Spring Harbor Association Board, the remarks were:

> ". . . not intended for public consumption Watson was being mischievous. Anyone can tell this . . . He was South Park before there was South Park. He's an equal opportunity critic. He'll say something purposefully outrageous just to see if you'll say, 'Bullshit, Watson!' and if you don't he'll get bored and walk away. He just says things impulsively and he'll sometimes catch himself doing it; catch himself

[21] C. Hunt-Grubbe, "The Elementary DNA of Dr Watson," *Sunday Times Magazine* (14th October 2007).
[22] *CNN*, "Nobel-winning biologist apologizes for remarks about blacks" (18th October 2007), https://edition.cnn.com/2007/WORLD/europe/10/18/nobel.apology/index.html
[23] Hunt-Grubbe, "The Elementary DNA of Dr Watson," *op. cit.*

being naughty. He misjudges, he doesn't realise that people won't realise he's being humorous. He doesn't mean to hurt people."

For this long-time friend, the publication of these remarks meant that Hunt-Grubbe, who did not respond to my request for an interview, was "Judas and Benedict Arnold combined. She knew better. It was so upsetting."[24]

Already in London, Watson hosted a reception at the Royal Society but then cancelled his book tour and returned to the US, not least because the Science Museum and venues in Bristol and Edinburgh had cancelled his talks because of his remarks. Watson told newspapers he was "bewildered" and had no memory of saying what Hunt-Grubbe had attributed to him, though he did not deny that he may have said it.[25] This implies that he knows he has a habit of telling the truth, as he sees it, when asked. When Soref wrote a letter of complaint to *The Sunday Times* about the article, Robin Morgan (b. 1955), the editor of the *Sunday Times Magazine,* replied to her: "Dr Watson DID use those words AND MORE. They were not put in his mouth, they are not misquotes, they were not invented."

As a result of the publication of the remarks, Watson was not only branded "racist" by the Labour Mayor of London, Ken Livingstone (b. 1945), but by numerous scientists. He was condemned in the pages of the prestigious scientific journal *Nature* for being "crass" and lacking "sensitivity." As English evolutionary psychiatry researcher Bruce Charlton noted, there was no attempt in *Nature* to actually scientifically interrogate the veracity or otherwise of Watson's claims. "The editorial included such comments as: 'his notorious propensity for making outrageous statements,' 'a track record of making distasteful remarks,' 'on many previous occasions voiced unpalatable views tinged with racism and sexism,' 'his views have finally been deemed beyond the pale,'

---

[24] Cathy Soref, Interview with the author, 31st July 2024, by telephone.
[25] S. Connor, "Watson makes humiliating return to US after row over race comments," *The Independent* (20th October 2007).

'demonstrates a sheer unacceptable offensiveness,' 'unpleasant [...] utterances,' and 'crass comments.'"[26]

Watson's successor, in 2003, as President of the Cold Spring Harbor Laboratory, was Australian scientist Bruce Stillman (b. 1953). In 2007, Stillman also became its CEO with Watson being Chancellor and working for the laboratory as a fundraiser. In that same year, due to the furore, Watson resigned from his position as Chancellor of the Cold Spring Harbor Laboratory and trustee. According to Stillman, Watson was "appointed as Chancellor Emeritus, Professor Emeritus and Honorary Trustee in 2008. However, he remained an employee of CSHL through 2018, devoting time and effort to the compilation and annotation of historically significant and scholarly materials from throughout his illustrious career as a scientist and author at CSHL - services that CSHL recognizes as significantly important to its history."[27] Stillman was, according to Cathy Soref, in a "no win situation," meaning he could not simply defend Watson. Stillman publically declared that the laboratory's Board of Trustees, "vehemently disagree with [Watson's] statements and are bewildered and saddened if he made such comments."[28] "So the lab's Board of Trustees voted for Watson to step down, feeling it was the only way to save the lab," continued Soref. Some members of the Board of Trustees, who make large donations to the laboratory, told me that they defended Watson, though none of them wished to go public lest they be thrown off the board.

Nevertheless, Watson felt compelled to stand down. This was despite the fact that by all accounts, Watson, a superb fundraiser "is credited with having converted an almost bankrupt, dilapidated laboratory into a 'DNA Town' with a research, teaching and conference center; community outreach programs; a publishing house; and new buildings, including hosting facilities."[29] In other words, Cold Spring Harbor Laboratory

---

[26] B.G. Charlton, "Editorial," *Medical Hypotheses,* 70 (2008): 1077-1090. Quoting, Editorial, "Watson's Folly," *Nature* (2007): 449:948.

[27] Bruce Stillman, 29th January 2025.

[28] W. Dunham, "Scientist Watson quits post after race remarks," *Reuters* (25th October 2007), https://www.reuters.com/article/lifestyle/science/scientist-watson-quits-post-after-race-remarks-idUSN25200619/

[29] [29] P. Abir-Am, "Watson's World," *American Scientist* (May-June 2003).

wouldn't amount to much if it wasn't for Watson's hard work and ability. Not only that but, according to Soref, years earlier Watson had financially contributed to the construction of a house on lab property in which he could live but which would be owned by the lab, an assertion Stillman substantiated. Watson had contributed, claimed Soref, because he wanted the house to remain as it had been when he had lived in it, as a kind of museum but also as a place in which "a top scientist could live and entertain" and maintain a kind of scientific "salon." This was naïve. It assumed he'd be on good terms with the lab for the rest of his life.

It should be noted that Hunt-Grubbe wrote a follow up article to her *Sunday Times Magazine* piece in which she implored that Watson should not be condemned for his remarks.

> "I am not trying to destroy a brilliant scientist and I am genuinely horrified by the response. We need to squeeze every last drop of brilliance from this man if we are to continue hoping to unravel the genetic causes of disease. He strives to help young people in their careers. My biggest concern is that, by helping me, he has damaged himself. I could not hope more, that I am wrong."[30]

However, she did have Watson's original remarks on tape, he presumably knew he was being taped,[31] and it seems unlikely that she didn't realise that there would be at least some kind of furore if the remarks were published.

And it Gets Worse . . .

This turn of events was highly significant, more significant than it was understood to be at the time. It marked a turning point in the history of Western civilization. There had been hints of this development for a long time. Ten years earlier Watson had been condemned by gay rights and anti-abortion campaigners for saying that a woman should be allowed to have an abortion for whatever reason she liked, including if it could be shown that the child would likely be homosexual and she was saddened

---

[30] C. Hunt-Grubbe, "Science always has and should be open to debate," *Sunday Times* (21st October 2007).
[31] McCormick, "King Lear and Dr Watson," *op. cit.*

by the prospect of not having grandchildren as a result of the child's likely homosexuality. This evoked an hysterical reaction in which it was implied that Watson wanted to use genomic research to eliminate homosexuality.[32]

Watson wasn't sensitive enough in 1997, and was merely *criticised*, but this was 2007. Watson was *cancelled*; ostracised. This demonstrated just how much things had already changed, and it was a marker of how things would be different in the future. Returning to Clare College, Cambridge in 2011 (where Watson had been a post-doc when he discovered the structure of DNA in 1953) to give a lecture, a group of students organised a silent protest with the organiser proclaiming: "This is a man who does not reflect Clare's ideals of inclusiveness and diversity and should not be allowed to speak at the College."[33] In other words, by 2011, at Cambridge University, certain dogmas were far more important than the pursuit of truth.

In 2019, the already-cancelled Watson was simply defenestrated. According to Cathy Soref, she met, by chance, the woman who was in charge of the PBS television show *American Masters,* having taken Watson to a salon to see the Somali-Dutch politician Ayaan Hirsi Ali (b. 1969) of whom he was an enormous fan. Talking to the PBS producer, Soref leapt upon the opportunity to try to rehabilitate Watson. "I didn't want his obituary to say 'Watson: Racist' because he's not. I wanted them to make a documentary that would reveal the real Watson; the Watson I know." According to Soref, this is an anti-racist, a life-long Democrat who voted for Obama twice and who "didn't care that he was half-black," and who is also "the greatest humanitarian;" obsessed with trying to find a cure for cancer.

The project took many years and, while it progressed, the interviewer with whom Watson was working, James Redford (1962-2020), became seriously ill and had to stand aside. Replaced by another man, alas, the new interviewer, not really understanding the purpose of the project, "threw in the zinger" (asked about Watson's views on race and whether

---

[32] S. Boggan, G. Cooper and C. Arthur, "Nobel winner backs abortion 'for any reason,'" *The Independent* (17th February 1997).
[33] S. Sharman, "Silent Treatment for Nobel Laureate," *Varsity* (6th March 2011).

they'd changed) and Watson repeated his remarks on race differences in intelligence in even more explicit terms:

> "Not at all. I would like for them to have changed, that there be new knowledge that says that your nurture is much more important than nature. But I haven't seen any knowledge. And there's a difference on the average between blacks and whites on IQ tests. I would say the difference is genetic."

A journalist for *The New York Times* asked of readers, "How should such fundamentally unsound views be weighed against his extraordinary scientific contributions?"[34]

In response, Cold Stream Harbor Laboratory told newspapers that Watson's remarks were "unsubstantiated and reckless" and "reprehensible, unsupported by science." They also stripped him of his honorary titles, specifically "chancellor emeritus, Oliver R. Grace professor emeritus and honorary trustee."[35] The following year, during the Black Lives Matter protests of that summer, they even decided to change the name of their graduate school because it was named after Watson.[36]

When I asked Bruce Stillman, who has been president of the Cold Spring Harbor Laboratory since 2003, to explain why this had happened, he asserted: "Jim Watson has made major contributions to science and society, and focusing on his statements that were influenced by his declining health is not productive. In addition, much of what has been written about this era is incorrect."[37] He later added that Watson "remained an employee and Honorary Trustee of CSHL until 2019. There are two portraits of Jim hanging in buildings on the CSHL campus and a bust of

---

[34] A. Harmon, "James Watson Had a Chance to Salvage His Reputation on Race. He Made Things Worse," *New York Times* (1st January 2019), https://www.nytimes.com/2019/01/01/science/watson-dna-genetics-race.html

[35] *BBC News,* "James Watson: Scientist loses titles after claims over race" (13th January 2019), https://www.bbc.com/news/world-us-canada-46856779

[36] E. Cahan, "Amid protests against racism, scientists move to strip offensive names from journals, prizes, and more," *Science* (2nd July 2020), https://www.science.org/content/article/amid-protests-against-racism-scientists-move-strip-offensive-names-journals-prizes-and

[37] Bruce Stillman, email, 29th July 2024.

him is in our library. He still lives on CSHL's campus with his family."[38] When I asked Stillman why, if Watson is genuinely so venerated that he deserves a bust and portraits, his other honours have not been restored to him, I did not receive a reply.

According to Cathy Soref, there was nothing wrong with Watson's health when he gave the interview to *American Masters* and Stillman's assertion is completely untrue. Reading between the lines, Stillman's response is fascinating. Stillman implies that what has been written is incorrect but, nevertheless, he does not wish to take an opportunity to correct it; the furore should simply be forgotten about. He also seems to imply that Watson made the remarks he made due to poor mental health; presumably senility. If this was the case, and Watson was not responsible for his actions, it rather begs the question of why he should be punished for making the remarks. Thus, the tactic is to deal with the problem of a highly eminent person making such remarks by dismissing him, implicitly, as senile; but, nevertheless, to punish him, implying that he is not senile, in order to satisfy the Woke mob. In a sense, in this ersatz religious context, it's as though his remarks were so egregious that even if he was senile – which he wasn't, in late 2018 he was still driving a car, as we will see later, and the remarks that were broadcast in 2019 were made before this - he had to be sacrificed to atone to the offended Woke gods. I put these criticisms to Bruce Stillman and did not receive a reply.

In 2003, the English historian of science Robert Olby (1933-2020) wrote of Watson, "His gaffes were overlooked and his snide remarks forgiven, for it was accepted that Watson had remarkable intuition, vision and drive."[39] By 2007, and certainly by 2019, these talents were no longer sufficient; in a context of much more pronounced ersatz religious ardour. Cathy Soref informed me that it is likely that the lab had hired a PR expert and that he had advised Stillman that the situation could best be dealt with by blaming Watson's remarks on his age. "Bruce was trying to save the lab," said Soref. "He was in an untenable position, because of the politically correct social milieu. For Bruce, dealing with Watson was sometimes like a parent having to protect the family heirlooms from an

---

[38] Bruce Stillman, 29th January 2024.
[39] R. Olby, "Too young for gardening," *Nature,* 426 (2003): 229-230.

unruly child who is running around, and their heirloom was the lab." Stillman disputes this: "CSHL did not need saving at that time. It was then, and remains today, a very strong and world-leading research and education institution," he told me.[40]

The 2019 furore, it should be noted, occurred in a near-hysterical context in which many academics were being cancelled for expressing the most parsimonious summary of data with regard to race. One of the most significant "moral panics" over "eugenics" in academia occurred in 2018 with the "discovery" of the "London Conference on Intelligence" which had been taking place each year at University College London (UCL) since 2015. It was organized by English psychologist James Thompson (b. 1948), who was an honorary Senior Lecturer at UCL, and it included papers on race differences in intelligence. The university conducted an inquiry into how this could have happened and considerable media attention was garnered.[41] As a direct result of attending the conference, and of the consequent mini-moral panic about eugenics and race research that it provoked, a number of the academics involved were "cancelled." English psychologist Richard Lynn (1930-2023) was stripped of his Emeritus Professorship in the Psychology Department at the University of Ulster (a department he had founded in 1972),[42] English political scientist Noah Carl (b. 1990) was fired from Cambridge University in part for attending the conference and for publishing alongside some of its more "controversial" academics,[43] German biochemist Gerhard Meisenberg (b. 1953) was sacked from his Professorship of Biochemistry at Ross University in Dominica,[44] and James Thompson resigned from his

---

[40] Stillman, 29th January 2025.

[41] For more detail see, E. Dutton, *Breeding the Human Herd: Eugenics, Dysgenics and the Future of the Species* (Perth: Imperium Press, 2023).

[42] R. Lynn, *Memoirs of a Dissident Psychologist* (London: Ulster Institute for Social Research, 2020), 226–227.

[43] N. Carl, "How Stifling Debate Around Race, Genes and IQ Can Do Harm," *Evolutionary Psychological Science,* 4 (2018): 399–407.

[44] A. Ellwanger, "An Open Letter on Campus Culture," *American Mind* (12th October 2020), https://americanmind.org/salvo/an-open-letter-on-campus-culture/

honorary senior lectureship at UCL.[45] An analysis showed that the cancelling of academics - ranging from condemnation by their university to being fired - sky-rocketed from 2015 onwards and especially did so in the wake of the furore over the conference.[46]

Heretic Status Thrust Upon Him

To misquote Shakespeare, "some achieve heretical status and some have heretical status thrust upon them." Watson's views have not changed, they are simply the most parsimonious understanding of the available evidence, but the world around him has changed, especially as, by the year 2007, he was already 79 years old and had, therefore, been educated in a very different academic universe. By the year 2007, the world had become enveloped by an ersatz religion with all of the dogmatism, fervour and irrationality of the most extreme forms of eighteenth century Anglicanism, though without the overt belief in a metaphysical universe, God or the need to uncover the nature of the world as God's revelation. "Wokeness," is, in a number of key respects, a Church, and Watson is a blasphemer. In that we can define ourselves, and even change sex because we say we have, we are all, in a sense, gods, sparks of divine light; though there are evil gods who don't accept that we can do so and who proclaim hurtful notions such as objective reality.[47] Watson is one of these evil gods.

Where Isaac Newton was an anti-Trinitarian and so an "atheist" or a "heretic,"[48] Watson is a "racist" and a "sexist." These words have the same function that "atheist," "heretic" or "papist" once did. "Racist" and "sexist" are emotionally charged insults; they are not neutral terms. As

---

[45] A. Fazackerley, "UCL eugenics inquiry did not go far enough, committee say," *The Guardian* (28th February 2020), https://www.theguardian.com/education/2020/feb/28/ucl-eugenics-inquiry-did-not-go-far-enough-committee-say

[46] N. Carl and M.A. Woodley of Menie, "A scientometric analysis of controversies in the field of intelligence research," *Intelligence*, 77 (2019): 101397.

[47] For a more detailed discussion of the religious dimensions to Wokeness see E. Dutton and J.O.A. Rayner-Hilles, *The Past is a Future Country: The Coming Conservative Demographic Revolution* (Exeter: Imprint Academic, 2022).

[48] S.D. Snobelen, "Isaac Newton, Socianism and 'The One Supreme God'" in M. Muslow and J. Rohls, (Eds.), *Socinianism and Arminianism: Antitrinitarians, Calvinists, and Cultural Exchange in Seventeenth-century Europe* (Leiden: Brill, 2005).

American philosopher Marcus Singer (1926-2016) has noted, the word ". . . 'racist' is not just a highly emotive term. It is a bludgeon word."[49] It is so potentially socially damaging to be accused of "racism" that fear of the accusation will make all but the bravest hold their tongues and avoid espousing anything termed "racist" by influential people. This is despite the fact that "racist" is an indefinite term, meaning that it can be stretched to reprove those who deviate even slightly from the path of orthodoxy. As Australian historian Alexandra Walsham has put it in her book *Church Papists*: "They were categories of deviance to which individuals who were even marginally departed from prescribed ideals might be assimilated and thereby reproved."[50]

Watson's punishment was not legal nor was it physical. He would not be burned at the stake for heresy, as was possible in English Law until 1677, the last person having been burned in 1612.[51] Watson's punishment was social; to be shunned, to be left out of the group; to be whispered about in negative terms, to not be invited to the birthday parties of the popular girls at school, consistent with the influence of female values in Western societies which we will explore later.[52] This shunning, however, can have serious financial consequences. In 2014, Watson auctioned off his Nobel Prize medal in order, so he said, partly to raise money for the Cold Spring Harbor Laboratory and also to invest the money in a painting by David Hockney (b. 1937). He told the *Financial Times* that he had been "unpersoned" due to his remarks on race and that he was selling his medal because he needed the money, due to having been ousted from the boards of assorted companies. Watson would make various bequests and keep the rest of the money raised.[53]

The reality, according to Cathy Soref, was that Cold Spring Harbor Laboratory had made it clear to Watson that when he died his wife, who

---

[49] M. Singer, *The Ideal of a Rational Morality: Philosophical Compositions* (Oxford: Clarendon Press, 2003), 172.

[50] A. Walsham, *Church Papists: Catholicism, Conformity and Confessional Polemic in Early Modern England* (Woodbridge: The Boydell Press, 1999), 108.

[51] See, S. Banks, *The British Execution, 1500-1964* (London: Bloomsbury, 2013).

[52] See, J. Benenson, *Warriors and Worriers: The Survival of the Sexes* (Oxford: Oxford University Press, 2014).

[53] A. Hartocollis, "By Selling Prize, a DNA Pioneer Seeks Redemption," *New York Times* (3rd December 2014).

is twenty years younger than him, and his adult son Rufus (b. 1970), who is schizophrenic and unable to work, would have two years to get out of the house and find somewhere else to live. Recall, that this is the house the construction of which Watson partly funded. Watson's medal was purchased by Russian billionaire Alisher Usmanov (b. 1953) for £2.6 million at an auction at Christies in New York. Usmanov declared that he would return the medal to Watson, adding: "In my opinion, a situation in which an outstanding scientist has to sell a medal recognising his achievements is unacceptable. James Watson is one of the greatest biologists in the history of mankind and his award for the discovery of DNA structure must belong to him." He further stated that Watson could keep the medal but that Watson must "donate the proceeds of the sale to the research institutions that had 'nurtured him,' including the universities of Cambridge, Chicago and Indiana."[54] It is noteworthy that it was a non-Westerner who came to Watson's rescue; who still valued "truth" above "feelings."

Not Even "Honest Jim" Was Safe . . .

October 2007 was the point at which the ruling ideology - administered by bureaucrats and the media (including academic journals) - achieved true mastery over the older scientific criteria of truth and accomplishment. This domination was exercised by dishonest and cruel slander, by shunning and by suppression. The "Watson Affair" can be seen as an indicator of broad scientific and social trends. Watson served as a very public victim, as a warning to others who might be tempted to dissent from the prevailing ideology. If it could happen to somebody as eminent as Jim Watson, it could happen to anyone: "Be careful! Think very carefully before you dare to question the dogmas of the Woke, who are now thoroughly ensconced in power!"

The Watson Affair demonstrated how Western society had changed to the point of inversion; from being broadly supportive of genius, and providing various protected niches for those of great ability, such as

---

[54] I. Sample, "Billionaire bought James Watson's Nobel prize medal in order to return it," *The Guardian* (9th December 2014), https://www.theguardian.com/science/2014/dec/09/russian-billionaire-usmanov-james-watson-nobel-prize-return-scientist

universities, to something almost the opposite. By 2007, Western society was actively hostile to genius. This is because, as we will see, there is a definite flipside to genius and that is a tendency to offensively tell the truth. By seeking out and persecuting those who displayed the characteristics of the genius-type, most of those who were, or who had the potential to be, geniuses were now targeted. Furthermore, as we will see, the kinds of ideas typical of a genius were also excluded and attacked whenever they dissented from mainstream ideology in any way. Moreover, anyone who defended these ideas, no matter how tentatively or reasonably, was, likewise, condemned.

In this book, focusing on the case of Jim Watson, we will see that the genius is typically a package-deal. He combines extreme creative ability with a difficult personality. The nature of that difficult personality varies between geniuses, but often includes multiple "problems" ranging across social, ideological and professional behaviour, as we will see in the case of Watson. But because the difficult personality is part of the genius package, indeed it leads to his genius breakthroughs, when the genius personality type is suppressed, then so is genius achievement. The persecution and exclusion of Watson marked the point at which the person and reputation of even the most famous living scientific genius would be sacrificed with the near-unanimous agreement of the global scientific bureaucracy, research institutions, and the media. Even being a genius could not save you. In fact, your exclusion should be all the more fervent precisely because people might take "heresy" seriously if it is expounded by someone like you; a genius. This is dangerous for society, because it is the genius who moves things forward; who solves our problems.

In order to understand why the Watson Affair was so salient and why it occurred, we will answer a number of key questions. We will begin with, "What is a Genius?" Having established this, we will ask, "How is Watson a genius?" and we will demonstrate this to be so. "What are the key psychological traits of a scientific genius?" will be our next question and we will show that Watson possesses all of them. As part of this we will wonder, "What are the causes of genius?" We will then ask, "Why did we once protect genius?" and we will demonstrate that this protection was a consequence of very specific historical circumstances. Having established this, we will move onto, "Why do we now persecute genius?" But we will commence by setting out what a genius is.

Chapter Two

Is James Watson a Genius?

What is a Genius?

I am able to sit here and write, and easily edit, this book because of a genius; the man who invented the computer, English mathematician Charles Babbage (1791-1871).[55] I am able to research this book far more swiftly than would ever previously have been possible as a consequence of the genius who invented, or heavily developed, the internet, the English computer scientist Sir Tim Berners-Lee (b. 1955).[56] You are able to read it in relative comfort because of the geniuses who pioneered the assorted electronic devices by which both of us are surrounded. These are only possible because of the geniuses behind the Industrial Revolution. Are you using electric light in order to read this book? Are you reading it on an airplane or on a holiday which you have reached via an airplane or even by using a motor car? Did you order the book over the internet?

Geniuses are the Promethean movers and shakers of the world. Like Icarus, they fly as high as possible and sometimes they are burned as a consequence; scientific geniuses are prospectors, searching for "scientific gold," as Watson himself has put it.[57] In some cases, historically, their ideas have been found so offensive to those with vested interests in the *status quo* that they have come perilously close to literally being burned as heretics, such as Galileo (1564-1642) who had to face the wrath of the Roman Inquisition in 1633 for the heresy of defending the Copernican

---

[55] D. Swade, *The Cogwheel Brain: Charles Babbage and the Quest to Build the First Computer* (London: Little Brown, 2000).
[56] L. Green, *The Internet: An Introduction to New Media* (Oxford: Berg, 2010), 34.
[57] "Interview with James Watson: Nobel Prize in Physiology or Medicine, 1962," *Nobel Prize* (2019).

model of the solar system.[58] In fact, Italian Dominican friar Giordano Bruno (1548-1600) *was* burnt at the stake for his cosmological theories, such as that stars were distant suns surrounded by planets that might even harbour life.[59] To a significant degree, geniuses have much in common with heretics. The genius comes up with something that is commonly agreed to be highly original and ground-breaking. In the world of science, on which we will focus in this book, it will usually be a world-changing invention, a ground-breaking discovery or a brilliant theory that makes sense of a whole array of data in a beautifully parsimonious way, such that the field in which the genius is a researcher is fundamentally altered. They differ in that religious heretics hold to certain dogmatic beliefs and hold to them ardently, whereas the scientist employs the empirical method and logic, avoiding, or hopefully avoiding, holding to dogma.

Geniuses, these rare people in terms of the development of humanity, are nuggets of gold where the rest of us are mere sand. However, other aspects of their character may be best summarised using far less flattering metaphors: they are petty criminals where the rest of us are law-abiding, they cause offence and ruin the atmosphere at the party either because they are socially clumsy or because they just don't care; they let you down at the last minute because they're suddenly feeling "depressed" where *you* can always be relied upon to turn up for that beer. In fact, one researcher has made a direct comparison between geniuses and criminals, arguing that both reflect high levels of testosterone and the need for males to be highly competitive when they are young in order to attain resources and to attain females.[60] We have to understand the nature of such people because, as we will see later, we are producing fewer and fewer of them per capita; there are fewer and fewer people who are generally being recognised as scientific geniuses and in this book we will explore a number of reasons why this might be the case.

---

[58] T. Mayer, *The Roman Inquisition: Trying Galileo* (Philadelphia, PN: University of Pennsylvania Press, 2015).

[59] A. Martinez, *Burned Alive: Bruno, Galileo and the Inquisition* (London: Reaktion Books, 2018).

[60] S. Kanazawa, "Why productivity fades with age: The crime–genius connection," *Journal of Research in Personality,* 37 (2003): 247-272.

A genius, to labour the point, is a person who is widely recognised as having made an extremely important contribution to their field; a contribution of ground-breaking significance. How do we conclude that this is the case? Is this not merely subjective? The answer is "No." Analyses of bibliographies indicate that there is widespread agreement among writers on which people are "geniuses," on which people are extremely important to their field. This is known as "convergent bibliography." A person's significance is essentially a function of how they are regarded by their peers and this can be modelled by examining the prominence and prevalence of particular names across historical works.[61] If one does this, certain names emerge and these can be regarded as geniuses. Some people argue that this method is subjective because it is based on the ratings of mere people and these may be coloured by prejudice, meaning that certain potential geniuses are ignored. It can be countered that genius is a form of behaviour, just as tool use among chimpanzees is a form of behaviour. We know that tool use among chimpanzees is real only because multiple raters have observed this. Similarly, we know that a person behaves as a genius (by having a huge impact on everything around him) because multiple raters have observed this.

With the concept of "genius" defined, then, the next question is, "Does James Watson qualify as a genius?" Before we answer this, let's take a brief overview of his life.

Watson's Life: A Brief Overview

James Dewey Watson was born on 6th April 1928 in Chicago, the only son of a businessman also called James Dewey Watson (1897-1968). His parents also had a daughter, Betty, who was born in 1930. This is consistent with studies showing that scientific geniuses, though not political geniuses, tend to be either first-borns or only-children, perhaps because this provides them with greater childhood intellectual

---

[61] D.K. Simonton, *Genius, Creativity and Leadership* (Cambridge, MA: Harvard University Press, 1988).

stimulation,[62] or because childhood isolation somehow causes them to develop their creativity.[63] Jim's mother's parents had emigrated from Glasgow, and his maternal grandmother was of Irish ancestry, meaning that Watson was raised Roman Catholic. Watson grew up on Chicago's South Side, attending the Horace Mann Elementary School and the South Shore High School, both of them "public schools," in the American sense of "non-fee-paying;" what the British would call "state schools." In 1943, at the age of just 15, Watson was awarded a scholarship to the University of Chicago, under a special scheme which we will explore later, where he concentrated on Zoology. Watson graduated in 1947, at the age of 19, living at home during his studies. He went on to be a PhD student at the University of Indiana, being awarded his doctorate in 1950, at the age of just 22.

Watson was then a post-doctoral researcher at the University of Copenhagen, before transferring to Clare College at Cambridge University. In 1953, he and the English biologist Francis Crick (1916-2004), at the Cavendish Laboratory, worked out the structure of DNA. In this endeavour, they worked with British-Jewish chemist Rosalind Franklin (1920-1958) who was at Kings College London and then at Birkbeck College London, changing her position due to frequent disagreements with her director, which, as we will see below, Watson put down to Franklin's "feminist" qualities and "moods." Franklin worked out some of the key properties of DNA, using X-ray diffraction. Franklin died of ovarian cancer aged just 37. In addition, they collaborated with New Zealander biophysicist Maurice Wilkins (1916-2004) who shared the Nobel Prize with Watson and Crick and who was Franklin's director.

In November 1953, Watson and Crick were inspired by Franklin's idea that DNA was helical, an idea about which she later became sceptical. It has been suggested that a student of Franklin's, Raymond Gosling (1926-2015), took an X-ray of DNA, known as Photograph 51, which Wilkins showed to Watson. He had the right to do this, as Franklin's findings legally belonged to his laboratory and she was soon to leave to

---

[62] R. Ochse, *Before the Gates of Excellence: The Determinants of Creative Genius* (Cambridge: Cambridge University Press, 1990), 64.
[63] Ochse, *Before the Gates of Excellence, op. cit.,* 78.

Birkbeck, so her findings had to be handed over to Wilkins.[64] Watson immediately realised that DNA forms a double helix. However, letters have since come to light indicating that Franklin understood what her data meant and willingly shared it with Watson and Crick. It seems that Franklin understood her data, even though Watson concluded that she did not, but did not quite comprehend its full significance; as if it didn't interest her. Indeed, an article written for *Time* magazine, which was never published, had presented Franklin as one of the co-discoverers of the structure of DNA, implying that she was perfectly content with her treatment at the hands of Watson.[65] This is consistent with Watson's summary in one of his memoirs. He recalls that Wilkins telephoned to say that both he and Franklin had found that their X-ray data supported the double helix. Her immediate acceptance of Watson and Crick's model at first astounded Watson because, "I had feared that her sharp, stubborn mind, caught in her self-made antihelical trap, might dig up irrelevant results that would foster uncertainty about the correctness of the double helix." She had anyway been increasingly moved towards thinking the structure must be helical. "Her past uncompromising statements on this matter thus reflected first-rate science, not the outpourings of a misguided feminist."[66]

In January 1953, the Britain-based researchers recognized that they were competing against American chemist Linus Pauling (1901-1994) to solve the structure of DNA, as they had got hold of a pre-print of his triple helix model, which Pauling didn't realise was erroneous. In February, Watson and Crick realised that DNA was shaped as a double helix with Crick proclaiming in the Cambridge pub *The Eagle* that they had "found the secret of life."[67] The experiments at Kings College London were vital because they corroborated their data. Franklin was reluctant to go ahead

---

[64] H. Markel, "The Ugly Truth Behind the Discovery of DNA," *Washington Post* (13th September 2021).

[65] T. Saey, "What was Rosalind Franklin's true role in the discovery of DNA's double helix?" *Science News* (26th April 2023). See, M. Cobb and N. Comfort, "What Rosalind Franklin truly contributed to the discovery of DNA's structure," *Nature* (25th April 2023).

[66] J.D. Watson, *The Double Helix: A Personal Account of the Discovery of the Structure of DNA* (London: Weidenfeld and Nicolson, 1968), Ch. 28.

[67] Watson, *The Double Helix, op. cit.*, Ch. 26.

and publish the results until there was more data, so she and Wilkins were merely acknowledged in Watson and Crick's seminal study which presented their findings; they were not co-authors.[68]

Leaving Cambridge, Watson worked at the California Institute of Technology ("Cal Tech") before transferring to Harvard, as a biologist, in 1955. He was Professor of Biology at Harvard between 1961 and 1976. Awarded the Nobel Prize for Physiology or Medicine for his earlier research at Cambridge in 1962, in 1968, Watson became the director of the Laboratory of Quantitative Biology at Cold Spring Harbor on Long Island and resigned from his Harvard professorship in 1976 in order to concentrate on his work on Long Island. Cold Spring Harbor Laboratory, a privately funded institution, was established in 1890 and was the home of the Eugenics Records Office between 1910 and 1939.[69] In 1994, Watson became the laboratory's president and was its chancellor until 2007, at which point he was "cancelled" as we discussed earlier. Between 1990 and 1992, Watson began and was in charge of the Human Genome Project, to sequence the human genome.[70] In 1997, President Bill Clinton (b. 1946) awarded Watson the National Medal of Science and, in 2002, the British government bestowed upon him an honorary knighthood.

How Does Genetic Selection Operate?

It is difficult to argue that Watson is anything other than a genius; bearing in mind the importance of his breakthrough. To fully understand his discovery, however, we must take a bit of a detour.

We must familiarise ourselves, first, with how selection operates. *Natural Selection* is the process whereby an organism is adapted - both physically and mentally - to a particular kind of ecology. A gene is composed of two alleles. In the process of procreation, with most genes, an infant inherits one allele from each parent. Sometimes something will go wrong, and one of these genes will not copy correctly. This leads to a

---

[68] J.D. Watson and F.H.C. Crick, "Molecular Structure of Nucleic Acids: A Structure for Deoxyribose Nucleic Acid," *Nature,* 171 (1953): 737-738.

[69] On the history of eugenics, see: Dutton, *Breeding the Human Herd, op. cit.*

[70] H. Markel, *The Secret of Life: Rosalind Franklin, James Watson, Francis Crick, and the Discovery of DNA's Double Helix* (New York: W.W. Norton, 2021).

defective gene, a "mutation." Under the harsh conditions of Darwinian selection, organisms are fine-tuned to their environment. Therefore, any mutation that has any effect on gene function at all will almost always make the gene less functional, and the organism less well-adapted to its environment. Each child is born with anywhere from 40 to 80 new mutations, depending on the age of the father, as these increase with paternal age. Most are in the realm of junk DNA and cause no harm, but an unknown fraction causes mild impairment, and a few are bad enough to cause a disease or disability, such as Huntington's Disease or Achondroplasia, which leads to dwarfism.[71]

Accordingly, the carriers of these mutations will be selected against, because they are more likely to die young, or are less likely than others to have many children even if they survive. Sometimes, a mutation will actually give the carrier an advantage in its particular environment. Pale skin, for example, would have given the first pale-skinned mutant an edge in a cloudy northern climate because he or she would have been able to absorb more sunlight and convert it into Vitamin D, especially in an agricultural context in which there was reliance on corn and less access to fruit and vegetables.[72] When this kind of mutation manifests in the right kind of environment then the allele will be selected for because the carrier will be less likely to be disabled by rickets and he will be more likely to end up with a large number of descendants. However, in general, mutations are selected against.

We all inherit mutations from our parents under our current conditions of weakened selection pressure. Each of us carries about three new mutations which neither of our parents carried. In most cases, these don't do us much harm.[73] It has also been estimated that the genome in modern Western countries, specifically in Iceland, acquires at least 60 new

---

[71] R.M. Pauli, "Achondroplasia: A Comprehensive Clinical Review," *Orphanet Journal of Rare Diseases*, 14 (2019): 1.

[72] See G. Cochran and H. Harpending, *The 10,000 Year Explosion: How Civilization Accelerated Human Evolution* (New York: Basic Books, 2009).

[73] M. W. Nachman and S. L. Crowell, "Estimate of the mutation rate per nucleotide in humans," *Genetics,* 196 (2000): 297–304.

mutations every generation.[74] Iceland is a useful place to conduct such studies due to the Icelandic being a small, isolated and homogenous population with universally accessible healthcare.[75] However, the rise in genome sequencing – which Watson, incidentally, oversaw in its early stages when he was in charge of the Human Genome Project between 1990 and 1992[76] - in recent years has meant that these results have been found in many countries, not just Iceland.[77] This process, of new mutations manifesting every generation, has two key consequences.

Firstly, there are simply more carriers of genes that cause severe defects and, thus, more people who suffer from these severe defects. But secondly, it means that almost all human genomes now contain both small and large defects. In some cases, genetic diseases are not due to having a specific faulty gene, but as a consequence of *locus heterogeneity*, meaning that a deleterious mutation in any one of a number of genes can lead to the increased risk of a disease. This is the case with Alzheimer's for example.[78] The many flaws that almost every human being has - both physical and mental - are to a large extent caused by the assortment of genetic defects that they carry. These defects work together to make every aspect of the carrier operate sub-optimally, resulting in increases in disease susceptibilities, intellectual limitation, minor physical defects, and minor mental defects. Under Darwinian conditions, most of these mutations would have been purged every generation due to high child mortality, of around 50 per cent until about 1800,[79] although mutations that caused only a very minor limitation could survive and become common in a particular area with a small, homogenous population due to "founder effect" (one

---

[74] A. Kong, M. Frigge, G. Masson et al., "Rate of de novo mutations and the importance of father's age to disease risk," *Nature*, 488 (2012): 471–475.

[75] J. Gulcher, A. Helgason and K. Stefansson, "Genetic homogeneity of Icelanders," *Nature Genetics,* 26 (2000): 395.

[76] T. Lee, *The Human Genome Project: Cracking the Genetic Code of Life* (New York, Springer, 2013).

[77] See, Sarraf, Woodley of Menie and Feltham, *Modernity and Cultural Decline, op cit.*

[78] L. Hernandez and D. Blazer, (Eds.), *Genes, Behaviour and Social Environment* (Washington, DC: National Academies Press, 2006), Ch. 3.

[79] T. Volk and J. Atkinson, "Is Child Death the Crucible of Human Evolution?" *Journal of Social, Evolutionary, and Cultural Psychology,* 2 (2008): 103–116.

fertile founder heavily influences a small population) or "genetic drift" (when allele frequencies simply change in chance ways across time). In general, though, such mutations were selected out. This process has broken down due to medical advances, inoculation, better living conditions and cheaper food, leading to an increasing "mutational load" with each new generation.

How Do Mutations Arise?

Mutations arise as copy errors during DNA replication (we will define DNA below), either with or without damage to the DNA. They can be expressed in four ways, because there are four kinds of genetic variants, or alleles: additive, recessive, dominant and X-linked.

Dominant alleles affect the trait which they impact when the allele is present in one copy besides the alternative "normal" allele, because they dominate the normal allele. *Recessive* alleles are expressed only when they are present in two copies. *Additive*, or intermediate, inheritance means that the effects of the alleles add up. Most complex traits, such as height, blood pressure and intelligence, are *polygenic*. This means that natural variations in them are caused by many different genes working together to produce the relevant trait. As a highly polygenic trait, intelligence is easily disrupted by mutations because mutations in a very large number of different genes, a few thousand of them, can interfere with its expression.

Epistastic Effects: Bipolar Disorder

The effects of some mutant alleles are only triggered if another mutant allele in a different gene is also inherited. This is known as *epistasis*. Many studies have found that certain psychiatric disorders, such as schizophrenia and bipolar disorder, sometimes manifest due to the *epistatic effects* on a complex trait of two different alleles both being present in one individual.[80] This would mean that both parents could be psychologically normal, though, between them, carry both of the alleles that lead to an epistatic effect if they are both inherited.

---

[80] C. Webber, "Epistasis in Neuropsychiatric Disorders," *Trends in Genetics,* 33 (2017): 256–265.

For example, a mutation in one gene may put its carrier at risk of manic-depressive (bipolar) disorder, but *only* if that person also carries a mutation in a *different* gene. If both mutations happen to be inherited by a child, the child will grow up to develop bipolar disorder. This is a form of depression characterized by oscillating between periods of extreme happiness and energy ("mania") and periods of abject despair. A famous sufferer is the English comedian and writer Stephen Fry (b. 1957). He attempted suicide in 2012 and had previously come close to it a number of times.[81]

Recessive: Sickle Cell Anemia

There can also be a significant effect if you inherit two mutant *recessive alleles* of the same gene, one from each parent, so that no normal copy of the gene is present. Sometimes, this is sufficient to cause specific genetic disorders. For example, research in northern Finland, where there are elevated rates of mild mental retardation compared to the rest of the country, has highlighted a defect in a gene known as *CRADD,* a defect which is 50 times more frequent in Finland than elsewhere in Europe. It is a recessive allele, and if both parents carry a copy of the defective *CRADD* allele then there is a 25 per cent chance that any child will be mildly mentally retarded through inheriting two copies of it.[82] Carrying one copy of the allele does no harm because, being recessive, it is not expressed unless the other allele is present.

There are, however, cases where a genetic disease stays in the population because inheriting one copy of the mutant allele benefits health but inheriting two copies damages health. For example, people who suffer from sickle cell anemia, which is most prevalent among Sub-Saharan Africans, have two copies of the same mutant allele in a gene encoding

---

[81] S. Cable, "A downcast Stephen Fry appears the day after he reveals he tried to commit suicide last year with a 'huge a number of pills and vodka,'" *Mail Online* (5th June 2013), https://www.dailymail.co.uk/news/article-2336406/Stephen-Fry-tried-commit-suicide-year-large-number-pills-vodka-saved-producer-unconscious-body.html.

[82] M. Kurki, E. Saarentaus, O. Pietiläinen et al., "Contribution of rare and common variants to intellectual disability in a sub-isolate of Northern Finland," *Nature Communications,* 10 (2019): 410.

hemoglobin. However, those who carry only one copy are not only healthy, but have improved immunity to malaria.[83] Improved malaria resistance has been strongly selected for in human populations that were exposed to this disease in the past, while the offspring with sickle cell anemia would rarely have lived long enough to reproduce. This is because sickle cell anemia is a life-threatening condition, the symptoms of which include a low number of red blood cells, recurrent episodes of vascular occlusion with severe pain and tissue infarction, frequent infection, delayed growth, delayed puberty, and vision problems in some patients.[84] American Jazz musician Miles Davis (1926–1991), who suffered from sickle cell anemia, died of pneumonia, which had plagued him throughout his life, aged 65.[85]

Dominant: Huntingdon's Disease

By contrast, some conditions arise from a single mutant *dominant allele*. Dominant alleles dominate in the sense that a single mutant allele, when paired with the normal one, will always cause a disease. Huntington's Disease is a neurodegenerative disorder that starts in young or middle-aged adults with subtle behavioral changes, then progresses to a severe movement disorder with involuntary overshooting movements accompanied by progressive dementia, problems swallowing, speaking, and breathing, and death about 20 years after the onset of the first symptoms.

Symptoms usually start to manifest between the ages of 30 and 50. It is a dominant condition. If one of your parents has Huntington's disease, this parent will have a normal and a mutant allele, and you will have a 50-50 chance of inheriting either the normal or the mutant allele.[86] The American folk musician Woody Guthrie (1912–1967) - writer of "This Land is Your Land," among other hits - died of Huntington's Disease aged

---

[83] L. Luzatto, "Sickle cell anaemia and malaria," *Mediterranean Journal of Hemotology and Infectious Diseases,* 4 (2012): e2012065.
[84] See, P. Jones, *Genes and Sickle Cell Disease* (New York: Chelsea House, 2008).
[85] J. Szwed, *So What? The Life of Miles Davis* (New York: Random House, 2012).
[86] See, T. Visser, *Huntington's Disease: Etiology and Symptoms, Diagnosis and Treatment* (Hauppage, NY: Nova Science Publishers, 2010).

55. He inherited the condition from his mother.[87] However, one might, of course, develop such a condition due to a *de novo* mutation passed on by a parent, which happens in 10 per cent of cases of Huntington's Disease, usually via the father.[88]

X-Linked: Hemophilia and Turner Syndrome

X-linked alleles are the exception. They do not come in pairs. They are on the X chromosome, and they are passed from parent to child. A chromosome is an aggregate of genes all of which, together, control a series of functions. For example, the sex of an organism is dictated by it having either two X chromosomes (female) or an X and a Y chromosome (male). A normal human has 23 chromosomes. One of the most well-known X-linked conditions is the blood-clotting disorder hemophilia, which affected many of the inter-married royal families of Europe in the nineteenth and twentieth centuries, specifically the British, German, Spanish, and Russian Royal Houses. Hemophilia renders the blood very slow to clot, resulting in excessive bleeding. It appears that hemophilia must have entered these royal families via the British Royal Family as a *de novo* mutation on the sperm of Prince Edward, Duke of Kent (1767–1820). Prince Edward was one of the younger sons of King George III (1738–1820). As a result of this mutation, Prince Edward's daughter, Queen Victoria (1819–1901), was a "carrier" of hemophilia.[89]

With X-linked conditions, the mother is a "carrier" but never displays any symptoms. Her daughters have a 50 per cent chance of carrying the disease, of which they will display no symptoms, and a 50 per cent chance of being normal. Her sons have a 50 per cent chance of *suffering* from the disease and a 50 per cent chance of being normal. If these male hemophiliacs have children, then they will pass on the hemophilia mutation only to their daughters, who will all be carriers, as the affected

[87] K. Coombs, *Woody Guthrie: America's Folk Singer* (Minneapolis, MN: Carolrhoda Books, 2002).
[88] G. Houge, O. Bruland, I. Bjørnevoll et al., "De novo Huntington disease caused by 26–44 CAG repeat expansion on a low-risk haplotype," *Neurology,* 81 (2013): 1099–1100.
[89] D. M. Potts, *Queen Victoria's Gene: Haemophilia and the Royal Family* (Stroud: History Press, 2011).

male will always pass on one X chromosome to a daughter. This is what occurred with Queen Victoria's hemophiliac son Prince Leopold, Duke of Albany (1853–1884). Prince Leopold's daughter, Princess Alice, Countess of Athlone (1883–1981), was a carrier.[90] More importantly, Queen Victoria's daughter, Princess Alice, Grand Duchess of Hesse (1843–1878), was a carrier, as was Alice's own daughter, Alexandra, Tsarina of Russia (1872–1918). The result was that the Russian Crown Prince, Alexey (1904–1918), suffered from hemophilia, an issue which destabilized Russia's absolute monarchy, contributing to revolution, civil war, and the takeover of Russia by the Bolsheviks.[91]

Sometimes, one of the two X chromosomes is not passed on to the female or it is only partially passed on. When this happens, the female develops Turner Syndrome. This is marked by sterility as well as by a number of physical abnormalities including a short and wide neck, a broad chest with widely spaced nipples, short stature, limited or no sexual changes at puberty, low-set ears and downward-slanting eyes. Sufferers have normal intelligence, but they tend to have impairments in aspects of visio-spatial skills and mathematics.[92]

What is Deoxyribonucleic Acid (DNA)?

Now that we are clear on the nature of selection and of genes, we can turn to DNA itself. Some genes instruct the body to make certain proteins so that it functions properly. Some genes help control other genes. Either way, these genes are composed of DNA. DNA contains the information to encode the proteins. RNA (Ribonucleic acid) carries the information from the DNA and transforms that information into proteins that perform most cellular functions. A nucleotide is the basic building block of nucleic acids. These are composed of a nitrogen base, a sugar molecule and a phosphate group which links the sugar molecule of one nucleotide to the next, forming the backbone of the nucleic acid strand. A "base pair" refers to

---

[90] R. K. Massie, *Nicholas and Alexandra: The Classic Account of the Fall of the Romanov Dynasty* (New York: Random House, 2000), 147.

[91] D. M. Potts, *Queen Victoria's Gene: Haemophilia and the Royal Family* (Stroud: History Press, 2011).

[92] P. Fechner, *Turner Syndrome: Pathophysiology, Diagnosis and Treatment* (New York: Springer, 2020).

two nitrogenous bases, one from each strand of the DNA "double helix," that are bonded together by hydrogen bonds. Base pairs are essential for the double-stranded structure of DNA. So, while nucleotides are the basic building blocks of nucleic acids, base pairs are specific pairings of nucleotides that hold the two strands of DNA together in a double helix. Nucleotides come in four forms: adenine (A), thymine (T), guanine (G), and cytosine (C). The question, answered by Watson and Crick, is, "How do they fit together?" The answer is like a kind of 3-D jigsaw: A fits to G and T fits to C in two chains of molecules; a double helix, where there are two chains of molecules running in opposite directions. This is how genetic information is stored and replicated.[93]

The information in DNA is encoded into these base pairs. Genes vary in size from a few hundred DNA base pairs to more than 2 million of them, and variations in the form of a gene which you possess will influence the instructions it gives. In a gene, the specific sequence of nucleotides will be repeated various numbers of times, known as "repeats." If there are a large number of repeats then we have the "long form" of the gene and if there are a small number of repeats then we have the "short form" of the gene. With many genes, there are multiple forms based on the number of repeats; it is not simply binary. To give an example, a gene called DRD4 7-repeat – a form of a gene with seven repeats – has been shown to be associated with inquisitiveness, intellectual curiosity and impulsivity. It codes for dopamine receptors in the central nervous system, which induce positive feelings. Almost all alleles in East Asian populations are 2- and 4-repeats, while 7-repeats are found in about 20 to 30 per cent of Europeans, Africans, and Polynesians. In some Amazonian tribes, 50 per cent of the tribe carry the very long-form allele. The fewer repeats there are then the less inquisitive, on average, the carrier appears to be, and it has been argued that this may explain why Northeast Asians have relatively few per capita Nobel Prizes for science despite being more intelligent than Northern Europeans.[94] As noted earlier, between 1990 and 2003, the Human Genome Project worked to sequence all the DNA in a

---

[93] J.D. Watson and A. Berry, *DNA: The Secret of Life* (New York: Knopf, 2003).
[94] K. Kura, J. te Nijenhuis and E. Dutton, "Why do Northeast Asians Win So Few Nobel Prizes?" *Comprehensive Psychology,* 4 (2015).

human; known as the human genome. The genome contains 19,900 genes which are used to produce proteins.[95]

It is difficult to over-state how important Watson's discovery of the structure of DNA, as a double helix, has been. If nobody had made that discovery we would not understand how DNA flows to RNA; we wouldn't know how DNA replicates or how genes are transcribed into RNA. In the absence of this knowledge, gene-mapping (identifying where a gene sits on a chromosome) and gene-sequencing would be all but impossible, meaning we would be far less able to identify genes associated with complex traits, such as heart disease or diabetes, or work out which genes are associated with particular conditions. This would make designing medicines to target specific genes extremely difficult, just as it would identifying people who required preventative medicine due to certain genetic dispositions, such as towards certain kinds of cancer. To give an example, I once knew an Australian lady whose grandmother had died of breast cancer and whose mother had nearly died of it. It was found that she carried a specific gene which made it extremely likely that she would develop breast cancer, regardless of any environmental factors. Accordingly, pre-emptive action was taken to address this. In the absence of Watson's discovery this would have been impossible and she may well have died prematurely of breast cancer. In the absence of Watson's discovery, it would also be much more difficult to manufacture recombinant proteins, such as insulin. Genetic Engineering, allowing the creation of modified organisms for medical and agricultural purposes, would be extremely hard, as would the identification of the workings of novel pathogens. We could not compare different genomes and, in terms of crime prevention, we certainly couldn't engage in DNA identification; there could be no DNA Database of the kind that exists in the UK.

In addition, Watson's significance also derives, as one journalist has summarised, from his "remarkable ability to recruit and shape the careers of the next generation of scientists and from his various projects for spreading DNA literacy through outreach, education and publishing." Also "he is credited with having converted an almost bankrupt, dilapidated

---

[95] T. Strachan and A. Read, *Human Molecular Genetics* (Boca Raton, FL: CRC Press, 2019)

laboratory into a 'DNA Town' with a research, teaching and conference center; community outreach programs; a publishing house; and new buildings, including hosting facilities,"[96] as we noted earlier.

What Would Life Be Like Without Watson's Discovery?

In everyday terms, if Watson hadn't made his breakthrough there would be many people you know who would no longer be with us because they had died, prematurely, of heart attacks, cancer and diabetes, to name just three relevant conditions. People with any such significantly genetic disorders would face fatal delays in identification and in treatment, as it would be so much more difficult to produce targeted therapies.

Without such therapies, the singer Elton John (b. 1947) would have died of prostate cancer in about 2017, the comedian and writer Stephen Fry (b. 1957), whom we met earlier, may have died of prostate cancer around 2018, the singer and actress Olivia Newton-John (1948-2022) would likely have died of breast cancer in 1992 rather than 30 years later, journalist and broadcaster Victoria Derbyshire (b. 1968) would have died of breast cancer in about 2015, journalist and broadcaster George Aliagiah (1955-2023) would likely have died of bowel cancer in about 2014, and writer and broadcaster Nigella Lawson (b. 1960) would have died of breast cancer in the late 1990s. Many more people would have committed suicide, suffering from profound depression, or would have trudged through miserable lives, spreading misery in the process, there being a contagious element to depression.[97]

The murder-rate, which has fallen considerably because it is so difficult to get away with murder and due to medical advances allowing lives to more easily be saved,[98] would be considerably higher, reliant on "old fashioned policing" rather than on forensics. DNA technology has been crucial to solving numerous murders and without it these murderers

---

[96] Abir-Am, "Watson's World," *op. cit.*
[97] T.E. Joiner, "Contagious depression: existence, specificity to depressed symptoms, and the role of reassurance seeking," *Journal of Personal and Social Psychology,* 67 (1994): 287–296.
[98] E. Dutton and M.A. Woodley of Menie, *At Our Wits' End: Why We're Becoming Less Intelligent and What It Means for the Future* (Exeter: Imprint Academic, 2018).

would be walking the streets, free to kill again.[99] To give an example, on 23rd April 1968, a 14-year-old schoolboy called Roy Tutill (1954-1968) thumbed a lift, something perfectly normal in those days, in Chessington in Surrey, while making his way home from school in Kingston to his home in Brockham. He wanted to save his bus fare because he was saving up to buy a new bicycle. His body was found three days later in the village of Mickleham. Tutill had been raped and strangled. Despite some clues – he was seen getting into an Austin Westminster Mark II and there was a vague description of the driver – Tutill's murder went unsolved.

In 1996, a partial DNA sample was extracted from Tutill's trousers and kept in a freezer. Then, in September 1999, a gardener called Brian Field (1936-2024) was arrested for drunk driving in Birmingham and his DNA was taken via a saliva swab, as was then routine. In the year 2000, it was found that Field's DNA matched the DNA on Tutill's trousers. He confessed to police the following year and spent the rest of his life in prison. Between 1968 and his arrest for murder, Field had built up a long criminal record for sexually assaulting young boys: In 1969 in Wrexham, in 1972 in Aberdeen, in 1982 in Oswestry, in 1983 in Shrewsbury and in 1986 in Stafford. He served three jail sentences for these offences.[100] There is evidence that he may have committed other child murders in the meantime as well.[101]

Without Watson's breakthrough, the ability to breed animals and crops would be heavily impaired, meaning that food would be far more expensive. Any novel pathogens would spread rapidly, killing millions of people because their genetic dynamics could not be identified and a target medicine could, therefore, not be produced. But, most obviously, unable to sequence the human genome, our ability to combat disease would be

---

[99] See, S. Wade, *DNA Crime Investigations: Solving Murder and Serious Crime Through DNA and Modern Forensics* (Barnsley: Pen and Sword, 2009).
[100] *Evening Standard,* "Paedophile gets life for 1968 killing" (12th April 2012), https://www.standard.co.uk/hp/front/paedophile-gets-life-for-1968-killing-6335710.htmlm- See also: B. Graham and B. Taylor, "Science reaches into the past and brings justice for boy who never came home," *Mail Online* (16th November 2001), https://www.dailymail.co.uk/news/article-84553/Science-reaches-past-brings-justice-boy-came-home.html
[101] S. Madden, "Schoolboy murderer Brian Field dies in prison," *BBC News* (24th April 2024), https://www.bbc.com/news/articles/c51nxn5yq9go

massively diminished. Put simply, we would be in a far harsher world if Watson hadn't discovered that DNA was shaped like a double helix. All of these important factors were understood by the Nobel Prize Committee in 1962, with Watson and Crick being awarded the Nobel Prize as a consequence.

With it reasonably established that Watson is a genius, the next question we must answer is: "What are the key traits of genius?" We will divide this into two sub-questions; the first relating to intelligence and the second relating to personality.

Chapter Three

What is the Intelligence Profile of the Genius?

How Are Geniuses Different from Normal Scientists?

Analyses of highly successful creative scientists have noted a number of key traits which they all seem to share. These were neatly summarised in the 1963 book *Scientific Creativity* by American psychologists Calvin Taylor (1915-2000) and Frank Barron (1922-2002). The creative scientist is:

> "(1) of superior measured intelligence; (2) exceptionally independent in judgment and resistant to group-endorsed opinions; (3) marked by a strong need for order and for perceptual closure, combined with a resistance to premature closure and an interest in what may appear as disorder, contradiction, imbalance, or very complex balance whose ordering principle is not immediately apparent; (4) unusually appreciative of the intuitive and non-rational elements in their own nature; (5) distinguished by their profound commitment to the search for aesthetic and philosophic meaning in all experience."[102]

This summary implies sensation-seeking, extremely high openness, autism and aspects of psychopathy, terms we will define below. It can, perhaps, be simply reduced down to three key factors: outlier high intelligence, autism, and psychopathy. Evidence, in fact, indicates that autistic traits in children are associated with later creativity and high

---

[102] C.W. Taylor and F. Barron, *Scientific Creativity: Its Recognition and Development* (New York: Wiley, 1963).

openness.[103] In order to understand these, we must first familiarise ourselves with the research on personality.

What Are the Big 5?

Personality is, in essence, "our general way of being." Differences in personality predict differences in how people will respond in a certain situation. Personality evaluations are usually measured by questionnaires: How close to you does a car moving at a certain speed have to be before you judge that it is too dangerous to cross the road in front of it? How many annoying things have to happen to you in a day before you lose your temper and raise your voice? How strongly do the emotions of others impact how you feel?

Different people will give different answers to these questions, in part because of variation in their personality. Typically, people are asked whether a certain behaviour, or like or dislike, is present or absent in them; or else they are asked to rate its strength. Multiple such questions can be analysed and averaged to yield a few personality "traits" which cluster together. The exact number of these traits used by psychologists depends on the purpose of the personality evaluation. The number can be as few as one general master trait (e.g. pro-social versus anti-social), or dozens of specific traits such as aggression, or courage – but usually, for convenience, the number of traits used for describing personality have been between about two and five.

Many psychologists currently suggest that personality can best be understood in terms of five essential personality characteristics: these are the "Big 5" and can be remembered with the acronym OCEAN.

(1) *Extraversion*: Extraversion is a need for external stimulation – especially social stimulation. It involves feeling positive feelings strongly. Introversion is sufficient internal stimulation and, therefore, independence from external stimuli.

---

[103] R. Smees, L. Rinaldi and J. Simner, "Autism-Linked Traits and Creativity: Empathy and Sensory Sensitivities in Children Predict Creative Activities and Openness," *Creativity Research Journal* (2024): 1-15.

(2) *Neuroticism:* Neuroticism relates to emotional instability – especially negative moods such as anxiety, depression, and shyness.

(3) *Conscientiousness*: Conscientiousness refers to responsiveness to social norms, usually leading to organised, rule-following, and self-disciplined behaviour. In essence, it is impulse control.

(4) *Agreeableness*: Agreeableness shows itself in a high interest in other people, what they are thinking and how they feel. In other words, it is altruism and empathy; detecting and understanding the feelings of others.

(5) *Openness-Intellect*: Openness references intellectual curiosity and a preference for novelty, creativity (in some sense of the word), hypnotisability and unusual psychological experiences. Openness weakly but significantly (0.3) correlates with intelligence, as it is measuring some of the same things.

These five personality traits are (except for Openness-Intellect) regarded as independent of IQ scores (at least within normal IQ ranges); and our placing on them predicts how we behave. For example, high Conscientiousness as a child predicts greater success in education and employment; Agreeableness weakly predicts educational success and, of course, social success; high Neuroticism predicts problems with mood swings, anxiety and depression. High Openness-Intellect will tend to result in being a novelty-loving, impractical, perhaps artistic, academic or spiritual dreamer. A moderately high score, however, is a predictor of artistic success, or at least, it is on some measures of artistic success that focus on the production of novelty. Differences in personality traits are between 50 per cent[104] and 70 per cent genetic,[105] but 50 per cent is widely accepted.

There are consistent sex differences in personality. Females score higher in Conscientiousness, Agreeableness, Neuroticism (especially anxiety), Openness and Extraversion. It is theorised that this makes them better able to raise children and better able to compete in the highly social

---

[104] D. Nettle, *Personality: What Makes You Who You Are* (Oxford: Oxford University Press, 2007).

[105] R. Lynn, *Dysgenics: Genetic Deterioration in Modern Populations* (London: Ulster Institute for Social Research, 2011).

female world that we will explore below.[106] There are also age differences in personality. Conscientiousness and Agreeableness increase with age while Extraversion and Neuroticism decrease, apart from a blip in adolescence where this is reversed,[107] possibly to help transition to independence from one's parents and to be more vigilant to the threats involved in finding the right mate.[108]

What is the General Factor of Personality?

The Big Five were developed from the Big Three traits defined by psychologist Hans Eysenck (1916-1997), who arrived in England from Germany in the 1930s and became the most important personality in British academic psychology. The Big Three are Extraversion, Neuroticism and Psychoticism. In effect, the Big Five dimensions of Conscientiousness and Agreeableness are the opposites of various aspects of Eysenck's Psychoticism; and Openness takes some aspects of Psychoticism and blends them with behaviours characteristic of modern intellectuals.[109]

Many psychologists have shown that the Big Five are all co-correlated, and could all, therefore, be collapsed into a single personality variable, which he called the General Factor of Personality (GFP).[110] GFP can be conceptualised as the single dimension of personality – from pro-social to antisocial – which underlies the more specific personality traits,

---

[106] Y. Weisberg, C. DeYoung and Jacob Hirsch, "Gender Differences in Personality across the Ten Aspects of the Big Five," *Frontiers in Psychology*, 2 (2011): 178.

[107] C. Soto, O. John, S. Gosling and J. Potter, "Age Differences in Personality Traits from 10 to 65: Big Five Domains and Facets in a Large Cross-Sectional Sample," *Journal of Personality and Social Psychology*, 100 (2010): 330-348.

[108] On the development of adolescent personality, see: W. Meeus, R. Van de Schoot, L. Keijsers et al., "On the progression and stability of adolescent identity formation: A five-wave longitudinal study in early-to-middle and middle-to-late adolescence," *Child Development*, 81 (2010): 1565-1581.

[109] H. Eysenck, "Creativity and personality: Suggestions for a theory," *Psychological Inquiry*, 4 (1993): 147-178.

[110] J.P. Rushton and P. Irwing, "A General Factor of Personality from two meta-analyses of the Big Five," *Personality and Individual Differences*, 45 (2008): 679-683; D. van der Linden, C. Dunkel and K. Petrides, "The General Factor of Personality (GFP) as Social Effectiveness: A Literature Review," *Personality and Individual Differences*, 101 (2016): 98-105.

analogously to how general intelligence or "*g*" underlies all the specific cognitive abilities, as we will see below. So, the General Factor of Personality can be conceptualised as the degree to which a personality is pro-social; in other words, the degree to which someone has the kind of personality type and behaviours that underpin many socially desirable traits, the degree to which someone approximates to the type of person that makes for friendliness, helpfulness, being a "good neighbour." The GFP describes a basic personality dimension, high levels of which may have evolved as an adaptation in complex and stable societies so that people would "get along well together." A person with high GFP would be sociable, extraverted, concerned with the feelings of others, and self-disciplined in pursuit of socially-approved goals. He'd also have stable emotions, and be open to new ideas.[111] GFP predicts higher salary, attaining a leadership position and working in a relatively sociable job.[112] This would contrast sharply with a person who has autism.

What is Autism?

What, then, is autism? There are fundamental average differences between the male and female brain. The extreme male brain is strongly focused on systematizing but it is empathy blind; in other words, it is autistic; it is high in systematizing but low in empathy, meaning it is hyper-focused on solving problems. The extreme female brain is the opposite; it is very high in empathy but it is system-blind.[113] In this sense, the autistic is low in cognitive empathy, which is an aspect of Agreeableness.

It should be noted that there is slightly more to autism that high systematizing and low empathy, traits which manifest as a strong desire for order, a dislike of change, a focus on objects over people, obsessiveness, a tendency to be blunt and socially clumsy and a tendency not to understand social rules. Autism also involves heightened sensory

---

[111] Rushton and Irwing, "A General Factor of Personality from two meta-analyses of the Big Five," *op. cit.*

[112] D. van der Linden, C. Dunkel and E. Dutton, "The General Factor of Personality (GFP) is Associated with Higher Salary, Having a Leadership Position, and Working in a Social Job," *Acta Psychologica,* 234 (2023): 103847.

[113] S. Baron-Cohen, "The extreme male brain theory of autism," *Trends in Cognitive Sciences,* 6 (2002): 248-254.

awareness, such that sufferers can easily become overwhelmed by environmental stimuli, and extreme emotions, possibly due to feelings one's own bodily sensations to such an extreme degree. Consequently, autistics tend to suffer from anxiety, an aspect of Neuroticism, which may be allayed by obsessiveness and order; a desire for order also being a component of Conscientiousness. In addition, as they are highly sensitive to stimuli, they will experience the world as uncontrollable and swirling chaos, which will induce anxiety.

They will also tend to cope very badly with change; it will make them anxious and depressed as they have a strong desire for order. Lacking social skills, they are also likely to experience childhood adversity, such as bullying. In other words, the world will tell them they are "bad" at a formative age, meaning that they may fail to develop an innate sense of self-worth. The result may be a collapse into depression later in life. Also, negative feelings may be so overwhelming that a negative spiral may commence.[114] The consequence of this may be the development of Narcissistic traits as a coping mechanism; you deal with your intense negative feelings by telling yourself that you are special. This might explain why creative people appear to have a high sense of self-worth and even a sense that they are on a unique mission.[115] There is evidence that people with autistic traits are elevated in aspects of psychopathy, such as callousness.[116] In addition, autism is associated with Borderline Personality Disorder (BPD).[117] This disorder can involve periods of Narcissism and periods of despair and can be comorbid with Narcissistic Personality Disorder.[118] It should be emphasised that Narcissistic or

---

[114] L. Hull, L. Levy, M.-C. Lai et al., "Is social camouflaging associated with anxiety and depression in autistic adults?" *Molecular Autism,* 12 (2021).

[115] See, Aslinger et al., "The Influence of Narcissistic Vulnerability and Grandiosity on Momentary Hostility Leading up to and Following Interpersonal Rejection," *op. cit.*

[116] K. Maguire, H. Warman, F. Blumenfeld and P. Langdon, "The relationship between psychopathy and autism: a systematic review and narrative synthesis," *Frontiers in Psychiatry* (2024).

[117] G. Richards, S. Kelly, D. Johnson and J. Galvin, "Autistic traits and borderline personality disorder traits are positively correlated in UK and US adult men and women," *Personality and Individual Differences,* 213 (2023): 12287.

[118] S. Hörz-Sagstetter, D. Diamond, J. Clarkin et al., "Clinical Characteristics of Comorbid Narcissistic Personality Disorder in Patients With Borderline Personality Disorder," *Journal of Personality Disorders,* 32 (2017): 1-17.

Borderline Personality *Disorder* can be expected to be destructive to all aspects of life. However sub-clinical expressions of the same traits, or clinical expressions of only some of the traits where others are subclinical or absent, especially when balanced with high intelligence, may result in high socioeconomic success.

Borderline Personality Disorder is characterised by highly unstable and extreme moods, poor emotional regulation, a fundamental fear of abandonment and of being alone, extreme feelings of shame, intense and unstable relationships (including sexual risk-taking, perhaps due to a feeling that "love" may not come again) and unstable goals, due to being plagued by acute negative feelings (such as shame, anxiety, self-loathing and self-doubt), and a weak sense of self; an oscillation between extremes. Sufferers have a weak sense of self in the sense that our personalities sit within various ranges on scales, such as high to low psychopathy. Most people operate within relatively narrow ranges, depending on environmental factors, on these scales. A person with a weak sense of self will, especially under stress, dramatically swing to the extremes of these scales, meaning that they will seem like they are different people at different points; histrionic at one point, entirely avoidant a few days later.[119] About 20 per cent of sufferers also have bipolar depression, where they swing from mania to profound depression. Those who have both conditions have even more extreme BPD symptoms.[120]

In that they cannot regulate their emotions, sufferers cannot regulate their self-esteem; so it may swing between grandiose Narcissism and feelings of abject worthlessness. For the same reason, their identity and goals can radically change in accordance with these swings in self-esteem. When they are Narcissistic, they may decide to leave the boyfriend, upon whom they are parasitic and who they don't really love, for their high status lover. When they are feeling worthless and insecure, such a risk may seem intolerable, so they will continue with the original relationship which they may have only embarked on due to being lonely.

---

[119] See, Dutton and Rayner-Hilles, *Woke Eugenics, op. cit.*
[120] M. Zimmerman and T. Morgan, "The relationship between borderline personality disorder and bipolar disorder," *Dialogues in Clinical Neuroscience*, 15 (2013):79–93.

They will tend to idealise their partner; perceiving him as a special person who can rescue them from their torment. They do this to supress fears about rejection and it also reflects their extreme emotions. However, they will also engage in "splitting," where they will rapidly move from idealising to devaluing their partner. This may happen because they will have a very strong reaction to something negative that the partner does. This punctures the fantasy, so they cope with their conflicted feelings, and take power and control over the situation, by telling themselves that the partner is actually evil; he has wilfully caused these negative feelings. They may even wrongly infer that the partner will abandon them, leading to intense negative feelings, the view that the partner is wicked and the belief that they are under threat. This cathartic outlet of negativity can make them feel better and they will gradually return to idealisation.

Fearing abandonment, they may cause their partners to abandon them via their paranoid and aggressive reaction to minor indications of this possibility or they may pre-emptively abandon their partners, thus maintaining a sense of control. They will oscillate between abandonment-anxiety and intimacy-anxiety as, for them, intimacy is associated with abandonment and even abuse, as BPD may be a reaction to inconsistent parenting, subject to their parents' moods. Inconsistent parenting may lead to fear of abandonment and intense negative feelings, but also intense positive feelings, especially if the child is of an extravert temperament, because happy events provide euphoric relief from a dangerous world, because positive events feel so much stronger by comparison, because a deep need for affection is met and because they have a more reactive emotional system. In a sense, BPD can be understood to be a kind of specific adaptation to an unstable ecology, where you must react to unpredictable threats aggressively and where, due to the unpredictability, you may as well take risks, resulting in feeling positive feelings strongly such that you are rewarded with dopamine when risks pay off.[121] Under stress, they may dissociate and degenerate into psychosis; paranoid about all around them as a survival mechanism. They also feel some forms of

---

[121] This is a fast Life History Strategy, a concept which we will explore in more detail below.

disgust very strongly, especially disgust with themselves,[122] but others only very weakly.[123] It has been averred that this reflects abnormal sensory processing.[124] This may also be a matter of emotional dysregulation; in which there are only extremes and no middle ground in terms of disgust, something often found with children's tastes.

Due to their extreme emotions, which would reflect Neuroticism and even aspects of Extraversion, autistics, like those with BPD, tend to have an unstable sense of self; oscillating between extremes of personality traits whereas a normal person will have a narrower and more predictable emotional range meaning that "self" will appear more stable across time.[125] Due to bullying, autistics may be more likely to develop BPD. There is also some evidence that autistics experience passionate love more strongly, at least when the autism is comorbid with Attention Deficit Hyperactivity Disorder (ADHD), which we will discuss below.[126] We can see how autism might make people intellectually curious, as they will want to comprehend the true nature of the world, or, at least, find some kind of satisfying structure for it. We will see below that Neuroticism and Extraversion may themselves potentiate creativity.

In that autism reflects a stereotypical male brain, it is also associated with elevated testosterone and, consequently, with hyper-sexuality: autistics will have a stronger sex drive than controls and will more easily make sexual associations. Consequently, they are more likely than are

---

[122] A. Schienle, A. Haas-Krammer, H. Schöggl et al., "Altered state and trait disgust in borderline personality disorder," *Journal of Nervous and Mental Disease,* 201 (2013): 105-108.

[123] E. Kot, B. Kostecka, J. Radoszewska and K. Kucarska, "Self-disgust in patients with borderline personality disorder. The associations with alexithymia, emotion dysregulation, and comorbid psychopathology," *Borderline Personality Disorder and Emotional Dysregulation,* 10 (2023): 24.

[124] G. Arrondo, G. Murray, E. Hill et al., "Hedonic and disgust taste perception in borderline personality disorder and depression," *British Journal of Psychiatry,* 207 (2015): 79-80.

[125] S. Pires, P. Felgueiras, S. Borges and J. Jorge, "Autism Spectrum Disorder in Females and Borderline Personality Disorder: The Diagnostic Challenge," *Cureus,* 15 (2023): e40279.

[126] L. Soares, A. Alves, D. Costa et al., "Common Venues in Romantic Relationships of Adults With Symptoms of Autism and Attention Deficit/Hyperactivity Disorder," *Frontiers in Psychiatry,* 12 (2021): 593150.

controls to develop sexual fetishes or "paraphilias."[127] In addition, anxiety – which is associated with autism – potentiates sexual arousal in men which could lead to the development of unusual sexual associations, possibly independent of autism.[128] There is also a curvilinear relationship between anxiety and sexual arousal in women. This may be because a specific kind of anxiety – "state anxiety," involving feelings of apprehension - is associated with elevations in the sympathetic nervous system, which itself leads to sexual arousal.[129] For this reason, autogynephilous transsexuality – where a male is sexually aroused by the idea that he is a woman and is obsessed with this idea, such that he takes action to appear as though he is a woman – is associated with autism. Those who suffer from gender dysphoria are six times more likely than controls to be autistic.[130]

Similarly, there is a robust association between autism and sado-masochism,[131] presumably due to its object-focused and scripted nature, and the high testosterone power-play, and sense of control or certainty, involved. It is, thus, worth noting evidence of atypical sexuality among geniuses. According to German psychiatrist Felix Post's (1931-2001) study of 291 great men, 73 per cent of scientists had "normal" sexuality dropping to just 36 per cent among writers. Indeed, scientists were "abnormal" in terms of their low levels of sexual promiscuity, even by early twentieth century standards. Post found that 82 per cent of scientists had stable marriages, this being just 36 per cent among writers.[132]

---

[127] D. Schöttle, "Sexuality in autism: hypersexual and paraphilic behavior in women and men with high-functioning autism spectrum disorder," *Dialogues in Clinical Neuroscience,* 19 (2017): 381-383.

[128] M. Fox, M. Seto, N. Rafaie et al., "The Relation Between the Paraphilias and Anxiety in Men: A Case-Control Study," *Archives of Sexual Behavior,* 51 (2022): 4063-4084.

[129] A. Bradford and C. Meston, "The impact of anxiety on sexual arousal in women," *Behavioral Research Therapy,* 44 (2006): 1067-1077.

[130] V. Warrier, D. Greenberg, E. Weir et al., "Elevated rates of autism, other neurodevelopmental and psychiatric diagnoses, and autistic traits in transgender and gender-diverse individuals," *Nature Communications,* 11 (2020): 3959.

[131] J. Muller, "Are sadomasochism and hypersexuality in autism linked to amygdalohippocampal lesion?" *Journal of Sexual Medicine,* 8 (2011): 3241-3249.

[132] Post, "Creativity and psychopathology," *op. cit.*

What is Attention Deficit Hyper-Activity Disorder?

Sometimes the obsessiveness dimension of autism may reflect something even more specific. Geniuses are often hyper-focused on their problem, refusing to care about anything else, even about eating in the case of Archimedes (c. 287-c. 2012 BC), who would be so engrossed in solving his problems that he would forget to do so.[133] This hyper-focus is characteristic of ADHD and researchers have suggested that those who suffer from this condition may sometimes be more creative as a consequence.[134] There is an extent to which autism and ADHD tend to co-occur.[135] ADHD involves, in addition to periods of hyper-focus, trouble paying attention, impulsive behaviour and the need to constantly be active and to be doing something. Sufferers, at least of the sub-clinical form, are often good at pattern-spotting and at divergent thinking; meaning that they come up with novel solutions to problems. Even those with the clinical form display elevated creativity. They are more emotionally dysregulated, have reduced impulse control, require constant stimulation, and are easily distracted. This allows them to switch between different zones of thought and, accordingly, to make original connections.[136] We can easily see how this is congruous with the genius traits of sensation-seeking, relatively low impulse control, making original connections, and even obsessiveness, insomuch as that which is not intrinsically utterly captivating is simply boring. Alternatively, it has been argued that anxiety leads to obsessiveness, to the desire to structure a disordered world, and that anxiety also causes executive dysfunction and inattentiveness.[137] ADHD

---

[133] M. Fitzgerald and B. O'Brien, *Genius Genes: How Asperger's Talents Changed the World* (Shawnee Mission, KN: Autism Asperger Publishing Company, 2007), 26

[134] N. Boot, B. Nevicka and M. Baas, "Creativity in ADHD: Goal-Directed Motivation and Domain Specificity," *Journal of Attention Disorders,* 24 (2020): 1857-1866.

[135] Y. Leitner, "The Co-Occurrence of Autism and Attention Deficit Hyperactivity Disorder in Children – What Do We Know?" *Frontiers in Human Neuroscience,* 8 (2014): 268.

[136] M. Hoogman, M. Stolte, M. Baas and E. Kroesbergen, "Creativity and ADHD: A review of behavioral studies, the effect of psychostimulants and neural underpinnings," *Neuroscience and Biobehavioral Reviews,* 119 (2020): 66-85.

[137] A. Guzick, J. McNamara, A. Reid et al., "The link between ADHD-like inattention and obsessions and compulsions during treatment of youth with OCD," *Journal of Obsessive-Compulsive and Related Disorders,* 12 (2017): 1-8.

traits may even explain, as we will see below, why geniuses often do not perform amazingly at school or at university. They only begin to shine once they have found the subject that truly fascinates them.

The use of androgenic steroids has been shown to cause ADHD symptoms, implying that ADHD, like autism, is partly a reflection of androgens.[138] Similarly, females with elevated testosterone levels are more likely to have ADHD.[139] Moreover, ADHD appears to be part of a more general antisocial cluster. It has been found that people diagnosed with ADHD are 50 per cent more likely to have Dark Triad traits (see below) than are neurotypical people.[140] Consistent with this, there is also a strong overlap between Borderline Personality, Narcissistic Personality and ADHD.[141]

Making Sense of the Dark Triad

The second key component to genius appears to be psychopathy. This involves, among other traits, a high sense of self-worth, a constant need for stimulation, poor behavioural control, lack of emotional empathy, impulsivity, cheating and lack of remorse. In essence, it combines aspects of low Agreeableness, low Conscientiousness and high Neuroticism. It is part of the so-called "Dark Triad" which also includes Machiavellianism (being power-hungry) and Narcissism, the three of which inter-correlate. Dark Triad traits are associated with adultery, exploitation and sexual risk-taking.[142] It could be argued that if you are high in this triad, and especially psychopathy, then you are low in trust, which will make you intellectually

---

[138] E. Kildal, B. Hassel and A. Bjørnebekk, "ADHD symptoms and use of anabolic androgenic steroids among male weightlifters," *Scientific Reports,* 12 (2022): 9479.

[139] S. Herguner, H. Harmanci and H. Toy, "Attention deficit-hyperactivity disorder symptoms in women with polycystic ovary syndrome," *International Journal of Psychiatry of Medicine,* 50 (2015): 3.

[140] L. Cumyn, L. French and L. Hechtman, "Comorbidity in adults with attention-deficit hyperactivity disorder," *Canadian Journal of Psychiatry,* 54 (2009): 673-683.

[141] M. Ferrer, O. Andion, J. Matali et al., "Comorbid attention-deficit/hyperactivity disorder in borderline patients defines an impulsive subtype of borderline personality disorder," *Journal of Personality Disorders,* 24 (2010): 812-822.

[142] M. Apostolou, "The association of Dark Triad personality traits with infidelity: Evidence from the Greek-cultural context," *Culture and Evolution,* 20 (2024): 137-143.

curious. Machiavellianism is a personality disorder centrally characterised by strongly desiring power; in other words, by being extremely ambitious and manipulative to that end. Such people are also cunning, ruthlessly pragmatic, exploitative and low in altruism. One of the key predictors of Machiavellianism is Neuroticism.[143] If you experience the world as a frightening place, you may wish to take control of it and, accordingly, you will need to comprehend it.

Narcissism is characterised by entitlement, arrogance, exploitation and a desire for praise. There are two kinds of Narcissism. Grandiose Narcissism is associated with low Agreeableness and with selfishness. It is also associated with Extraversion; Grandiose Narcissists will gain Narcissistic supply through social activity. Where it is a disorder, meaning it is highly pronounced, it is also associated with Neuroticism.[144] Grandiose Narcissists are entitled, have aspects of high self-esteem, see themselves as unique and special, are overconfident and delusional, and they are willing to exploit people. To challenge a person with Narcissistic Personality Disorder, and his conception of himself as perfect and even as morally superior, is to assert power over him, and he feels all-powerful. Also, it is to puncture his fantasy. His fantasy is vital because, to the extent his condition is environmentally caused, it has often developed as a means of dealing with trauma and other emotional problems, reflective of Neuroticism.[145] Thus, such a challenge, if it is sufficiently severe, will injure and infuriate him, potentially resulting in a hostile reaction,[146] and even in "Narcissistic Rage,"[147] such that his self-esteem maintaining

---

[143] S. Jacobwitz and V. Egan, "The Dark Triad and Normal Personality Traits," *Personality and Individual Differences,* 40 (2006): 331-339.

[144] E. Aslinger, S. Lane, D. Lynam and T. Trull, "The Influence of Narcissistic Vulnerability and Grandiosity on Momentary Hostility Leading up to and Following Interpersonal Rejection," *Personality Disorders,* 13 (2022): 199-209.

[145] C. Montoro, P. de la Coba, M. Moreno-Padilla and C. Galvez-Sanchez, "Narcissistic Personality and Its Relationship with Post-Traumatic Symptoms and Emotional Factors: Results of a Mediational Analysis Aimed at Personalizing Mental Health Treatment," *Behavioral Sciences,* 12 (2022): 91.

[146] C. O'Reilly and N. Hall, "Grandiose narcissists and decision making: Impulsive, overconfident, and skeptical of experts–but seldom in doubt," *Personality and Individual Differences,* 168 (2021): 110280.

[147] On Narcissistic Rage see, Z. Krizan and O. Johar, "Narcissistic Rage Revisited," *Journal of Personality and Social Psychology,* 108 (2015): 784–801.

fantasy can continue. If he is an extremely pronounced Narcissist, and the challenge is sufficiently triggering, he might break-down, as such people have been found to oscillate between grandiosity and vulnerability in a way that is not true of subclinical Narcissists.[148] People with high self-esteem have the confidence associated with Grandiose Narcissism but lack the grandiosity, entitlement and demeaning attitude towards others.[149] Narcissism is partly heritable: Grandiosity is about 23 per cent heritable while entitlement is roughly 35 per cent heritable.[150]

Vulnerable or covert Narcissism, like Grandiose Narcissism, involves an inflated sense of self-importance, but it is markedly different. It is a coping mechanism for negative feelings – they live in a fantasy of superiority - but, unlike Grandiose Narcissists, such people are introverts and are avoidant, they require constant reassurance from others and will fish for compliments, they are overtly insecure and they are extremely sensitive to rejection, meaning they will crumble at the slightest perceived insult and become vengeful, rather than aggressive. They are also highly self-conscious.[151] They are low in Agreeableness and high in Neuroticism.[152] Such people will often adopt a parasitic lifestyle in which they subtly manipulate others into believing that they (the covert Narcissist) are uniquely vulnerable but also special; a misunderstood victim in need of care. They seem, and to some extent are, anxious and hyper-sensitive but, deep down, they feel superior and crave Narcissistic

---

[148] E. Jauk, E. Weigle, K. Lehmann et al., "The Relationship between Grandiose and Vulnerable (Hypersensitive) Narcissism," *Frontiers in Psychology,* 8 (2017): 1600.

[149] C. Hyatt. C. Sleep, J. Lamkin et al., "Narcissism and self-esteem: A nomological network analysis," *PLoS One*, 13 (2018): e0201088.

[150] J. Luo, H. Cai and H. Song, "A Behavioral Genetic Study of Intrapersonal and Interpersonal Dimensions of Narcissism," *PLoS One,* 9 (2014): 93403.

[151] E. Jauk, E. Weigle, K. Lehmann et al., "The Relationship between Grandiose and Vulnerable (Hypersensitive) Narcissism," *Frontiers in Psychology,* 8 (2017): 1600.

[152] Aslinger et al., "The Influence of Narcissistic Vulnerability and Grandiosity on Momentary Hostility Leading up to and Following Interpersonal Rejection," *op. cit.*

supply.[153] Signalling that you are a virtuous victim, a common left-wing tactic, is associated with Narcissism of this kind.[154]

The Grandiose Narcissist reacts aggressively to a threat to his ego. He is low in Agreeableness and high in Extraversion. Thus, he reacts very strongly to the "positive feeling" of being worshipped and, low in emotional empathy, he must destroy competitors who challenge him. He believes he is special and worthy of worship. The extreme Grandiose Narcissist seems to mix Extraversion and Neuroticism, as implied by the emotional oscillation we discussed earlier. The vulnerable Narcissist, who is more likely to be female, reacts to fear of abandonment. She is Neurotic and low in Agreeableness.[155] If someone induces negative feelings in her then, feeling that she is superior (a sense she has cultivated in part to cope with negative feelings), she must take vengeance on them and, being Neurotic, she will be paranoid and, so, highly sensitive to perceived insults. In that sense, she oscillates between superiority and inferiority. Perhaps we can say that where a Grandiose Narcissist craves large-scale power and glory and really feels superior most of the time, the covert Narcissist craves control and to be looked after and more frequently doubts the sense of superiority.

What is Intelligence?

With our personality terms examined, we must now be clear on the nature of intelligence. Intelligence is defined as the ability to solve cognitive problems combined with how quickly you can solve them. The quicker you can solve a problem and the harder it has to be before you are stumped, then the more intelligent you are. Intelligence can be conceived of as rather like a pyramid. At the base of the pyramid there are numerous "specialised abilities" that are only very weakly associated with intelligence, such as

---

[153] E. Bell, C. Kowalski, P. Vernon and J. Schermer, "Political Hearts of Darkness: The Dark Triad as Predictors of Political Orientations and Interest in Politics," *Behavioral Sciences,* 11 (2021): 169.

[154] E. Ok, Y. Qian, B. Strejcek and K. Aquino, "Signaling virtuous victimhood as indicators of Dark Triad personalities," *Journal of Personality and Social Psychology,* 120 (2021): 1634-1661.

[155] Aslinger et al., "The Influence of Narcissistic Vulnerability and Grandiosity on Momentary Hostility Leading up to and Following Interpersonal Rejection," *op. cit.*

the ability to tie your shoe laces or catch a ball. Moving up the pyramid, there are the three main forms of intelligence, which are more strongly associated with how smart you are: mathematical, verbal and spatial intelligence. People vary on how highly they score on tests of these. Some people are more verbally-tilted, such as people who study Humanities subjects, while others are more mathematically-tilted, such as those who study the sciences. But, in general, those who score high on one score high on all, so we can conceive of a factor which underpins all of them. This is "general intelligence," known as *g,* which is at the pinnacle of the intelligence pyramid. In general, when we speak of someone as being "intelligent" we mean that they have high "general intelligence."[156]

One very occasionally meets people who have high verbal intelligence but are not especially high in "general intelligence": think of the stereotypical postmodern social scientist, or even a "Woke" hard scientist, and the pseudo-profound but vacuous and illogical work that they produce. Sometimes, you'll meet the opposite: the tongue-tied physicist who is fantastic at Maths. But, in general, people who are high in one kind of intelligence are high in the others. Some people argue that there are "multiple intelligences," including "emotional intelligence,"[157] but this weakly correlates with "intelligence" as normally defined.[158]

Intelligence is important in, and is prized in, all cultures, with negative correlates of intelligence, such as criminality, being disliked in all cultures.[159] Intelligence is associated, often strongly, with numerous salient issues: socioeconomic status born into, socioeconomic status achieved, educational attainment, criminality (negatively), income, mental and physical health, longevity, emotional sensitivity, memory, social skill, moral reasoning and much else.[160] People with low intelligence, which is strongly genetic as we will see below, will severely struggle in life. It was

---

[156] For a far more detailed exploration see: Jensen, *The g Factor, op. cit.*

[157] H. Gardner, *Frames of Mind: The Theory of Multiple Intelligences* (New York: Basic Books, 1983).

[158] S. Kaufman, C. DeYoung, D. Reiss and J. Gray, "General intelligence predicts reasoning ability for evolutionarily familiar content," *Intelligence,* 39 (2011): 311-322.

[159] Jensen, *The g Factor, op. cit.*

[160] Jensen, *The g Factor, op. cit.*

with this humanitarian consideration in mind that Watson remarked in a 2003 Channel 4 documentary: ""If you are really stupid, I would call that a disease. The lower 10 per cent who really have difficulty, even in elementary school, what's the cause of it? A lot of people would like to say, 'Well, poverty, things like that.' It probably isn't. So I'd like to get rid of that, to help the lower 10 per cent."[161] He was suggesting the development of some kind of gene therapy to combat low intelligence. He'd made such remarks to the Cambridge Union Society in 1996.[162]

What is IQ?

Your IQ ("Intelligence Quotient") is how well you score in IQ tests compared to others of your age. The ability to solve cognitive problems increases up to middle age, meaning that intelligence can be ascertained by comparing people to those of their own age. These scores are "normally distributed" on a bell curve. Most people have an IQ of around 100, the average, and smaller and smaller percentages have higher or lower IQs. The "normal range" is between 70 and 130. Those with an IQ score of below 70 (2.5 per cent of the UK population) are mentally retarded. The 2.5 per cent with an IQ score above 130 are extremely bright. A score of 100, the average, would be the expected score for a policeman, fireman or typical office worker, 85 might be a security guard or someone who works in a supermarket stacking shelves, while 80 would be the long-term unemployed or casual labourers. At the other end, a high school science teacher might have an IQ of 115, a lawyer or doctor of about 120 and a university science professor of around 130.[163]

The scores achieved on IQ tests are strongly associated with other measures of cognitive ability, such as academic attainment, as well as with concrete measures such as your reaction times – the quicker you react to stimuli, the quicker you solve problems[164] – and brain size; the brain being

---

[161] S. Bhattacharya, "Stupidity should be cured, says DNA discoverer," *New Scientist* (28th February 2003).
[162] *Wolverhampton Express and Star,* "Don't be Stupid!" (20th February 1996).
[163] R. Herrnstein and C. Murray, *The Bell Curve: Intelligence and Class Structure in American Life* (New York: Free Press, 1994).
[164] This implies that a significant component of intelligence is a high functioning nervous system.

a thinking muscle. Modern IQ tests are "culture fair" because groups that score poorly in them, such as African-Americans, score the most poorly on the most "culture fair" components of the test, which are actually the best measures of intelligence. In addition, groups that are far more divorced from American cultural norms than blacks, such as Native Americans on reservations, outscore, for example, blacks in the Southern States.[165] In addition, these tests can hardly be said to reflect "white culture" as Northeast Asians outscore whites to a significant degree. Furthermore, the notion of "stereotype threat" – that groups stereotyped to do poorly on IQ tests perform badly on them due to the stress of the stereotype that their group does badly – has been comprehensively refuted. Some groups primed with the idea that they will do badly do better than expected, and there is clear publication bias, with university theses that don't substantiate the thesis not being published.[166] It is important to note that race differences in IQ are paralleled by race differences in reaction times and in cranial capacity and that these are in the expected direction, only further underscoring the fairness of these IQ tests. In addition, Northeast Asians are found to be mathematically tilted while blacks are found to be verbally tilted.[167] If the tests were flawed, why would they pick up on this subtle difference which everyday experience tells us is clearly true?

Intelligence is strongly genetic. It has been estimated that it is about 0.8 heritable in adulthood based on identical twin studies and twin adoption studies. This means that about 80 per cent of differences in intelligence between adults are a matter of genetics. The heritability of intelligence in childhood is low, around 0.2, because the child is not creating his own environment. This is being created by the parents and other adults and it reflects their IQ, which may be higher or lower than their child's. Only when he becomes an adult does he start creating an

---

[165] Jensen, *The g Factor, op. cit.*
[166] E. Dutton and M.A. Woodley of Menie, *At Our Wits' End: Why We're Becoming Less Intelligent and What It Means for the Future* (Exeter: Imprint Academic, 2018); C. Ganley, L. Mingle, A. Ryan et al., "An examination of stereotype threat effects on girls' mathematics performance," *Developmental Psychology*, 49 (2013): 1886-1897.
[167] R. Lynn, *Race Differences in Intelligence: An Evolutionary Analysis* (Augusta, GA: Washington Summit, 2006).

environment consistent with his own innate IQ, resulting in a heritability of 0.8.[168] The key environmental component to intelligence is a cognitively stimulating environment. This will push your intelligence to its phenotypic maximum. However, the more intelligent you are, the more interested you will be in analytic issues and the more intelligent will be your friends, family and colleagues. Consequently, the more intelligent you are, the more likely you will be to push yourself to this maximum.[169]

Sheldon Cooper: Diminishing Returns

People may be highly critical of the television series *The Big Bang Theory,* which is about four scientists at Cal Tech who are friends and colleagues and their relationship with the socially intelligent, though not especially academically intelligent, waitress and actress Penny. But the one thing it portrayed well - until it tried to become the replacement for *Friends,* focusing on "relationships" and giving everybody girlfriends – was the genius-type. Socially-awkward, blunt, eccentric and extraordinarily intelligent, Sheldon Cooper is that type.

Consistent with being that type, he struggles with things that people of about average intelligence, such as Penny, have no trouble with at all. He is physically inept, he cannot drive or is, at least, very bad at driving a car such that he relies on his friend Leonard to ferry him to and from work, and he has poor social skills. He can be surprisingly stupid for such a highly intelligent person. The nature of genius intelligence is unusual, partly because it is extremely high based on estimates of the IQs of recognised scientific geniuses. In general, they are estimated to be in the top 0.5 per cent of the population.[170] It has been shown that as people become more intelligent – as IQ goes up – the relationship between the different cognitive abilities becomes weaker. This is termed *Spearman's Law of Diminishing Returns*, after English psychologist Charles Spearman (1863-1945) who first described this effect in 1927.[171] In other words, as

---

[168] R. Plomin and I. Deary, "Genetics and intelligence differences: five special findings," *Molecular Psychiatry,* 20 (2015): 98-108.

[169] See, J.R. Flynn, *Does Your Family Make You Smarter: Nature, Nurture and Human Autonomy* (Cambridge: Cambridge University Press, 2015).

[170] D.K. Simonton, *Genius, Creativity and Leadership, op. cit.*

[171] C. Spearman, *Abilities of Man: Their Nature and Measurement* (London:

people become more intelligent, they become more specialized in the nature of their intelligence. So, a person who is of roughly average intelligence will be "okay" in terms of their linguistic, spatial and mathematical scores but they will be relatively equally okay in each one. By contrast, somebody who has much higher intelligence may be better on all of these measures, but they won't be equally better.

They are likely, for example, to have much higher mathematical scores, with their linguistic scores being only moderately higher. But the mathematical scores are so much higher that, overall, the Physics student, or whatever he may be, will have a much higher average IQ.[172] Spearman's Law of Diminishing Returns does not refute the concept of *g* – this being present in the ability scores of even those with the highest-levels of intelligence. The *g* factor is however somewhat *weaker* among such individuals; as specialized abilities become more specialized and autonomous, playing a bigger role in influencing cognitive performance.

Geniuses, who have extraordinarily high IQs, will therefore tend to have an even weaker relationship between their different cognitive abilities. What this means, in practice, is that though they are super-intelligent overall, they may actually be below average when it comes to certain tasks that are towards the base of the "intelligence pyramid" and, so, only weakly correlate with *g*. This, along with their moderately high psychopathy and autism, would help to explain their often less than outstanding academic performance at university and, indeed, their stereotypical "nutty professor" behaviour patterns. Einstein supposedly once got lost close to his home in Princeton, New Jersey. He walked into a shop and said, "Hi, I'm Einstein, can you take me home please?" He couldn't drive a car, and many other tasks that most people take for granted were simply too difficult for him.[173] This is, probably, the best example of somebody of extraordinary intelligence being, really, quite stupid, albeit in a specialized sort of way.

Macmillan, 1927).
[172] M.A. Woodley, "The social and scientific temporal correlates of genotypic intelligence and the Flynn Effect," *Intelligence,* 40 (2012): 189-204.
[173] B. Hoffmann, *Albert Einstein: Creator and Rebel* (London: Hart-Davis, 1972).

Needing a Manager

Bruce Charlton and I have highlighted many other examples of this in *The Genius Famine,* in which we explored the decline of genius and possible reasons for the decline. Like Sheldon, the genius will often be deficient in terms of social skills, meaning that he has few friends and never gets married. Often, geniuses – whether scientific or ground-breaking in the arts - are incapable of the basics of everyday life; they cannot look after themselves. As Dutton and Charlton observe, the American reclusive poet Emily Dickinson (1830-1886) was "managed" by Colonel T.W. Higginson; Jane Austen (1775-1817) flourished in the obscurity of her family and the critic and social philosopher John Ruskin (1819-1900) was sheltered and nurtured by his parents, then a cousin. Thomas Aquinas (1225-1274) was looked after by his brother Friars; Genetics-founder Johann Mendel (1822-1884) was secluded in a monastery; Pascal (1623-1662) was looked after by his aristocratic French family.

Also, many geniuses were sustained by a capable wife – Kurt Gödel (1906-1978) depended on his, older, wife Adele; and would only eat food prepared by her; so that when she was hospitalized, Gödel literally starved. When there is a close-knit and idealistic community, this may also help – for example, the community of mathematicians looked after Hungarian Paul Erdos (1913-1996), who never had a home, possessed only the contents of a small suitcase, and camped-out in the house of one mathematics professor after another for decades, while collaborating on research papers. The Indian genius mathematician Srinivasa Ramanujan (1887-1920) was discovered and protected by the Cambridge Professors G.H. Hardy (1877-1947) and John Littlewood (1885-1977) – although he died, weakened by his inability to eat adequately due to Brahmin dietary restrictions that were too severe for English life.[174]

The Intelligence of James Watson

There is some evidence that this kind of skewed intelligence is found in Watson. James Watson's childhood is also indicative of late development, a trait which is associated with intelligence and also autism, especially

---

[174] Dutton and Charlton, *The Genius Famine, op. cit.*

with regard to intellectual development. An obvious example of this is Isaac Newton; a mediocre undergraduate who performed relatively poorly in his final exams at Cambridge, to the extent that his performance, according to a later student, the antiquarian William Stukeley (1687-1765), had been "looked upon as disgraceful."[175] Francis Crick failed to obtain a scholarship to an Oxbridge college and he achieved a second class degree, an issue to which we will return below.[176] Charles Darwin dropped out of Edinburgh University's medical school and received a fourth class degree (a non-honours degree) in Divinity from Cambridge University, because he wasn't sufficiently interested to even try for the honours degree.[177]

This delayed development may be because they respond differently to experiences, meaning that experience-dependent mechanisms of development illicit different responses, causing idiosyncratic developmental delays. For example, because autistics will socialise differently, the brain will be stimulated differently and will grow differently.[178] Certainly, Watson's physical development was delayed. He informs us: "I was then acutely conscious of my size, only five feet tall when entering high school, and shorter than my sister, who went through puberty early and reached her final height of five feet three inches while I was still only five foot one."[179] There is evidence that autism is associated with irregular puberty timing, due to hormonal interference. There is a tendency for it to occur either relatively early or relatively late and it

---

[175] G. Christianson, *Isaac Newton and the Scientific Revolution* (Oxford: Oxford University Press, 1996).
[176] J. Glynn, *My Sister Rosalind Franklin* (Oxford: Oxford University Press, 2012), 58.
[177] N. Barlow, P. Barrett and R. Freeman (Eds.), *The Works of Charles Darwin* (Abingdon: Routledge, 2016).
[178] G. Vivanti, J. Barbaro, K. Hudry et al., "Intellectual Development in Autism Spectrum Disorders: New Insights from Longitudinal Studies," *Frontiers in Human Neuroscience,* 7 (2013): 354.
[179] Watson, *Avoid Boring People, op. cit.,* 14.

appears that Watson was in the latter category.[180] Eventually, Watson reached the height of 6 foot 2.[181]

People with very high intelligence are often ill-served by IQ tests because their intelligence tends to be highly skewed, meaning they may even score poorly on sub-tests that would be no problem for a more average person. In this regard, it is fascinating that Watson writes:

> "I always liked going to grammar school and twice skipped a half grade, graduating when I was just thirteen. Somewhat down-casting were the results of my two IQ tests, discovered by stealthy looks at teachers' desktops. In neither test did I rise much above 120. I got more encouragement from my reading comprehension scores, which placed me at the top of my class."[182]

Evidently, then, there is some sort of delay, or deficiency, or a combination of these, in Watson's non-verbal reasoning. Alas, we cannot discern any more detail than that from this information, though we later learn, when he is given a physical exam, "My hopes went up when I failed the exam on machine tools and did poorly on recognizing upturned shapes." He also has trouble passing his driving test.[183] So there appear to be deficiencies in spatial intelligence. This is evidently reflective of the skewed intelligence that we would expect of a genius. Crick, for example, commented that Watson was extremely clumsy, to the extent that he had trouble peeling an orange.[184]

Was Watson an Intellectual Late Bloomer?

Despite outward appearances, Watson was not outstanding academically when he was very young. He was a late bloomer. This late, or unusual,

---

[180] S.-J. Tsai, Y.-W. Lue, C.-H. Yu et al., "Autism and risk of precocious puberty: A cohort study of 22,208 children," *Research in Autism Spectrum Disorders,* 114 (2024): 102390.

[181] J.D. Watson *Genes, Girls and Gamow: After the Double Helix* (New York: Knopf, 2002), Ch. 22.

[182] Watson, *Avoid Boring People,* 11.

[183] Watson, *Genes, Girls and Gamow, op. cit.*

[184] Hargittai, *The DNA Doctor, op. cit.,* 191. Quoting, F. Crick, "The Double Helix: A Personal View," *Nature*
(26th April 1974), 776-771.

intellectual development might be argued to be seen in Watson's university entrance, as he did not even attempt to go to a highly prestigious institution, such as one of the Ivy League colleges, in particular Harvard. This, however, rather misunderstands American higher education in the 1940s. It cannot be easily compared to the English system in which, as in Francis Crick's case, University College London was clearly less prestigious than Cambridge University when he attended the former. In 1952, students at Harvard were, to a great extent, from the region around where Harvard is situated – they were from Massachusetts and New York - and from a number of exclusive boarding schools. Around two thirds of applicants were accepted and 90 per cent of applicants whose fathers had attended were accepted. By 1960, it had been transformed into a truly elite college, attracting the brightest students from throughout the nation. As testimony to this, in 1952 the average verbal SAT score of a Harvard student was 583. By 1960, it had risen to 678. When Watson started at university, there was still a strong tendency for highly intelligent Americans to attend the best university in or near their state.[185]

In addition, Watson's university entrance was also rather idiosyncratic. Watson effectively admits that it is unlikely that he got into the University of Chicago, his local university, on merit alone. His father knew the university's president and his father had been at Oberlin College when the president's own father worked there. Nevertheless, Watson received a full scholarship, after an exam and an interview in which he discussed various books he had read. This scholarship involved starting university as part of an "exciting plan for admitting students who had only finished two years of high school and whose brains had not already been rotted out by the banality of high school life."[186]

Watson was only 15 years-old when he commenced his degree, whereas most undergraduates would have started their degree at the age of 18. However, the program was aimed at highly intelligent pupils of his age; it did not imply that he was outstandingly intelligent. Chicago would admit the students two years before they would normally have graduated from high school and then provided a special degree program for them in

---

[185] Herrnstein and Murray, *The Bell Curve, op. cit.*
[186] Watson, *Avoid Boring People, op. cit.,* 16.

which every student was obliged to take parts of all of the courses that were available: literature, science, mathematics, philosophy and so on. As American historian of science Horace Judson (1931-2011) has summarised: "To be fifteen at the University of Chicago was not prodigious, hardly a matter for remark."[187] Indeed, Watson graduated in 1946 from this degree but stayed at Chicago for a further year to achieve a full degree in Zoology; a proper degree.[188]

In the eighteenth and nineteenth centuries, it was common, in Scotland, to start university at the age of 14, as did the economist Adam Smith (1723-1790) when he began at Glasgow University,[189] and Charles Darwin (1809-1882) when he began at Edinburgh University.[190] When I was a postgraduate at Aberdeen University in 2002, I knew a number of undergraduates who were only 16. In fact, Watson's sister was part of the same program, herself going to the University of Chicago at 15. "I was a keen reader with a much better-than-ordinary memory," was Watson's explanation for being accepted onto the program.[191]

But returning to Watson's intelligence, as we have discussed, geniuses appear to take time to intellectually shine and to find their "calling" and, accordingly, they tend to be late intellectual developers for this reason. Watson's undergraduate life reflects this. He does not get the best grades. He is "very good," rather than excellent, though it is striking that he even recalls the grades he used to receive in the mid-1940s. "Much of the time I couldn't tell what was required of me, and my self-esteem fell when I received a B on my exam at the end of the summer term. Fortunately, only the results of the comprehensive exam taken at the end of the full year's work would appear on my official record. But I got a B on that too."[192] This issue is ruminated on again and again: "With my interest in birds drawing me toward a career in biology, I was disappointed when I got yet

---

[187] H.F. Judson, *The Eighth Day of Creation: Makers of the Revolution in Biology* (Cold Spring Harbor, NY: Cold Spring Harbor Laboratory Press, 1996), 28.
[188] Judson, *The Eighth Day of Creation, op. cit.*, 29.
[189] G. Kennedy, *Adam Smith: A Moral Philosopher and His Political Economy* (Basingstoke: Palgrave Macmillan, 2016), 16.
[190] S. Herbert, *Charles Darwin, Geologist* (Ithaca, NY: Cornell University Press, 2005), 29.
[191] McElheny, *Watson and DNA, op. cit.*
[192] Watson, *Avoid Boring People, op. cit.*, 23.

another B on the comprehensive exam that August."[193] Rather like Darwin, it seems that Watson is far more interested in naturalism than in actually concentrating on his degree: "I remained all through my college years a fervent ornithologist, especially during the spring and fall migrations, when I frequently went by myself, sometimes extending the reach of public transportation by hitchhiking, to prime birding areas."[194] Consistent with this, studies have found that scientific geniuses do not tend to especially shine in terms of their educational attainment; they shine when they are left alone to pursue their quest.[195]

This "late blooming" may also be related to the nature of autism itself. There is some evidence autistics tend to be relatively "late bloomers." The period in which their brain is highly plastic is longer than that of controls and the end of that period appears to be delayed by a year in relation to controls. In effect, they develop more slowly but can then rapidly catch-up, at least among child samples.[196] If the autism is a consequence of brain damage brought about by some form of developmental instability, such as a difficult birth, then we would expect delayed intellectual development as the brain gradually repairs itself, co-opting other parts of the brain to undertake the functions normally undertaken by the damaged areas.[197] However, the research on child samples appears to imply that delayed intellectual development may be an intrinsic quality of autism. For example, autistics tend to focus on parts rather than wholes, despite their focus on systematizing; a tendency that would need to be overcome in order to successfully solve problems.[198] In addition, it has been found that the volume of "gray matter in several regions of the cortex across the parietal, occipital and frontal lobes declines earlier than usual during

---

[193] Watson, *Avoid Boring People, op. cit.,* 24.

[194] Watson, *Avoid Boring People, op. cit.,* 25.

[195] Ochse, *Before the Gates of Excellence, op. cit.,* 90.

[196] S. Kim and C. Casari, "Brief Report: Longitudinal Trajectory of Working Memory in School-Aged Children on the Autism Spectrum: Period of High Plasticity and 'Late Bloomers,'" *Journal of Autism and Developmental Disorders* (2023).

[197] See E. Dutton, *Sent Before Their Time: Genius, Charisma and Being Born Prematurely* (Melbourne: Manticore Press, 2022).

[198] E. Knight, T. Altschuler, S. Molholm et al., "It's all in the timing: Delayed feedback in autism may weaken predictive mechanisms during contour integration," *bioRxiv* (2024).

adolescence in the brains of people with autism than in controls. Adolescents with autism also show an abnormal delay in the increase of white matter volume in the cortex."[199]

This is interesting because it may imply that otherwise intelligent autistics may fall back a bit, relative to their peers, during adolescence before overtaking them later. This would be consistent with an obvious genius, like Francis Crick, being rejected from his attempts to attain Oxbridge scholarships and getting a second class degree. Watson writes of Crick's academic record: "There he liked science but never pulled out the grades required for Oxford or Cambridge. Instead he studied physics at University College London, afterward staying on for a Ph.D. financially sponsored by his uncle Arthur."[200] In those days it wasn't especially competitive to get in to Oxford or Cambridge if you were a public school boy like Crick as there was a great deal of nepotism,[201] but all but the very wealthy needed scholarships - and Crick's parents couldn't afford the tuition fees. Crick's Latin also wasn't good enough; Latin being a requirement to get into Oxbridge until 1960.[202] Accordingly, he had to find somewhere cheaper and that didn't require Latin.[203] That Crick should

---

[199] N. Zeliadt, "Brains of people with autism show altered growth with age," *The Transmitter* (11th December 2014); N. Lange, B. Travers, E. Bigler et al., "Longitudinal volumetric brain changes in autism spectrum disorder ages 6-35 years," *Autism Research,* 8 (2015): 82-93.

[200] Watson, *Avoid Boring People, op. cit.,* 97.

[201] See, Abbott, *Student Life in a Class Society, op. cit.* Highly intelligent students would obtain scholarships to Oxford or Cambridge but, for those who had to pay the fees, the majority, entrance was not especially taxing if they had been to the correct schools (public schools) and had the necessary qualification in Latin, a subject studied at all public schools, though frequently not at state schools. For example, Britain's sometime Deputy Prime Minister Michael Heseltine (b. 1933), who attended the public school Shrewsbury, recalled that he was an "undistinguished schoolboy" and that when he went to Oxford University, in 1951, there was neither an entrance exam nor even an interview by college tutors. The school simply sent a letter to the college recommending Heseltine for a place and he was accepted. See, M. Heseltine, *Life in the Jungle: My Autobiography* (London: Hodder and Stoughton, 2000), 26.

[202] J. Brooke-Smith, *Gilded Youth: Privilege, Rebellion and the British Public School* (), 117.London: Reaktion Books, 2019).

[203] R. Olby, *Francis Crick: Hunter of Life's Secrets* (Cold Harbor, NY: Cold Harbor Spring Laboratory Press, 2011), 38-29.

have a problem with Latin would be congruous with Spearman's Law of Diminishing Returns.

Nevertheless, this is all followed by a further delay in truly shining academically. As with Crick, though at a postgraduate rather than undergraduate level, Watson was rejected from his first choice of postgraduate university, California University of Technology, and though Watson was accepted by Harvard, they were not prepared to offer him any financial assistance, meaning it was impossible to take-up the offer.[204] In 1978, they gave him an honorary degree.[205] Watson, however, was offered a stipend from the University of Indiana to study for a doctorate in Zoology, with the admissions tutor making it perfectly plain, in a hand written post-script, that Watson could essentially research whatever happened to interest him. This was perfect because, for Watson, you should narrow-down your interests while still an undergraduate. If you fail to, then: "In such circumstances I might have grown bored with my thesis research and been obliged to wait until after my Ph.D. was completed, some three or four years, before experiencing true intellectual excitement. And by then I would have left the most thrilling problem of all— the DNA structure— for others to solve."[206] During his doctorate Watson, anyway, spent a summer informally studying at Cal Tech,[207] and even later, after his breakthrough discovery of the structure of DNA, formally working there, and then working at Harvard.[208] With the nature of genius intelligence established, we will now turn to genius personality and why such a personality is necessary for genius to manifest.

---

[204] Watson, *Avoid Boring People, op. cit.,* 31.
[205] V. McElheny, *Watson and DNA: Making a Scientific Revolution* (Hoboken, NJ: John Wiley and Sons, 2003), "James Dewey Watson: A Brief Chronology."
[206] Watson, *Avoid Boring People, op. cit.,* 37.
[207] Watson, *Avoid Boring People, op. cit.,* 84.
[208] Watson, *Avoid Boring People, op. cit.,* 122.

Chapter Four

Why Does Genius Require Autism and Psychopathy?

The Neglected Child in All of Us

Returning to Watson's cancellation in 2007, where he honestly discussed his views on the future of development in Sub-Saharan Africa, this series of events gives us a deep insight into him and the nature of genius itself. We all know, deep down, that what he was saying was empirically accurate and reasonable and, to those who doubt this, its accuracy will be demonstrated later.

Some of us have dealt with the cognitive dissonance this has induced – with reality not being how we would like it to be – by telling ourselves, based on fallacious arguments, that Watson is wrong, but our emotional reaction to what he said only proves that, deep within us, we know he is correct. We don't like to acknowledge this because we see ourselves as morally superior people and what makes us morally superior is our Wokeness; our belief that all people (except those who disagree with us) are somehow equal. We have adopted this sense of moral superiority to cope with the negative feelings by which we are overwhelmed, so if Watson takes that away from us then we are just that neglected child, fearing abandonment, that nobody seems to love, and we will be publicly proved to be dishonest, stupid or both, feelings we might be unable to deal with. But all of us know that, due to the new ideology that has gradually taken hold, you just mustn't *say* what Watson said. It will hurt the sensitivities of the New Church Ladies, wherein purple hair has replaced blue rinse. So what kind of person says it anyway? The answer is the genius type and it is that same tendency which allows him to come up with and present his genius ideas.

What Does It Take to Break the Rules?

Returning to our discussion of personality, Dutch psychologist Dimitri Van der Linden and I have explored the way that whereas the average scientist – who might build on the insight made by the genius – would combine high intelligence with high Agreeableness and high Conscientiousness,[209] the genius would have a much more complicated psychological profile. Experts on genius such as American psychologist Dean Simonton and Hans Eysenck, whom we met earlier, concur that high-intelligence is a necessary component for genius, but nowhere near a sufficient one; genius being an emergent property of rare combinations of environment, personality and intelligence. The scientific genius is extremely high in intelligence, but is moderately *low* in Conscientiousness and Agreeableness. As we saw earlier, we might better reduce this to autism and psychopathy.

This is crucial to genius because genius involves coming up with and presenting a ground-breaking and highly original idea. Frequently, it involves solving a very difficult problem and working to solve this – to the exclusion of most other things – for years on end. True originality will always offend vested interests. It will, at first at least, be met with ridicule and at worst with open hostility. True originality will also involve breaking the rules; thinking the unthinkable, contemplating something that is so "out there" that it would seem ludicrous to ordinary people. It would be unthinkable to those who are high in rule following.

This is why geniuses require the personality profile which they have. As they are relatively low in Conscientiousness, they are happy to disregard the rules and they have the ability to think outside of them. This permits them to notice patterns which other people fail to notice and there is a degree to which noticing patterns and relationships is the essence of creativity, even in the artistic realm. Combined with extremely high intelligence, this means that they have the ability to think in a highly original way and, so, to solve incredibly difficult problems.

---

[209] See: E. Dutton and D. Van der Linden, "Who are the 'Clever Sillies'? The intelligence, personality, and motives of clever silly originators and those who follow them," *Intelligence,* 49 (2015): 57-65.

Their moderately low Agreeableness will have two consequences. Firstly, it will help them to dedicate themselves to their work, as they find dealing with other people extremely difficult and tiresome. Aspects of low Agreeableness, such as Narcissistic traits in which you have very strong self-belief,[210] can be associated with high self-esteem, so they are likely to bounce back quite well from any discouragements which they experience while trying to solve their chosen problem. Once they've solved it, they will have no difficulty in telling the wider world about it. This is because, moderately low in Agreeableness, they won't care about the offence they may cause and, being low in cognitive empathy, they would have trouble anticipating that their work would cause offence even if they did care.

This lack of concern with the feelings of others reflects two traits, as we have seen: psychopathy and autism. Primary psychopathy, thought to be mainly genetic, is characterised by low anxiety and high impulsivity whereas secondary psychopathy, thought to be more environmental, is characterised by high anxiety.[211] Indeed, one study found that secondary psychopathy is characterised not just by low Agreeableness and high Neuroticism but also by relatively high Conscientiousness, with the lack of impulse control specifically associated with primary psychopathy. Primary psychopaths are callous and fearless; secondary psychopaths, though capable of very nasty behaviour, can be frightened and remorseful and emotionally dysregulated, with the potential for some empathy.[212]

Dean Simonton observes that as we move from mathematics, through the sciences and humanities into the arts, then levels of depression increase, as do levels of psychopathy. However, the most original members of each category – for example, original mathematicians – have a psychology which is more similar to the average psychology in the subject lower down the logical hierarchy; further towards the arts. If they

---

[210] Aslinger et al, "The Influence of Narcissistic Vulnerability and Grandiosity on Momentary Hostility Leading up to and Following Interpersonal Rejection," *op. cit.*
[211] A. Sethi, E. McCrory, V. Puetz et al., "Primary and Secondary Variants of Psychopathy in a Volunteer Sample Are Associated With Different Neurocognitive Mechanisms," *Biological Psychiatry,* 12 (2018): 1013-1021.
[212] S. Jakobwitz and V. Egan, "The 'Dark Triad' and normal personality traits," *Personality and Individual Differences*, 40 (2006): 331–339

combine this with very high intelligence, amazing innovation is potentially the result.[213]

Can Psychopathy Lead to Greatness?

Felix Post, whom we met earlier, conducted a character-trait analysis of 291 world famous men. He found that 17.8 per cent of world famous scientists are severely psychopathic, compared to 30.8 per cent of composers, 17.4 per cent of politicians, 37.5 per cent of artists, 26 per cent of thinkers, and 46 per cent of writers. About 1 per cent of people in Western populations are severely psychopathic.[214] Hence, clearly, psychopathy, when optimally combined with high intelligence, helps to bring about genius. Such people do not care about the controversies they stir-up; in fact they may well rather enjoy them, not least because it gives them a feeling of power; a sadistic delight as they watch all the NPCs struggling to cope.

These kinds of traits can be seen in Watson. Firstly, he does not follow the social rules. For Watson, "Francis, however, did not worry about these skeptics. Many were cantankerous fools who unfailingly backed the wrong horses. One could not be a successful scientist without realizing that, in contrast to the popular conception supported by newspapers and mothers of scientists, a goodly number of scientists are not only narrow minded and dull, but also just stupid."[215] These included Rosalind, his colleague, of whom he wrote, "The real problem, then, was Rosy. The thought could not be avoided that the best home for a feminist was in another person's."[216] Even so, Watson essentially admits that he may have fancied her, remarking on one of her presentations: "She spoke to an audience of about fifteen in a quick, nervous style that suited the unornamented old lecture hall in which we were seated. There was not a trace of warmth or frivolity in her words. And yet I could not regard her as totally

---

[213] D. K. Simonton, "Varieties of (Scientific) Creativity: A Hierarchical Model of Domain-Specific Disposition, Development, and Achievement," *Perspectives on Psychological Science,* 4 (2009): 5.
[214] Post, "Creativity and psychopathology: A Study of 291 World Famous Men," *op. cit.*
[215] Watson, *The Double Helix, op. cit.,* Ch. 3.
[216] Watson, *The Double Helix, op. cit.,* Ch. 2

uninteresting. Momentarily I wondered how she would look if she took off her glasses and did something novel with her hair."[217]

Watson's bluntness and failure to follow the rules seems to cause him assorted problems in life, including eviction by his Cambridge landlady: "My main crime was not removing my shoes when I entered the house after 9:00 P.M., the hour at which her husband went to sleep. Also I occasionally forgot the injunction not to flush the toilet at similar hours and, even worse, I went out after 10:00 P.M. Nothing in Cambridge was then open, and my motives were suspect."[218]

How Agreeable is Watson?

It is the low Agreeableness and low Conscientiousness of the genius academic that marks him out. The run-of-the-mill scholar is high in these traits. He combines being socially-skilled, and, to some extent, pro-social, with the kind of normal range high IQ which precipitates social conformity. Intelligence is associated with norm-mapping and the effortful control necessary to force yourself to believe that which it is socially useful to believe, and to then competitively signal it.[219] This militates against "rocking the boat" and against the questioning of accepted dogmas. This is not the case with Watson. In his memoir *Avoid Boring People,* Watson directly attacks what he regards as nonsensical theories, such as William Sheldon's (1898-1977) somatotype model, wherein body type is supposedly associated with personality type. He calls this "obvious crap."[220] I am not sure whether it is "obvious crap." There is a growing body of evidence for the veracity of physiognomy, an issue I have explored elsewhere.[221] Indeed, a more recent study has found a weak relationship between an ectomorphic (skinny) body type and Neurotic traits, such as

---

[217] Watson, *The Double Helix, op. cit.,* Ch. 10.
[218] Watson, *The Double Helix, op. cit.,* Ch. 6.
[219] M.A. Woodley of Menie and C. Dunkel, "Beyond the Cultural Mediation Hypothesis: A Reply to Dutton (2013)," *Intelligence,* 49 (2015): 186-191.
[220] Watson, *Avoid Boring People, op. cit.,* 65.
[221] E. Dutton, *How to Judge People By What They Look Like* (Oulu: Thomas Edward Press, 2018).

depression.[222] But there was, certainly, very limited evidence for it in the 1940s. The key point is that Watson is sufficiently low in traits of Agreeableness to directly state what he thinks about what he regards as a faulty model.

What Does It Mean to Think Intuitively?

A related aspect of genius we have highlighted is intuitive thinking. What does it mean to think intuitively? Intuition involves understanding something instinctively rather than consciously; it involves following your gut-feeling. This kind of thinking has been summarised in greater depth as (1) Rapid, spontaneous and a-logical (2) Holistic; mainly concerned with the whole situation instead of its parts (3) Tacit: Hard to verbalize or articulate (4) Made with a high degree of confidence. When a problem is highly novel, after all, there will be no clear pathway to solving it, meaning that (correct) intuition must play a part.[223]

It does seem rather counter-intuitive that something like mathematical genius could possibly be associated with "instinct;" with "thinking quickly."[224] Perhaps this works if you have a certain kind of mind. We can imagine that if you can spot patterns and imbibe a vast amount of information extremely quickly then the result will be correct intuitions. Intuitions will come to you, drawing on all of the information which you have absorbed, as though they are divine revelations and there is an elevated probability that they will be correct. Consequently, you will learn to trust your instincts – in the mathematical though perhaps not social world - and to carefully listen to them. In addition, the fact that you are low in Conscientiousness will mean that you will be relatively in touch with your instincts; you may even lack the effortful control necessary to suppress them. Further, your low Agreeableness, and even your Narcissistic traits, will mean that you might think to yourself, "Why on

---

[222] G. Nizam, M. Tariq and A. Ijaz, "Co-relational study of body types and fundamental neurotic reactions among adolescents of urban sector of Peshawar, Pakistan," *Journal of Social and Psychological Sciences,* 30 (2010): 1.

[223] J. Petevari, M. Osman and J. Bhattacharya, "The Role of Intuition in the Generation and Evaluation Stages of Creativity," *Frontiers in Psychology,* 7 (2016).

[224] D. Kahneman, *Thinking, Fast and Slow* (New York: Farrar, Straus and Giroux, 2011).

earth should I suppress how I feel about this matter?" But, being the genius that you are, you are likely to be instinctively correct about it in a way that somebody else might not be. We might even suggest that, as a rule, successful academic research involves suppressing your instincts.

As American philosopher Thomas Kuhn (1922-1996) demonstrated in *The Structure of Scientific Revolutions,* science does not progress via the gradual accumulation of new information, as, in an ideal world, it should. Instead, a particular scientific paradigm becomes the orthodoxy in the "guild of scientists," and professional scientists become invested in this orthodoxy. As careerists, they will want to signal how cooperative they are with regard to the orthodoxy and most scientists are careerists operating within a guild, rendering them highly resistant to those who challenge the orthodoxy, as their careers, to a significant extent, depend on accepting it. Eventually, however, the anomalies in the orthodoxy become so clear that the orthodoxy is over-turned in a "scientific revolution" and a new orthodoxy takes its place.[225] It might, therefore, be argued that being a successful career scientist partly involves suppressing your intuition and making a point of ignoring it.

However, it may, nevertheless, be the case that some people are more likely to have correct intuitions in certain areas than are others. "Woman's intuition" involves being able to read a room and "just know" something is, for example, a problem without quite knowing what the problem is. Women may learn to listen to their intuition because they are high in empathy and, thus, will be absorbing and processing large amounts of social information without consciously realising it. They may begin to learn that their "woman's intuition" is often correct with regard to potential social problems. We would expect the same to occur with geniuses and intuition. Furthermore, the very fact that geniuses tend to be high in openness and to be highly contrarian would perhaps mean that if they are in a scholarly environment which is highly sceptical of intuition then they will be interested in it for that reason alone. In summary, autism and intelligence may result in certain kinds of correct intuition.

---

[225] T. Kuhn, *The Structure of Scientific Revolutions* (Chicago: University of Chicago Press, 1962).

Is Watson Obsessive?

We have seen, then, the importance of aspects of psychopathy. But what about the more specific dimensions of autism? In this regard, American psychologist Gregory Feist has done a great deal of work.[226] In general, indeed, scientists score higher in Agreeableness (specifically altruism) than other scholars but they also score higher in autistic traits. This is especially true if their area is Mathematics or Engineering.[227] Clearly, autism aids original achievement because it makes a person obsessive, it causes them to take in more information, it causes them to be focused on ideas and systems, it makes them, to some extent, introverted (they can eschew company in pursuit of their ideas) and they won't anticipate that their original ideas will cause offence.[228]

At the age of eleven, just after he was confirmed, Watson stopped attending mass on Sundays "in order to accompany my father on his Sunday morning bird walks. Even as a small boy I was fascinated by birds."[229] This is precisely the kind of "special interest" which we would expect a person with autistic traits to develop. Indeed, a study of committed "birders" found that they were relatively high in Autism Spectrum Disorder.[230] Watson's birding has all the markers of a special interest, especially the level of commitment it involves; being up before sunrise in autumn to spot specific birds, for example.

In *Avoid Boring People,* Watson seems to assume that his readers will be sufficiently interested in this subject that they will want to know of the obscure breeds of bird which he can distinguish and even that we might

---

[226] G.J. Feist, "Personality, behavioral thresholds, and the creative scientist," in G.J. Feist, R. Reiter-Palmon and J.C. Kaufman (Eds.), *The Cambridge Handbook of Creativity and Personality Research* (Cambridge: Cambridge University Press, 2017).
[227] S. Baron-Cohen, S. Wheelwright, R. Skinner et al., "The Autism-Spectrum Quotient (AQ): Evidence from Asperger syndrome/high-functioning autism, males and females, scientists and mathematicians," *Journal of Autism and Developmental Disorders*, 31 (2001): 5–17.
[228] G. Feist, "How Development and Personality Influence Scientific Thought, Interest, and Achievement," *Review of General Psychology,* 10 (2006): 163-182.
[229] J. Watson, *Avoid Boring People,* 8.
[230] J. Essayli, *The Psychology of Extreme Birders: Parallels to Other Extreme Behaviors, Anorexia Nervosa, Addiction, and Autism Spectrum Disorder* (PhD Thesis: University of Hawaii at Manoa, 2013).

wish to see a page of his father's notebook on birds. He tells us that in the summer after he graduated from grammar school, he went on a scout camp: "Nonetheless, I came home content to have spotted thirty-seven different bird species."[231] Even with Watson's mother, there is at least evidence of a passionate interest in certain issues. The family didn't merely *vote* Democrat. Watson's mother was the "captain of the seventh ward precinct." In this regard, it is worth quoting Watson's exact words:

> "Our basement became the local polling station, earning us ten dollars per election, and my mother made another ten manning the polls. At the 1940 Democratic National Convention, held in Chicago, we rooted, to no avail, for Paul McNutt, Indiana's handsome governor then bidding to be chosen as Roosevelt's running mate."[232]

Indeed, when Watson returned from London in October 2007 after having been cancelled, Cathy Soref tried to cheer him up by bringing him a cake. Devastated by the accusations of racism, Watson looked at her and plaintively enquired, "What would my parents think?" Returning to Watson's descriptions, however, note the unnecessary level of detail which Watson provides the reader. This is precisely what you would expect of someone high in autistic traits. They would have an excellent memory for detail and they would tend to focus on details. Watson also provides his reader with many other completely unnecessary particulars, such as his precise school grades or how, on 15th January 1941, he and his father spotted "the seldom seen white winged scoter off Jackson Park in Lake Michigan."[233]

How Socially Skilled is Watson?

By 1946, by which time Watson was an 18 year-old undergraduate, he has finally physically matured. He also notes that his social skills have markedly improved. This is something that generally occurs with those who are high in autistic traits. Low in cognitive empathy, they learn the correct way to behave via observation; they learn, in effect, to camouflage

---

[231] Watson, *Avoid Boring People, op. cit.,* 11.

[232] Watson, *Avoid Boring People, op. cit.,* 9.

[233] Watson, *Avoid Boring People, op. cit.,* 14.

their autism and they become adept at this over time, as they practice more and more. Thus, Watson recalls: "Now more than six feet tall, I no longer looked a physical misfit. For the first time I began to befriend peers who were not obvious oddballs, elected because no one else seemed keen to eat with me. Soon I was being called "Jimbo," a southernism quickly adopted by several young waitresses who were inspired by my youth to treat me as a kid brother."[234] His "improved social skills" inspire a friend to set Watson up on his first and last college date, a date which Watson felt he ruined due to "awkwardness."

Evidence of autistic traits emerge much later when Watson decides to write a memoir about the discovery of the structure of DNA. Initially, he decides to call it "Honest Jim" because, "Honest Jim was my way to face head-on the controversial question prompting Seeds's cynicism, over whether Francis and I had improperly used confidential King's College data in working out the structure of DNA."[235] When he sent off the manuscript for colleagues to read, it became clear that he was rather too honest, to the extent of causing offence. He was asked to remove lines about someone practicing "screwy Chemistry" and "looking like an ass." Of this, Watson notes:

> "These were phrases I knew good taste would lead me to delete before the manuscript went to the printer. But since they were true, I was loath to remove them before absolutely necessary. In a similar vein, I never should have sent out a manuscript saying that Francis had never been a member of any college because he was thought to pinch other people's ideas. By this I only intended to convey the reason why King's, to their great loss, had not made Francis a fellow despite his unquestioned brilliance."[236]

Watson, in other words, appears not to quite understand the offence that such remarks are likely to have caused, as might the proposed title, as it implies that Watson did most of the work leading to the discovery. This is exactly how Crick felt, so the working title was changed to "Base Pairs."

---

[234] Watson, *Avoid Boring People, op. cit.,* 29.
[235] Watson, *Avoid Boring People, op. cit.,* 221.
[236] Watson, *Avoid Boring People, op. cit.,* 229.

Even so, Crick, and others involved in their research, were so appalled by the manuscript that they had a lawyer write to Watson saying that his clients felt that the book libelled them.[237] Watson presents us with a list of Crick's objections to a revised manuscript which Crick conveyed to him in a letter. Some of the criticisms seem to display a kind of cognitive dissonance. Crick is so emotional that one wonders whether Watson is correct and Crick simply has trouble accepting this because this correctness punctures Crick's self-importance: "Your view of the history of science is found in the lower class of women's magazines." However, Crick may have a point when he notes: "The fact a man is well known does not excuse his friends from respecting his privacy while he is alive."[238] In other words, the manuscript is breaking confidences and spreading "gossip," even if it is true, and this is hardly a tactful thing to do. For instance, it includes these lines on Crick:

> "His concern was not without reason. Although he knew he was bright and could produce novel ideas, he could claim no clear-cut intellectual achievements and he was still without his Ph.D. He came from a solid middle-class family and was sent to school at Mill Hill. Then he read physics at University College, London, and had commenced work on an advanced degree when the war broke out."[239]

This is in 1968. In Watson's 2007 memoir, *Avoid Boring People,* we find almost exactly the same sentences, but they include the fact that Crick didn't do very well at school and was unable to get into Oxford or Cambridge. It seems likely that Crick objected to Watson publishing this information, told to Watson in confidence. Crick's own memoir does not mention it.[240] Watson reveals other personal information, such as about Crick's marital arrangements, which would have been rather taboo in 1968 when *The Double Helix* was published: "Francis' first marriage did not last long, and a son, Michael, was looked after by Francis' mother and aunt."[241] Also, Watson is portrayed as the careful one whereas Crick is

---

[237] Watson, *Avoid Boring People, op. cit.,* 228.
[238] Watson, *Avoid Boring People, op. cit.,* 231.
[239] Watson, *The Double Helix, op. cit.,* Ch.8.
[240] Crick, *What Mad Pursuit, op. cit.*
[241] Watson, *The Double Helix, op. cit.,* Ch. 9.

impulsive: "But now, to my delight and amazement, the answer was turning out to be profoundly interesting. For over two hours I happily lay awake with pairs of adenine residues whirling in front of my closed eyes. Only for brief moments did the fear shoot through me that an idea this good could be wrong."[242] As Watson' biographer summarised, of the reaction to his savagely frank memoir: "How could a man of 40, of such transcendent achievement and influence, fail to exhibit mature judgment and kindness in describing the lightning strike of 1953? Would Jim ever grow up, and put aside the brutality of the young?" He also notes: "He spoke to the students with such light-hearted and brutal frankness that one wondered if he mightn't be the most indiscreet scientist in the 300-year history of modern science."[243]

Even Watson's dress sense is indicative of autistic traits. He seems not to care or understand how extreme scruffiness makes him seem to people. A biographer has referred to his "shabby clothing."[244] For French biologist Francois Jacob (1920-2013), Watson was: "Tall, gawky, scraggly, he had an inimitable style. Inimitable in his dress: shirttails flying, knees in the air, socks down around his ankles."[245] Even Watson's way of speaking, in high-pitched rasps, is highly idiosyncratic.

The Relationship between Testosterone and Genius

Psychopathy and autism are both associated with androgens; with masculine hormones such as testosterone. Testosterone makes men aggressive and gives them drive and it also makes them "male-brained": low in empathy, high in systemizing and belligerent. On this basis, we should be able to show a relationship between androgens and genius and two studies have achieved this. National-level empirical data on scientific productivity, in terms of numbers of publications, and science Nobel laureates was compared to seven national-level androgen indicators; namely androgenic body hair (specifically hair on the fingers), the length

---

[242] Watson, *The Double Helix, op. cit.*, Ch. 26.

[243] McElheny, *Watson and DNA, op. cit.*

[244] Hargittai, *The DNA Doctor, op. cit.*, 160.

[245] Hargittai, *The DNA Doctor, op. cit.*, 195. Quoting, F. Jacob, *The Statue Within: An Autobiography* (London: Unwin, 1988), 264.

of the CAG repeat on the androgen receptor gene, prostate cancer incidence, male and female 2D:4D finger ratio (male hands are more shovel-like), and sex frequency and number of partners. The majority of these indicators were associated in the expected direction with per capita number of scientific publications and Nobel prizes. Moreover, several indicators significantly interacted with national-level estimates of intelligence, such that androgen levels are related to measures of scientific achievement only when the level of intelligence is relatively high; that is when the countries assessed had an average IQ of at least 90, which takes in over 90 per cent of countries that have ever won a science Nobel Prize. The relationships were, in some cases, quite strong. Having women with feminine fingers correlated at -0.7 with the markers of per capita genius and androgenic hair correlated at 0.59.[246]

This was replicated using different markers. Left-handedness is associated with testosterone and autistics are more likely to be left-handed, as are males. Schizophrenia is associated with being right-handed and, in some of its components, is the opposite of autism. Schizotypal personality is a condition marked by disorganised and distorted thinking, unusual psychological experiences, an inability to experience pleasure, difficulty with relationships, being highly withdrawn and not enjoying company. Schizophrenia is a psychotic disorder which differs from the life-long pattern of the schizotypal personality. Schizophrenia involves delusions and hallucinations episodically which impair functioning completely. This is absent in the schizotypal personality. Schizophrenia is an extreme manifestation of these symptoms, tending also to involve paranoid delusions. Whereas autistics are not interested in external manifestations of internal states, schizophrenics over-detect these, perceive them in the world itself and, so, can become paranoid.[247]They also suffer from religious delusions, partly because they transpose their hyper-empathy onto the world itself, perceiving evidence of a mind acting behind it. Using countries with an IQ of at least 90, it was found that there was a strong

---

[246] D. Van der Linden, E. Dutton and G. Madison, "National-level Indicators of Androgens are Related to the Global Distribution of Scientific Productivity and Science Nobel Prizes," *Journal of Creative Behavior,* 54 (2020): 134-149.
[247] Nettle, *Personality, op cit.*

negative association between per capita scientific achievement, such as science Nobel Prizes, and per capita schizophrenia and also per capita right-handedness. It is countries with high levels of autism and left-handedness which, when you control for intelligence, produce scientific and even literary geniuses; partly because originality is an expression of psychopathy as well as autism.[248]

This relative absence of schizophrenia among geniuses is congruous with Felix Post's analysis of geniuses which found extremely low levels of schizophrenia among geniuses and their relatives; a finding that even held for artistic geniuses. Only 1.7 per cent of the sample had schizophrenia and only 4 per cent had schizophrenic or probably schizophrenic relatives. Roughly 71 per cent of those with such relatives were writers, though it should be stressed that Post's study is limited by the fact that it is based on biographies and subjective descriptions rather than formal medical analysis.[249] There is, however, evidence of a genetic overlap between autism, bipolar disorder and schizophrenia.[250] It should be noted that there is debate over how long schizophrenia has existed, with some scholars arguing that it suddenly manifested, as a collection of symptoms, at the beginning of the nineteenth century and others averring that there is evidence for its existence in the Middle Ages.[251]

Women as Watson's Special Interest

With regard to autism, and the related issue of elevated testosterone, Watson is extremely direct, one might even say obsessive, about his interest in women, which intensifies by 1948, as his confidence in his social skills increases. Even so, this was gradual. "I wasn't the sort of person you asked to go to a dinner party when I was 22. I would neither

---

[248] E. Dutton, D. Van der Linden and G. Madison, "Why Do High IQ Societies Differ in Intellectual Achievement? The Role of Schizophrenia and Left-Handedness in Per Capita Scientific Publications and Nobel Prizes," *Journal of Creative Behavior,* 54 (2020): 871-883.

[249] Post, "Creativity and psychopathology," *op. cit.*

[250] L. Carroll and M. Owen, "Genetic overlap between autism, schizophrenia and bipolar disorder," *Genome Medicine,* 1 (2009): 102.

[251] R.W. Heinrichs, "Historical origins of schizophrenia: two early madmen and their illness," *Journal of the History of Behavioral Sciences,* 39 (2003): 349-363.

amuse them [the other guests] nor put them at ease. The only thing I cared about was the gene—and girls," he told a journalist in 1989.[252] In *Avoid Boring People,* Watson presents us with a photograph of himself with the caption: "On the lookout for girls in Corona del Mar, California." People high in autistic traits tend to be late in starting sexual relationships, presumably due to their delay in acquiring the necessary social skills.[253] They are also more likely to develop fetishes, engage in inappropriate sexual behaviour, to fail to have sexual relationships at all,[254] and they experience love more passionately, due to their feelings and sensations being heightened. We, therefore, should not be surprised that Watson's first official girlfriend was not exactly a casual relationship:

> "Only in my last year at Indiana did I have a real girlfriend. She was a perky, dark-haired fellow graduate student in the Zoology Department, Marion Drasher. In early December, I took her to a local production of J. B. Priestley's play *An Inspector Calls.* Soon I was intensely in love, particularly after Christmas of 1949, when we were in New York City together . . . ." [255]

They broke-up in June 1950, Watson being unable to commit due to an anticipated research trip to Copenhagen. Naturally, as Watson was such a young PhD student, she was several years older than him, a difference which concerned her at first.

Watson seems to have a powerful interest in the opposite sex, and especially their physical attributes, and there are comments to this effect throughout *Avoid Boring People.* For example, when he is in Stockholm to receive his Nobel Prize he recalls, "Afterward our party moved on to a much smaller private affair that let me banter long with Ellen Huldt, a pretty dark-haired medical student, with whom I then arranged to have

---

[252] Quoted in McElheny, *Watson and DNA, op. cit.*

[253] M. Urbano, K. Hartmann, S. Deutsch et al., "Relationships, Sexuality, and Intimacy in Autism Spectrum Disorders" in M. Fitzgerald, (Ed.), *Recent Advances in Autism Spectrum Disorders, Volume I* (London: IntechOpen, 2013).

[254] M. Maggio, P. Calatozzo, A. Cerasa et al., "Sex and Sexuality in Autism Spectrum Disorders: A Scoping Review on a Neglected but Fundamental Issue," *Brain Science,* 12 (2022): 1427.

[255] Watson, *Avoid Boring People, op. cit.,* 84.

dinner the next night."[256] He experienced the Winter St Lucia ceremony while in Stockholm, in which a pretty teenage girl has the honour of leading a group of teenage girls, in white gowns, in a partly religious ceremony in honour of St Lucia. The lead-girl wears a crown of candles. Of this, Watson remarks: "Don't anticipate a flirtatious Santa Lucia girl."[257] During a period in the UK in 1965, Watson recollects: "A number of family friends were there, the youngest being the intelligent and statuesque Susie Reeder, about to receive her university degree at Sussex . . . The next evening we had dinner at Rule's Restaurant, just below Covent Garden. It was just a few minutes' walk away from the Aldwych Theatre . . ."[258]

The memoir is peppered with observations about attractive, young women: "I was still without a license when I spotted a tallish girl with possible real flair at The Greasy Spoon."[259] Of meeting a subsequent girlfriend at a party at her parents' home, he writes: "Again her face and voice made butterflies rumble through my stomach, but we parted as friends, not lovers . . ."[260] "More girl hope came after George Beadle told me that Gary Cooper's daughter, Maria, was thinking about being a biochemist and was coming with her parents to see Caltech the following week."[261]

Even in the tamer *The Double Helix* we find such remarks as, "The moment we edged through the door into the crush of half drunken dancers we knew the evening would be a smashing success, since seemingly half the attractive Cambridge au pair girls were there."[262] Watson mentions, "As long as Francis and I remained closed out from the experimental data, the best course was to maintain an open mind. So I returned to my thoughts about sex."[263] Indeed, Watson makes his views clear on the attractiveness

---

[256] Watson, *Avoid Boring People, op. cit.*, 189.
[257] Watson *Avoid Boring People, op. cit.*, 193.
[258] Watson, *Avoid Boring People, op. cit.*, 222.
[259] Watson, *Genes, Girls and Gamow, op. cit.*, 36.
[260] Watson, *Genes, Girls and Gamow, op. cit.*, 39.
[261] Watson, *Genes, Girls and Gamow, op. cit.*, 44.
[262] Watson, *The Double Helix, op. cit.*, Ch.16.
[263] *The Double Helix, op. cit.*, Ch. 20.

of Rosalind Franklin in his book on the discovery of DNA. It is so poetically written that it is worthy quoting in full:

> "I suspect that in the beginning Maurice hoped that Rosy would calm down. Yet mere inspection suggested that she would not easily bend. By choice she did not emphasize her feminine qualities. Though her features were strong, she was not unattractive and might have been quite stunning had she taken even a mild interest in clothes. This she did not. There was never lipstick to contrast with her straight black hair, while at the age of thirty-one her dresses showed all the imagination of English bluestocking adolescents. So it was quite easy to imagine her the product of an unsatisfied mother who unduly stressed the desirability of professional careers that it could save bright girls from marriages to dull men. But this was not the case. Her dedicated, austere life could not be thus explained she was the daughter of a solidly comfortable, erudite banking family. Clearly Rosy had to go or be put in her place. The former was obviously preferable because, given her belligerent moods, it would be very difficult for Maurice to maintain a dominant position that would allow him to think unhindered about DNA."[264]

Even in 1967, it was likely considered a tad sexist to write a paragraph like this, especially as a scientist talking about a female colleague. But evidently fascinated by sexuality and with a penchant for outraging people, Watson did not care. The exact paragraph has since been used to argue that Franklin was a victim of "gender-harassment" (which apparently means being demeaned because of your gender; a rather manipulative term due to its obvious resemblance to "sexual harassment") in the workplace,[265] and certainly of misogyny.[266]

---

[264] Watson, *The Double Helix, op. cit.,* Ch. 2.
[265] B. Benderly, "Rosalind Franklin and the damage of gender harassment," *Science* (1st August 2018), https://www.science.org/content/article/rosalind-franklin-and-damage-gender-harassment
[266] S. Delamont, "Review: Rosalind Franklin and Lucky Jim: Misogyny in the Two Cultures," *Social Studies of Sciences,* 33 (2003): 315-322.

Does Watson Display Attention Deficit Hyper-Activity Disorder?

We have seen that ADHD is germane to genius and significantly crosses over with autism. Watson displays evidence of this, in part, with regard to his attitude towards enjoyment. In his experience, you really should only keep doing something for as long as you enjoy it and, indeed, you should "leave a research field before it bores you." This may work with Watson because he is on a quest and when he realises that if something is unlikely to help him to reach the end of that quest then he is bound to stop enjoying it. He notes: "When I decided to abandon the genetic approach of the phage group in favor of learning X-ray crystallography to go after the three dimensional structure of DNA in Cambridge, I was in no way bored with the work of Max Delbruck and Salva Luria."[267]

You should always be open, argues Watson, to making a change that makes sense, rather than sticking with something, perhaps because the routine is comfortable or expected of you. It may be that precisely this kind of thinking, which implies moderately low Conscientiousness, is central to original thought. Watson summarises: "In fact, there is no good reason ever to be on the downward slope of experience. Avoid it and you'll still be enjoying life when you die."[268] In addition, it appears that Watson can be rather forgetful. In 1956, Watson simply forgot to renew his UK residence permit: "To my chagrin, I also got a summons to the Magistrates' Court at the Guildhall . . . I looked at my passport to discover that my permit had expired the week before. Going immediately to the police station, I hoped that my voluntary appearance would let my permit be routinely extended . . . After learning that I had ample money, lived in Clare, and worked at the Cavendish, my permit was extended until July 31. But I also was fined £5."[269] Watson observes a similar forgetfulness in Francis Crick, with the corridor outsider Crick's laboratory at Cavendish College, Cambridge becoming flooded: "Francis, with his interest in

---

[267] Watson, *Avoid Boring People, op. cit.,* 93.
[268] Watson, *Avoid Boring People, op. cit.,* 93.
[269] Watson, *Genes, Girls and Gamow, op. cit.,* Ch. 29.

theory, had neglected to fasten securely the rubber tubing around his suction pump."[270]

---

[270] Watson, *The Double Helix, op. cit.,* Ch. 1.

Chapter Five

Openness, Autism and Curiosity

Attracted to the Forbidden

In a world in which any discussion of racial differences can lead to you being socially ostracised and seriously damaged with the emotionally manipulative term "racist," many people, when confronted with research indicating that there are consistent national differences in IQ would simply refuse to even entertain it. Such research, questioning, as it does, the hallowed dogmas of Wokeness, would be dismissed out of hand, by many people, as "racist nonsense." Fallacious arguments that in all other circumstances would be seen through would suddenly become convincing.

But some people are not like that. For them, the very fact that something is "forbidden" is enticing, because it is likely where some hidden truth lies. The very fact that people dismiss something as "weird" or "bizarre" renders it all the more fascinating. Could there be some truth in it? This is what the genius is like; he is open-minded and intellectually curious and, as we have seen, this is associated with autism, presumably due to a burning desire to understand and structure the world.

The Genetics of Curiosity

At the national level this curiosity is also associated with scientific creativity. Certain kinds of behaviour have been found to be associated with forms of polymorphisms; alleles of which there are a variety. As we saw earlier, inquisitiveness, which inherently involves risk-taking, is predicted by the DRD4 7-repeat, psychological stability is associated with the 5HTTLPR long form while individualism is associated with the mu-opioid receptor gene; OPRM1 G allele. Northeast Asians tend to be lower in these psychological traits and they are also lower in these specific alleles. A study found that the two big contributors in per capita scientific genius, as assessed using science Nobel Prizes for example, are national level intelligence and also the prevalence of these alleles. This difference partly explains why Northeast Asians, and also Finns, have lower per capita scientific achievement than Europeans despite having markedly higher average intelligence.[271] They also seem to have a narrower intelligence range, which means fewer high IQ outliers.[272]

These alleles appear to militate in favour of intellectual curiosity. This can be regarded as part of the Openness-Intellect personality trait. Put simply, creative scientists, due to their intellectual curiosity, appear to have a very broad knowledge base compared to that of controls. Gregory Feist, in his meta-analysis, noted that creative scientists are characterised by being ". . . *more open to new experiences*, less conventional and less conscientious, more self-confident, self-accepting, driven, ambitious, dominant, hostile, and impulsive."[273] In other words, they are attracted to the breaking of norms and they are extremely open to superficially bizarre possibilities. The resulting broad knowledge base permits them to make connections between different domains and it has been argued that this is exactly how new ideas are generated; by seeing a connection between two domains of knowledge – a good example would be American biologist Edward O. Wilson (1929-2022) using his knowledge of ants to understand humans and, so, developing sociobiology, where human society is examined from a mainly biological perspective – which incrementalists, focused on their narrow area, simply don't perceive.[274]

Even as a child, we see evidence in Watson of the extremely high Openness that is associated with creative scientists. Consistent with high curiosity and, to some extent, high autism; he is simply fascinated by the world itself and desires to understand it in depth. As a 14 year-old, Watson

---

[271] Kura et al., "Why do Northeast Asians Win So Few Nobel Prizes?" *op. cit.*
[272] E. Dutton, J. te Nijenhuis and E. Roivainen, "Solving the puzzle of why Finns have the highest IQ, but one of the lowest number of Nobel prizes in Europe," *Intelligence,* 46 (2014): 192-202.
[273] G. Feist, "A meta-analysis of personality in scientific and artistic creativity," *Personality and Social Psychology Review,* 2 (1998): 290-309.
[274] E. O. Wilson, *Consilience: Towards the Unity of Knowledge* (New York: Alfred A. Knopf, 1998).

was, therefore, twice on national radio as a "Quiz Kid," where contestants competed in general knowledge tests, listened to by audiences of up to 20 million. He was let down by his relative lack of knowledge of Shakespeare plays and of the Old Testament, which be blamed on his Catholic upbringing. In describing this, Watson's highly competitive streak is clear. He feels deeply irked that there were "Quiz Kids" who were more successful than him.[275]

Is Watson the Outsider?

Geniuses are extremely intellectually curious, making it more likely that they will make the connections between disparate areas and so make a highly original connection. Congruous with this, highly creative scientists (maybe we can call them "semi-geniuses") will tend to make their main contribution in a subject other than the one in which they were formally trained, as a detailed analysis of them has demonstrated. Their formal training will tend to be, though will not always be, in a subject that is closer to Maths while their contribution will be in a subject that is lower down the logical hierarchy.[276] The Polish founder of social anthropology Bronisław Malinowski (1884-1942), who insisted that anthropologists conduct participant observation fieldwork, began his career studying Mathematics and Physics.[277] Franz Boas (1858-1942), who also made huge contributions to anthropology, was trained in Physics,[278] while Ernest Gellner (1925-1995), whose key contributions were in social science, began his career as a philosopher.[279]

James Flynn (1934-2020), after whom the psychological "Flynn Effect" (secular increases in IQ scores) is named, was trained as a political

---

[275] Watson, *Avoid Boring People, op. cit.,* 13.
[276] D. K. Simonton, "Varieties of (Scientific) Creativity: A Hierarchical Model of Domain-Specific Disposition, Development, and Achievement," *Perspectives on Psychological Science,* 4 (2009): 5.
[277] B. Średniawa, "The Anthropologist as a Young Physicist: Bronisław Malinowski's Apprenticeship," *Isis,* 72 (1981): 613-620.
[278] R. Zumwalt, *Franz Boas: The Emergence of the Anthropologist* (Lincoln, NI: University Nebraska Press, 2019).
[279] J. Hall, *Ernest Gellner: An Intellectual Biography* (London: Verso, 2014).

scientist.[280] Michael Woodley of Menie (b. 1984), after whom the "Woodley Effect" (evidence of declining intelligence) is named, was trained in Biology.[281] As we noted earlier, Edward O. Wilson, who founded sociobiology, was trained in the study of ants.[282] Charles Darwin's only formal qualification was in Theology.[283] Michael Ventris (1922-1956), who cracked the Linear B script, had no linguistic qualifications. He was a trained architect and he employed techniques from his architectural training to solve his problem.[284] This is an excellent example of making connections between different domains and the way in which it is this that brings about important new knowledge. Incrementalists are simply less able to do this. They are insufficiently high in Openness to look outside of their subject area.

This crossing of domains is true of James Watson. His passion was ornithology and his major subject as an undergraduate was Zoology, in which he received his degree. However, while he was still an undergraduate, as well as reading all manner of literature that was non-scientific as part of his idiosyncratic degree programme, he read Austrian physicist Erwin Schrödinger's (1887-1961) *What is Life?*[285] and became fascinated by genetics. A postgraduate at the University of Indiana, he was supervised by Italian microbiologist Salvador Luria (1912-1991). Watson studied the genetics of phages (viruses) and, in particular, the effects of X-rays upon them, this being the subject of his doctoral thesis.[286] Thus, Watson can be said to be a trained biologist. As a postdoc, Watson made his way to Copenhagen University and worked under the Danish biochemist Herman Kalckar (1908-1991) who was also working on

---

[280] E. Dutton, "Obituary: James Robert Flynn," *Mankind Quarterly,* 61 (2021): 773-779.
[281] A.J. Figueredo and M. Sarraf, "Michael A. Woodley of Menie, Yr.," *Encyclopedia of Evolutionary Psychological Science* (New York: Springer, 2020).
[282] E.O. Wilson, *Naturalist* (Washington, DC: Island Press, 1994).
[283] N. Barlow, (Ed.), *The Autobiography of Charles Darwin, 1809-1882* (New York: W.W. Norton, 1958).
[284] A. Robinson, *The Man Who Deciphered Linear B: The Story of Michael Ventris* (London: Thames and Hudson, 2012).
[285] E. Schrödinger, *What is Life? The Physical Aspect of the Living Cell* (Cambridge: Cambridge University Press, 1944).
[286] J.D. Watson, *The Biological Properties of X-Ray Inactivated Bacteriophage* (PhD Thesis: University of Indiana, 1951).

phages. However, Watson had decided that he wanted to explore the structure of DNA, so he spent much of his time there conducting experiments with a microbial physiologist. In 1951, Watson went to Cambridge as a postdoctoral researcher in what was, clearly, Chemistry, despite having no formal university qualification in this subject. He had taken Chemistry courses as an undergraduate but he was in no sense a qualified Chemist, and nor was Crick.

In this regard, Watson writes: "In every sense solving the double helix was a problem in chemistry. Alex Todd[287] facetiously told me that Francis and I were good organic chemists, not wanting to admit that a major objective in chemistry had been solved by nonchemists."[288] One of the people who was competing with Watson and Crick to work out the structure of DNA was the American chemist Linus Pauling. Of Pauling, Watson writes: "Much better to be the least accomplished chemist in a super chemistry department than the superstar in a less lustrous department. By the early 1950s, Linus Pauling's scientific interactions with fellow scientists were effectively monologues instead of dialogues. He then wanted adoration, not criticism."[289] In the end, the structure of DNA was discovered by two people were not trained chemists. This is, to a certain degree, what we would expect: the genius' key contribution – his ground-breaking, highly original work - is often in an area in which he is not formally trained. The incrementalist will make small contributions in his own area, but, in general, he will not accomplish anything particularly original or important. He may be left fuming with jealousy as an "outsider" who has failed to "play the game" makes an original contribution in *his* field.

Is Watson a Foreigner?

Gregory Feist has suggested that another correlate of being a creative scientist may even be being a foreigner; that you live or simply spend a period of time abroad. This may both reflect high curiosity and induce new ways of looking at the world mediated by new knowledge. Feist observes

---

[287] Alex Todd (1907-1997), Scottish biochemist.
[288] Watson, *Avoid Boring People, op. cit.,* 108.
[289] Watson, *Avoid Boring People, op. cit.,* 114.

that being a relatively recent immigrant to the US is weakly associated with scientific interest and talent.[290] Part of this may be because migration is associated with intelligence: intelligent people are more future-oriented and are more likely to have the financial resources necessary to migrate.[291] However, it may also be that, being from a different culture, they bring an outsider perspective. They have experienced another culture, and can, therefore, make connections which natives are unable to make: they have more knowledge upon which to draw.

It may follow that spending time abroad, all else being equal, would elevate the likelihood of creative achievement and, also, that creative types, being high in Openness and in risk-taking, would wish to spend periods of time abroad or even to emigrate. Consistent with this, Openness appears to predict migration, especially to very culturally distant countries. Agreeableness, Conscientiousness and emotional stability are negatively associated with migration.[292] This is because those who are high in Conscientiousness value security and order, those who are agreeable value social harmony and create strong social bonds, while those who are high in Neuroticism create weak attachments and have low quality friendships.[293] This research would imply that migration is associated with those who are intelligent and creative, but the fact of being an immigrant may also cause people to be more creative. In this regard, there is some evidence that living abroad is causally associated with creativity. Specifically, time spent living abroad (as opposed to travelling or holidaying) was strongly associated with creativity, to the extent that priming subjects with the idea of living abroad induced in them greater levels of creativity.[294]

---

[290] G. Feist, *The Psychology of Science and the Origins of the Scientific Mind* (New Haven, CT: Yale University Press, 2006), 74.

[291] Jensen, *The g Factor, op cit.*

[292] D. Fouarge, M. Özer and P. Seegers, "Personality Traits, Migration Intentions and Cultural Distance," *IZA Institute of Labor Economics* (2019).

[293] J. Décieux and T. Altmann, "The Relationship between Migration and the Big Five Personality Traits: Evidence from Probability-Based Samples," *Population, Space and Place,* 30 (2024): e2782.

[294] W. Maddux and A. Galinsky, "Cultural Borders and Mental Barriers: The Relationship Between Living Abroad and Creativity," *Journal of Personality and Social Psychology* 96 (2009): 1047-1061.

Watson's maternal grandfather was a Glasgow tailor while his maternal grandmother was the child of immigrants from County Tipperary, with the result that James Watson himself, though an atheist, is nominally Roman Catholic. His atheist father relented and allowed Watson to be raised Catholic, with Watson attending mass each Sunday until the age of eleven, at which point Watson abandoned Sunday mass for bird watching.[295] Immigrants tend to be of elevated intelligence compared to those whom they leave behind and they also tend to be risk-takers, relatively low in aspects of Agreeableness and Conscientiousness. In addition, as a Roman Catholic, of Scottish-Irish heritage on his mother's side, there is a degree to which Watson is an outsider, a foreigner, in the WASP-dominated United States of the 1920s;[296] he is able to perceive this world from an outsider perspective.

The time spent in Copenhagen, and then working at Cambridge University where Watson made his fundamental breakthrough, is also in line with the genius archetype. As we have discussed, there is some evidence that highly creative scientists are inclined to spend time abroad. On the one hand, this reflects traits such as high Openness, sensation-seeking and risk-taking; all of which are crucial elements of creativity. On the other hand, the fact of spending time abroad may feed into creativity insomuch as it will involve unusual experiences - new knowledge upon which to draw - and it will cause the sojourner to look at the world in a new way. This being so, a significant foreign sojourn, not merely a holiday in which a foreign culture is merely superficially experienced, may be a component of the creative process and, evidently, Watson underwent this experience twice; in the latter case for a number of years. Watson appears to be aware of this, asserting that, "Travel makes your science stronger."[297] Watson, however, makes this point in relation to travelling out of your own academic institution to give presentations and so meeting intelligent and useful people that may assist you with your own research. "By moving

---

[295] Watson, *Avoid Boring People, op. cit.,* 10.
[296] See, D. Brooks, *The Protestant Establishment: Aristocracy and Caste in America* (New York: Harper and Row, 1964).
[297] Watson, *Avoid Boring People, op. cit.,* 154.

out of your own turf, you are likely to spot clever graduate students and postdocs who might enhance your own environment."[298]

The Flipside of Genius Traits: Attraction to the Eccentric and Taboo and Breaking Academic Rules

However, there is a fascinating flip-side to this kind of personality which has been observed with many highly creative scientists. Put simply, their openness, and rejection of norms, may be so high that they will be attracted to, and at least be prepared to entertain, possibilities that most people will dismiss as manifestly ludicrous or as unutterably offensive and beyond the pale. There are many examples of this. Hans Eysenck was prepared to entertain the possibility that there might be something to astrology, a possibility that normal people would just dismiss out of hand.[299] American physicist William Shockley (1910-1989), who won the Nobel Prize for inventing the transistor radio, became extremely interested in dysgenics towards the end of his life and began to promote the highly taboo issue of eugenics.[300] Newton was obsessed with alchemy and many other eccentric ideas, such as finding hidden codes in the Bible. Scientists were amazed when Newton's many papers on alchemy resurfaced:

> "When Isaac Newton's alchemical papers surfaced at a Sotheby's auction in 1936, the quantity and seeming incoherence of the manuscripts were shocking. No longer the exemplar of Enlightenment rationality, the legendary physicist suddenly became "the last of the magicians."[301]

This attraction to the bizarre or to the taboo can be understood as the necessary flip-side of the genius. A norm-questioning, highly curious, semi-psychopathic, autistic personality will develop highly original, ground-breaking ideas, when combined with the necessary intelligence

---

[298] Watson, *Avoid Boring People, op. cit.*, 154.

[299] H. Eysenck and D. Nias, *Astrology: Science or Superstition?* (New York: Temple Smith, 1982).

[300] J. Shurkin, *Broken Genius: The Rise and Fall of William Shockley, Creator of the Electronic Age* (London: Macmillan, 2006).

[301] W. Newman, *Newton the Alchemist: Science, Enigma, and the Quest for Nature's "Secret Fire"* (Princeton, NJ: Princeton University Press, 2018).

and other traits. However, the same kind of personality will, therefore, be attracted to that which ordinary people will regard as offensive or wacky.

In much the same way, we might expect people with these traits to fail to precisely follow the "academic rules." Sub-clinically psychopathic, they will bend the rules or simply regard them, and other people's feelings, as not very important. For this reason, we shouldn't be surprised by evidence of academic misconduct such as plagiarism, even if of a minor kind involving not giving proper credit for ideas or information, in the case of Albert Einstein,[302] Charles Darwin,[303] and Hans Eysenck.[304] One can imagine that such people will take the view that the non-entity incrementalists whom they are accused of plagiarising are so unimportant that it surely isn't necessary to cite them. Not caring much about these rules themselves, they may wrongly assume that others won't really mind or they may take the view that the person's idea is so relatively insignificant that they are not worth bothering to cite. However, they may discover that "Hell hath no fury like a nobody scorned" and, moreover, their genius ideas will create for them enemies who will scrutinise all of their works in depth in search of any minor error that can be used against them. The work of incrementalist scientists is far less likely to be subjected to this level of scrutiny. Further, we would expect the mediocre, uncreative scientist to attempt to claw back a sense of self-worth by focussing on issues such as ethics. In general, there is some evidence that high status predicts behaving less ethically.[305] In much the same way, relatively unimportant nations tend to promote the idea that they are at least moral,[306]

---

[302] M. Wazeck, *Einstein's Opponents: The Public Controversy about the Theory of Relativity in the 1920s* (Cambridge: Cambridge University Press, 2014).
[303] J. Bergman, *The Dark Side of Charles Darwin: A Critical Analysis of an Icon of Science* (Master Books: Green Forest, AR, 2011).
[304] P. Corr, *Hans Eysenck* (London: Macmillan, 2015).
[305] P. Piff, D. Stancato, S. Côté et al., "Higher social class predicts increased unethical behaviour," *PNAS,* 109 (2012): 4086-4091.
[306] See, E. Dutton, *The Finnuit: Finnish Culture and the Religion of Uniqueness* (Budapest: Akademiai Kiado, 2009).

as do members of the middle class, in contrast to the upper class who actually have serious power.[307]

It would be germane, at this point, to take a slight detour from our examination of genius psychology to look at the precise taboo areas that such a psychology has led Watson to examine. In each case, we will show that he was empirically correct. We will then return to the broader exploration. It should be noted that even in 2008, some scientists were prepared to stand up and defend Watson. In an article in *Medical Hypotheses,* James Malloy explained that:

> "Dr Watson was correct on all accounts: (1) Intelligence tests do reveal large differences between European and sub-Saharan African nations, (2) the evidence does link these differences to universally valued outcomes, both within and between nations, and (3) there is data to suggest these differences are influenced by genetic factors. The media and the larger scientific community punished Dr Watson for violating a social and political taboo . . ."

They were, therefore, "lying to the public about numerous scientific issues to make Watson appear negligent in his statements; a gross abuse of valuable and fragile public trust in scientific authority."[308] The editor of the journal, Bruce Charlton (b. 1959), defended Watson for similar reasons in an editorial.[309] But far too few scientists had the courage to defend him.

---

[307] For further discussion of this tendency see Dutton and Rayner-Hilles, *The Past is a Future Country, op. cit.* and T. McEnery, *Swearing in English Bad Language, Purity and Power from 1586 to the Present* (London: Routledge, 2004).

[308] J. Malloy, "James Watson tells the inconvenient truth: Faces the consequences," *Medical Hypotheses,* 70 (2008): 1081-1091.

[309] B.G. Charlton, "Editorial," *Medical Hypotheses,* 70 (2008): 1077-1090.

Chapter Six

Are Fat People and
Southern Europeans More Sexual?

The Pursuit of Happiness

Although James Watson was "cancelled" in October 2007, these events were foreshadowed by furores over slightly less taboo-breaking comments, beginning in the year 2000. Watson was known for his scintillating lectures in which he would think out loud, often with regard to controversial topics. He had long acted in this way, but it suddenly became a problem in November of the year 2000 when he was giving a guest lecture at the University of California at Berkeley entitled, "The Pursuit of Happiness: Lessons from pom-C." Watson explained to his audience of 200 students and academics that a protein, pom-C, helps to create several different hormones: One of these determines skin colour ("melanin"); another increases a sense of well-being ("beta endorphins"); and the third plays a role in fat metabolism ("leptin").

Watson simply wondered aloud why evolution should have linked these hormones, which it clearly had because when traits are concomitantly selected for they become clumped together in a process known as "pleiotropy." Watson also mused on whether these compounds, which impacted mood and behaviour, might interact with sunlight, as this is what melanin does. It occurred to Watson that there may be a relationship between skin colour and sexual activity and between thinness and ambition.[310] After all, in pre-history, you passed on your genes if you had high status – if you were the alpha male with the large harem (we will

---

[310] T. Abate, "Nobel Winner's Theories Raise Uproar in Berkeley / Geneticist's views strike many as racist, sexist," *SF Gate* (13th November 2000), https://www.sfgate.com /science/article/Nobel-Winner-s-Theories-Raise-Uproar-in-Berkeley-3236584.php

look at this below) – and if you had a high sex drive. And somehow, being able to regulate your metabolism in a certain way had been selected for, as had dark skin.

To illustrate his point, Watson gave a number of amusing examples. With regard to exposure to sunlight and sexual urges, he quipped: "That's why you have Latin lovers. You've never heard of an English lover. Only an English patient." This was a reference to the film *The English Patient* which had come out in 1996. Watson displayed a slide of the English model Kate Moss (b. 1974), looking sad, to support his view that thin people are unhappy and therefore more ambitious. "Whenever you interview fat people, you feel bad, because you know you're not going to hire them," Watson observed. These remarks upset a number of students and lecturers; specifically females. We will look at the impact females have had on the university environment in a later chapter. According to a female student called Sarah Tegen, who was present and was deeply "offended" by Watson's lecture, Watson:

> ". . . started off describing an experiment by scientists at the University of Arizona, who injected male patients with an extract of melanin. They intended to test whether they could chemically darken the men's skin as a skin cancer protection, only to observe an unusual side effect - the men developed sustained and unprovoked erections."

The Nobel Prize winner "said this (melanin injection) is even better than Viagra because you don't even have to think about sex."[311] Tegen went on to become "Senior Vice President and Chief Publishing Officer, ACS Publications, at the American Chemical Society."[312] In other words, she does not appear to have gone on to be a creative scientist who has had made a profound breakthrough. According to another student, Jill Fuss, later the managing director of a charity which helps scientists,[313] so, again, not a creative scientist who has propounded a highly original theory:

---

[311] Abate, "Nobel Winner's Theories Raise Uproar in Berkeley / Geneticist's views strike many as racist, sexist," *op. cit.*

[312] "Sarah Tegen," *STM* (2024), https://www.stm-assoc.org/people/sarah-tegen/

[313] *Activate,* "From Fellow to Managing Director: Jill Fuss is a New Kind of Activate Success Story" (12th August 2022), https://www.activate.org/news/from-fellow-to-managing-director-jill-fuss-is-a-new-kind-of-activate-success-story

"Then he launched into this whole thing about the sun and sexual drive." He "showed slides of women in bikinis and contrasted them to veiled Muslim women, to suggest that controlling exposure to sun may suppress sexual desire and vice versa."

Watson went on to suggest that people who live in northern climates drink more alcohol in order to compensate for the unhappiness they suffer due to insufficient sunlight. He further remarked than thin people are likely to be more ambitious while fat people are likely to be more sexual, "because their bloodstreams contain higher levels of leptin, one of the hormones derived from pom-C."[314]

"Racist and Sexist Stereotypes"

As a consequence of Watson making his suggestions in a way that wasn't "sensitive" to people's "feelings," and, in particular, to the "feelings" of female students and academics, a biology lecturer called Susan Marqusee, later Professor of Molecular Biology at UC Berkeley, walked out of the lecture a third of the way through, presumably due to being unable to emotionally cope with listening to any more of it, congruous with a "stereotype," or rather an empirical fact, that females are more "emotional" than males due to being higher in Neuroticism, feeling negative feelings, especially anxiety,[315] induced, in particular, when their evolved desire for social conformity is interfered with.[316] She explained to reporters: "I was kind of in shock most of the time. He took a lot of what I consider sexist and racist stereotypes and claimed a biochemical basis without presenting any data."

Two female students told reporters how offended they were, as we saw earlier, and even Watson's supporters were mildly critical. "Doesn't a guy like Jim Watson have the responsibility to make this not ugly?" said UC Berkeley biologist Michael Botchan, a former student of Watson's. "Yes.

---

[314] Abate, "Nobel Winner's Theories Raise Uproar in Berkeley / Geneticist's views strike many as racist, sexist," *op. cit.*

[315] Y. Weisberg, C. DeYoung and Jacob Hirsch, "Gender Differences in Personality across the Ten Aspects of the Big Five," *Frontiers in Psychology,* 2 (2011): 178.

[316] A. Eagly and C. Chrvala, "Sex Differences in Conformity: Status and Gender Role Interpretations," *Psychology of Women Quarterly,* 10 (1986): 3.

But I cannot tell Jim Watson to change his ways." Berkeley genetics professor Thomas Cline said Watson's lecture "crossed over the line" from being "provocative" to being "irresponsible because the senior scientist failed to separate fact from conjecture."[317] Watson's various contentious remarks were reported in newspapers around the world and on *ABC News*.[318] When Watson won his Nobel Prize "A number of the next day's articles described me as a boyish-looking bachelor whom friends found lively and kindly."[319] Evidently, the liveliness had continued into old age.

Sunlight and Sex Drive

Of course, the only question that should have been in these people's minds, as genuine scientists, was, "Is what Watson is saying empirically accurate?" This is, after all, the only question that should concern any scholar.

The answer is, "Yes," Watson's "offensive" conjectures that November day in the year 2000 were indeed empirically accurate. They may have been slight simplifications, but this is not necessarily a bad thing in terms of helping people to understand complicated issues. As Watson has summarised, "Books, like plays or movies, succeed best when they exaggerate the truth. In communicating scientific fact to the non-specialist, there is a huge difference between simplifying for effect and misleading."[320]

Let us begin with the possibility that sunlight exposure might relate to sex drive. According to a study by Israeli geneticist Roma Parikh and colleagues, exposure to Ultra Violet B-light increases sex-steroid circulation levels in mice and humans, it enhances both female attractiveness and female receptiveness to males, it increases the length of female ovulation, and:

---

[317] Abate, "Nobel Winner's Theories Raise Uproar in Berkeley/Geneticist's views strike many as racist, sexist," *op. cit.*

[318] *ABC News,* "Laureate: Sex Drive Linked to Skin Color" (25th November 2000), https://abcnews.go.com/Technology/story?id=119772&page=1

[319] J.D. Watson, *Avoid Boring People: Lessons from a Life in Science* (New York: Knopf, 2007), 176.

[320] Watson *Avoid Boring People, op. cit.,* 169.

"Skin p53 regulates UVB-induced sexual behaviour and ovarian physiological changes." In other words, stimulating the skin with this light makes people sexually aroused. The authors summarise that, "In humans, solar exposure enhances romantic passion in both genders and aggressiveness in men, as seen in analysis of individual questionaries, and positively correlates with testosterone level."[321]

In essence, Watson's intelligent, evidence-based speculation was proven to be entirely correct 21 years later. Latin men have a higher sex drive than Englishmen, in part, due to greater exposure to the sun.

Skin Colour and Sex Drive

Watson's next suggestion was that there may be a relationship between skin darkness and sex drive, at least within race; possibly mediated by a relationship between testosterone and skin darkness. Testosterone is certainly correlated with sex drive. The higher someone's circulating testosterone, the higher, in general, is their libido.[322] Testosterone is indeed associated with darker skin,[323] which is one of the reasons why females tend to have lighter skin than males;[324] lighter skin signals the presence of the female hormone estrogen.[325] Testosterone is also associated with darker hair and even darker plumage, where there is a 0.88 correlation between darkness of plumage and testosterone level.[326] No wonder, then, that so many folk songs are based around "fair young maidens" and are

---

[321] R. Parikh, E. Sorek, S. Parikh et al., "Skin exposure to UVB light induces a skin-brain-gonad axis and sexual behaviour," *Cell Reports,* 36 (2021): 8.

[322] T. Travison, J. Morley, A. Araujo et al., "The relationship between libido and testosterone levels in aging men," *Journal of Clinical Endocrinology and Metabolism,* 7 (2006): 2509-2013.

[323] G. Sobral, C. Dubuc, S. Winters et al., "Facial and genital color ornamentation, testosterone, and reproductive output in high-ranking male rhesus macaques," *Scientific Reports,* 14 (2024): 2621.

[324] M. de Lurdes Carrito, I. Barbas dos Santos, C. Lefevre et al., "The role of sexually dimorphic skin colour and shape in attractiveness of male faces," *Evolution and Human Behavior,* 37 (2016): 125-133.

[325] B. Jones, A. Hahn, C. Fisher et al., "Facial coloration tracks changes in women's estradiol," *Psychoneuroendocrinology,* 56 (2015): 29-34.

[326] V. Bokony, L. Garamaszegi, K. Hirschenhauser and A. Liker, "Testosterone and melanin-based black plumage coloration: A comparative study," *Behavioral Ecology and Sociobiology,* 62 (2008): 1229-1238.

also set "in the month of May," when it tends to be sunny. Green eyes, in contrast to brown eyes, are associated with pre-natal estrogen exposure.[327]

A summary of the relevant studies notes that darker colouring is associated with greater aggressiveness in birds and lizards. In US states, darker skin was found to correlate with the murder rate at 0.55. Within Italy, the percentage of Italians with black eyes in an area correlated at 0.94 with the attempted murder rate, while the percentage with blue eyes correlated with the attempted murder rate at -0.45. Other research has found that, within race, brown-eyed children are more confident than blue-eyed children.[328] Self-confidence is itself correlated with pre-natal testosterone exposure.[329] All of this would imply that Watson was correct: dark skin and dark pigmentation in general is associated with testosterone, testosterone is associated with sex drive and drive more generally, so dark skin is very likely to be associated with sex drive.

Unhappiness, Ambition and Thinness

Watson also speculated that there may be a relationship between unhappiness and ambition. Subsequent research has demonstrated him to be correct in this regard. One of the key predictors of Machiavellianism is Neuroticism.[330] This personality trait involves experiencing negative feelings – such as sadness, fear, anger and resentment – intensely. It follows, as we have already discussed, that if you perceive the world as a frightening and unstable place then you will want to take power over it and, likewise, if you are full of resentment then you will desire power over other people. There appears to be relatively little research specifically on ambition and personality traits, but certainly work-engagement correlates

---

[327] P. Frost, K. Kleisner and J. Flegr, "Health status by gender, hair color, and eye color: Red-haired women are the most divergent," *PLoS One*, 12 (2017): e190238.

[328] D.I. Templer, "Rushton: The Great Theoretician and His Contribution to Personality" in H. Nyborg, (Ed.), *The Life History Approach to Human Differences: A Tribute to J. Philippe Rushton* (London: Ulster Institute for Social Research, 2015).

[329] P. Dalton and S. Ghosal, "Self-confidence, Overconfidence and Prenatal Testosterone Exposure: Evidence from the Lab," *Frontier in Behavioral Neuroscience*, 12 (2018): 5.

[330] S. Jacobwitz and V. Egan, "The Dark Triad and Normal Personality Traits," *Personality and Individual Differences*, 40 (2006): 331-339.

with ratings of personal ambitiousness and also with Neuroticism.[331] Evidently, then, unhappy people are more ambitious than are happy people in the sense that they work harder towards their socioeconomic goals.

Watson also speculated that people who are overweight will be less unhappy and thus less ambitious. In this regard, he was correct to some extent, but certain qualifiers need to be put in place. In personality psychology, experiencing negative feelings strongly – Neuroticism – is effectively an independent trait from feeling positive feelings strongly: Extraversion. To put it another way, the opposite of sadness is not happiness, it is a vague sense of everything being tolerable. Studies indicate that Extraversion predicts being overweight. This makes sense as Extraversion involves positive feelings and, accordingly, Extraverts will experience a great deal of pleasure from, for example, eating nice food. Neuroticism is associated, across time, with weight fluctuation. This implies that some Neurotic people go through periods of anxiety, where they don't eat much, and periods where they are more mentally stable, during in which they eat more.[332]

Interestingly, one of the side-effects of many anti-depressants, which are also used to treat anxiety, is increased appetite and consequent weight gain.[333] It has been implied that the American television personality Oprah Winfrey (b. 1954) may reflect this pattern, whereby her weight fluctuates with her fluctuating mood. When she is thin, she seems to lose ratings, perhaps because she is less ebullient. Ratings increase as she puts on weight, possibly because she is more confident.[334] There is some evidence that people who are depressed will tend to over-eat, perhaps in an attempt

---

[331] A. Furnham, C. Robinson and J. Haakonsen, "Hire Ambitious People: Bright- and Dark-Side Personality and Work Engagement," *Journal of Individual Differences,* 44 (2023): 47-56.

[332] A. Sutin, L. Ferrucci, A. Zonderman and A. Terracciano, "Personality and Obesity across the Adult Lifespan," *Journal of Personality and Social Psychology,* 101 (2011): 579-592.

[333] H. Gill, S. Gill, S. El-Halabi et al., "Antidepressant Medications and Weight Change: A Narrative Review," *Obesity,* 28 (2020): 2064-2072.

[334] M. Callahan, "The Oprah Syndrome," *New York Post* (24th January 2009), https://nypost.com/2009/01/24/the-oprah-syndrome/

to make themselves feel good, a process known as comfort eating.[335] Similarly, anxiety has been shown to be associated both with comfort eating and with uncontrolled eating, where people binge on huge amounts of food.[336] For example, the British television personality and author Richard Osman (b. 1970) has spoken of dealing with aspects of depression, such as a sense that his life has no direction, via compulsive binge-eating.[337] However, this is merely a correlation and there are differences at the extremes. Being extremely high in anxiety, such that it can be regarded as a disorder, is, indeed, associated with being extremely thin.[338] This is unsurprising, as everyday experience tells us that when you are plagued by worry about something then your appetite tends to be reduced.[339]

Thus, with certain qualifications, Watson was correct: thin people are, on average, unhappy and being unhappy makes you more ambitious. However, because we are dealing here with sometimes weak associations, it doesn't necessarily follow that thin people are likely to be more ambitious than fat people. For example, one study has found a correlation of 0.29 between Machiavellianism and BMI, meaning that people who are power-hungry are *more likely* to be overweight. According to the authors, "This is explained by the fact that Machiavellianism promotes an unhealthy lifestyle, resulting in a worse diet and less physical activity due to the Machiavellian nature of planning thoughtfully, which causes stress to some extent as immediate needs are suppressed for long-term goals."[340]

---

[335] L. Buratta, C. Pazzagli, E. Delvecchio, G. Cenci et al., "Personality Features in Obesity," *Frontiers in Psychology,* 11 (2020): 530425.

[336] L. Cifuentes, A. Campos, M. Silgado et al., "Association between anxiety and eating behaviors in patients with obesity," *Obesity Pillars,* 3 (2022): 100021.

[337] L. Whelan, "Richard Osman health: Pointless host on 'difficult journey' with addiction," *Daily Express* (22nd February 2022), https://www.express.co.uk/life-style/health/1569839/richard-osman-health-pointless-food-addiction

[338] L. Thornton, J. Dellava, T. Root et al., "Anorexia Nervosa and Generalized Anxiety Disorder: Further Explorations of the Relation Between Anxiety and Body Mass Index," *Journal of Anxiety Disorders,* 25 (2011): 727-730.

[339] R. Lynn, *An Introduction to the Study of Personality* (London: Macmillan, 1971).

[340] F. Brugger, E. Schönthaler, A. Baranyi et al., "Metabolic Syndrome in Affective Disorders: Associations with Dark Triad Personality Traits," *Metabolites,* 13 (2023): 956.

Of course, one of the problems here is that Machiavellianism is not only related to ambitiousness but, rather, to ambitiousness as a component of attaining power; there being a nuanced difference here. Is an ambitious writer, who accordingly manages to get his novel published, really trying to attain power? He is attaining status, and status may be said to give you a degree of power over other people, but is it the same thing as the writer managing to take over a publishing house via which many people are answerable to him? At best, publishing the novel is "soft power" rather than "hard power:" an extreme Machiavellian would not even care about fame; he would just yearn for power. Machiavellianism is also characterised, as we discussed earlier, by manipulativeness, deceitfulness, high levels of self-interest, and a tendency to see other people as a means to an end.

Is there another way of gaging ambitiousness? One possibility is looking at "Persistence." This "refers to the ability to maintain arousal and motivation internally in the absence of an immediate external reward. High P scores indicate hard-working, perseverance, ambitiousness, and perception of frustration as a personal challenge."[341] Accordingly, it is extremely close to "ambition," commonly defined as the desire and determination to achieve success. A significant component of persistence is "reward sensitivity;" as you are, after all, motivated by future rewards.[342] It has been found that there is an inverse relationship between reward-sensitivity and being over-weight or obese.[343]

Thus, there is at least a case for arguing that fat people are likely to be less ambitious. It does not follow that very low BMI, however, is associated with high reward sensitivity. Indeed, the same research found a weak positive correlation between BMI and reward sensitivity among people in the healthy weight range and found low reward sensitivity

[341] D. Laricchuita and L. Petrosini, "Individual differences in response to positive and negative stimuli: endocannabinoid-based insight on approach and avoidance behaviors," *Frontiers in Systems Neuroscience,* 8 (2014): 238.

[342] G. Frank, M. Schott, L. Sternheim et al., "Persistence, Reward Dependence, and Sensitivity to Reward Are Associated With Unexpected Salience Response in Girls but Not in Adult Women: Implications for Psychiatric Vulnerabilities," *Biological Psychiatry, Cognitive Neuroscience and Neuroimaging,* 7 (2022): 1170-1182.

[343] C. Davis and J. Fox, "Sensitivity to reward and body mass index (BMI): Evidence for a non-linear relationship," *Appetite,* 50 (2008): 43-49.

among the very thin. Such people, the authors argued, would be underweight due to the "subjectively diminished reward potential of food." But again, within certain caveats, there is a case, if no more than that, for arguing that fat people will be low in ambition and those within the normal weight range, though not the dangerously thin, will be higher in it.

What is Life History Strategy?

Before we discuss the issue of sexuality and being fat, it would be helpful to explore a potentially relevant theory. We all follow a relative Life History Strategy, sitting on a spectrum between "fast" and "slow." A fast Life History Strategy (LHS) is a suite of physical and mental traits that develop in an easy but unstable ecology, in which you must respond to sudden, unpredictable challenges by being extremely aggressive. A fast LHS is called an r-strategy, while a slow LHS is known as a K-strategy. Those people who are r-strategists "live for the now." They live fast and die young, because they could be wiped out at any moment: their environment is chaos. They, therefore, invest energy in copulation but invest little of their energy in their partners nor in nurturing their offspring. They do everything relatively early: they are born earlier, develop more quickly, go through puberty earlier, become sexually active younger, are more sexually promiscuous, enter the menopause earlier and die younger. In nature, r-strategy animals will have larger litters and even a higher number of nipples to feed these litters. They are low in Agreeableness, low Conscientiousness and high in Neuroticism.

K-strategists are adapted to a predictable yet harsh (and thus competitive) ecology, in which offspring who are insufficiently nurtured could all simply die. Thus, they "live slow and die old" and direct energy away from copulation and towards nurture, of both their partner and their offspring. Their offspring are more likely to survive if they are directed along the adaptive roadmap of life, such that they can better compete. So, the length of childhood increases such that they can be precisely taught about the narrow niche in which they must survive, indeed they are born essentially helpless, utterly reliant on their parents during early childhood. This ecology, being highly competitive, selects in favour of intelligence, as its harsh, competitive nature presents more problems to be solved. And, in that it requires nurture and cooperation, it selects for Agreeableness, Conscientiousness, social anxiety, but, in general, against Neuroticism, that is against strong negative feelings such as anger and jealousy. On every measure, such people live more slowly.[344] By contrast, an unstable ecology may require bursts of violent aggression. Clearly, the stereotypical single mother on a council estate surrounded by multiple children from multiple relationships is a fast Life History strategist when compared to the stereotypical female academic who married well into her thirties and has, perhaps, one child. The heritability of Life History Strategy is around 0.5.[345]

So Are Fat People More Sexual?

With all of this established, we can now turn to Watson's contention: Being obese is associated with fast Life History Strategy.[346] Indeed, obese women have been found to be more likely to report an unintended pregnancy, which would imply risky sexual behaviour consistent with a fast Life History Strategy.[347] Thus, all else controlled for, we would expect fat people to be more sexually-motivated, even if they might find, due to being perceived as unattractive, that they would be less able to obtain sex. Their low impulse control makes them fat and the same low impulse control is associated, due to Life History Strategy, with being highly sexually-motivated.

---

[344] J.P. Rushton, *Race, Evolution and Behavior: A Life History Perspective* (New Brunswick, NJ: Transaction Publishing, 1995)

[345] A.J. Figueredo, "The heritability of life history strategy: The *K*-factor, covitality, and personality," *Social Biology,* 5 (2004): 121-143.

[346] J. Maner, A. Dittmann, A. Meltzer and J. McNulty, "Implications of life-history strategies for obesity," *PNAS,* 114 (2017): 8517-8522.

[347] N. Bathos, K. Wellings, C. Labourde and C. Moreau, "Sexuality and obesity, a gender perspective: results from French national random probability survey of sexual behaviours," *British Medical Journal,* 340 (2010): 2573.

Chapter Seven

The Decline of Intelligence

The Rising Underclass

Watson's next controversy was in January 2007. In an interview with the magazine *Esquire* he asserted, "If there is any correlation between success and genes, IQ will fall if the successful people don't have children. These are self-obvious facts."[348] For this he was accused of being a eugenicist; one who wants to, in effect, breed humans such that their highly genetic qualities, such as intelligence, are improved and such that they are, in essence, healthier.[349]

Of course, he advocated no such thing, but people who are not especially intelligent or who are highly emotional engage in "fact-value conflation" where they infer that because you assert something is true, you must desire it to be true. Presumably this cognitive bias has developed as a way of shunning those who question group-norms because such people may interfere with the internal cooperation of the group causing it to be invaded by a more internally cooperative group. But it is, nevertheless, illogical for Wesley Smith (b. 1949) to have written in the magazine *First Things:* "Nobel Laureate James Watson, co-discoverer of the DNA double helix. Almost every time the curmudgeon opens his mouth—as in this January 07 *Esquire* interview—he reveals a stunted moral center. Indeed, based on the interview, Watson reveals himself to be a eugenicist . . ." The fact that Smith referred to Watson as a "curmudgeon" only highlights the extent to which his article was not a reasoned exercise.[350] Wesley Smith is

---

[348] Richardson, "James Watson: What I've Learned," *op. cit.*

[349] See, Dutton, *Breeding the Human Herd, op. cit.*

[350] W. Smith, "James Watson: Eugenicist and Potential Anti-Semite," *First Things* (1ˢᵗ February 2007), https://www.firstthings.com/blogs/firstthoughts/2007/01/james-watson-eugenicist-and-potential-anti-semite

a fellow at the Discovery Institute, a creationist think tank which espouses the teaching of "Intelligent Design" in US schools. Watson, as we will see, was correct.

Developed countries are breeding at below-replacement fertility, at least among the native populations. Nevertheless within these populations, there is a rapidly multiplying sub-demographic with far-above replacement level fertility; the underclass, those who are on welfare. They're roughly one fifth of the population in most Western countries at the moment. British readers will be familiar with the case of Mick Philpott (b. 1956) of Allenton in Derby in the English Midlands. In 2012, as part of an insurance fraud, Philpott set fire to his own house, with six of his young children – whom he'd intended to rescue from the flames - dying as a result. He lied to the public, appealing for help to find the people who had set fire to his house. Philpott, a long-term benefits recipient, is the father of seventeen children by assorted women; wives, girlfriends and a mistress,[351] children who will inherit the psychological traits that render their parents part of the underclass. Indeed, it is specifically the criminal underclass, rather than simply families who are on benefits, who have above replacement fertility in the UK, families on benefits that require police intervention.[352] Even prior to his conviction for manslaughter, Philpott had served time in prison for attempted murder, in 1978.[353] In 1991, Philpott was convicted of head-butting a colleague.[354] Noticing this tendency, for the socioeconomically unsuccessful to have high fertility, caused problems for James Watson.

---

[351] M. Paprota, *Constructing the Welfare State in the British Press: Boundaries and Metaphors in Political Discourse* (London: Bloomsbury Publishing, 2020), 76.

[352] A. Perkins, *The Welfare Trait: How State Benefits Affect Personality* (London: Palgrave Macmillan, 2016).

[353] S. Hare, "Derby fire deaths: Mick Philpott 'no right-minded father'" *BBC News* (2nd April 2013), https://www.bbc.com/news/uk-england-derbyshire-21953842

[354] *BBC News,* "Philpott sentencing: Derby fire deaths duo 'good' parents" (3rd April 2013), https://www.bbc.co.uk/news/uk-england-derbyshire-22011190

What is the Relationship
between Intelligence and Fertility?

There is sound evidence that the heritability of socioeconomic status across generations is extremely high, around 0.8. There are two reasons for this. Firstly, based on English data from parish records, wills and tracing families between 1600 and 2022, the heritability of the psychological traits which are associated with socioeconomic status – especially intelligence, which predicts socioeconomic status of origin and socioeconomic status achieved,[355] and personality – are very high; differences in them are mainly caused by genetics. Secondly, people tend to select for genetic similarity, especially with regard to highly genetic traits such as intelligence.[356] In addition, there are specific alleles that have been shown to be associated with high educational attainment, and thus with intelligence, and with socioeconomic success.[357]

Watson states that IQ will fall if these successful people don't have children. This is precisely what is occurring. Among females the correlation between intelligence and fertility it is around -0.2 while among males it is -0.089, attaining statistical significance.[358] Even controlling for education and earnings, IQ among Western females remains negatively correlated with fertility.[359] This negative IQ-fertility nexus is a "Jensen Effect": it is on the most genetically influenced IQ sub-tests, with some forms of intelligence being highly genetic and others being highly environmentally sensitive.[360] The male-female difference likely exists, in

---

[355] A. Jensen, *The g Factor: The Science of Mental Ability* (Westport, CT: Praeger, 1998).

[356] G. Clark, "The inheritance of social status: England, 1600 to 2022," *PNAS*, 120 (2023): e2300926120.

[357] A. Marees, D. Smit, A. Abdellaoui et al., "Genetic correlates of socio-economic status influence the pattern of shared heritability across mental health traits," *Nature Human Behavior*, 5 (2021): 1065-1073.

[358] G. Meisenberg, "The reproduction of intelligence," *Intelligence*, 38 (2010): 220–230.

[359] S. Kanazawa, "Intelligence and Childlessness," *Social Science Research*, 48 (2014): 157–170.

[360] M. A. Woodley and G. Meisenberg, "A Jensen effect on dysgenic fertility: An analysis involving the National Longitudinal Survey of Youth," *Personality and Individual Differences*, 55 (2013): 279–282.

part, because males do not have to make a trade-off, in the same way, between their fertility and their career and, of course, males remain fertile for longer. This negative relationship is increasingly being found in developing countries, such as China, as they continue to industrialize.[361]

Interestingly, highly egalitarian and developed societies, such as those in Scandinavia, appear to still have a very weak positive association between fertility and intelligence or between fertility and education level, at least among males, according to some studies.[362] In Sweden, among males, there is a positive IQ-fertility gradient based on army conscription data, partly due to very low IQ males having no children at all.[363] However, these studies are only on males, so there could be a negative IQ-fertility nexus overall, when females are also analysed. Moreover, it has been argued that Swedish conscription data is unrepresentative. One study found a positive association between income and fertility in the cohorts between 1920 and 1970 but as it was weak this could be driven by positive selection for certain personality traits, which we will explore later.[364] A Swedish cohort study, published in 1988, found that IQ and fertility correlated in Swedish men born up to 1924, after which there was no relationship.[365] Certainly, native Swedish reaction times are consistently slowing,[366] implying declining intelligence. We will explore reaction times in greater depth below.

---

[361] M. Wang, J. Fuerst and J. Ren, "Evidence of dysgenic fertility in China," *Intelligence*, 57 (2016): 15–24.

[362] G. Meisenberg and R. Lynn, "On-going trends of human intelligence," *Intelligence*, 96 (2023): 1017098.

[363] E. Gardner, M. Neville, K. Samocha et al., "Reduced reproductive success is associated with selective constraint on human genes," *Nature*, 603 (2022): 858–863; M. Kolk and K. Barclay, "Cognitive ability and fertility among Swedish men born 1951–1967: Evidence from military conscription registers," *Proceedings of the Royal Society B: Biological Sciences* (2019): 20190359.

[364] M. Kolk, "The relationship between life-course accumulated income and childbearing of Swedish men and women born 1940–70," *Population Studies* (2022).

[365] D. Vining, L. Bygren, K. Hattori, S. Nystrom and S. Tamura, "IQ/fertility relationships in Japan and Sweden," *Personality and Individual Differences*, 9 (1988): 931–932.

[366] G. Madison, M.A. Woodley of Menie and J. Sänger, "Secular Slowing of Auditory Simple Reaction Time in Sweden (1959–1985)," *Frontiers in Human Neuroscience* (2018).

What is the Flynn Effect?

Before we turn to the evidence that intelligence is in decline, we must examine the Flynn Effect. It should also be emphasised that the Flynn Effect—the secular rise in IQ scores across the twentieth century in Western countries—is entirely consistent with intelligence decline, as its putative discoverer,[367] American political scientist James Flynn (1934–2020), himself conceded.[368] As already discussed, intelligence can be conceived of as rather like a pyramid. At the base of the pyramid there are numerous "specialized abilities" that are only very weakly associated with intelligence. The documented rise in IQ scores has been found to have been on intelligence abilities at the base of the intelligence pyramid, and, in particular, on the subtest "similarities"—the ability to make associations. This ability is only a very weak measure of intelligence, but due to the fact that it has increased extremely rapidly, and due to the imperfect nature of IQ tests as means of measuring intelligence (certain personality sub-traits can also elevate your ability to solve problems) this has shown-up on the IQ tests as an overall IQ rise.

Flynn has argued that this occurred because we are an increasingly science-oriented society that increasingly teaches people to think in an analytic way; it makes them don "scientific spectacles."[369] This process has pushed these intelligence abilities to their phenotypic maximum, overwhelming an underlying decline in actual intelligence; in g. Once the phenotypic maximum in similarities is reached, then declining IQ would show up even on the IQ tests, and this is what began to happen in the West with cohorts born around the year 1980, according to some studies. This new trend is being widely referred to as the Negative Flynn Effect, connoting a phenotypic decline in IQ, and there is some evidence that this decline is actually driven by g; it is on the most genetic parts of the IQ test,

---

[367] R. Lynn, "Who discovered the Flynn effect? A review of early studies of the secular increase of intelligence," *Intelligence,* 4 (2013): 765–769.
[368] J. R. Flynn, and M. Shayer, "IQ decline and Piaget: Does the rot start at the top?" *Intelligence,* 66 (2018): 112–121.
[369] J. R. Flynn, *Are We Getting Smarter? Rising IQ in the Twenty-First Century* (Cambridge: Cambridge University Press, 2012), 15.

as we would expect.[370] A study of Norwegian military conscription data averred that the Negative Flynn Effect was entirely environmentally mediated, by comparing siblings.[371] But there are serious problems with this study, such as the methods employed being extremely opaque.

So, there is no inconsistency between intelligence decline and the Flynn Effect. Indeed, it may be that a hypothetical "Negative Flynn Effect" comes about, leading to accelerated reduction in IQ for environmental reasons. As people become less intelligent for genetic reasons, teachers will be less able to push the IQ of their pupils to its phenotypic maximum, meaning that the pupils' IQ will fall for both genetic and environmental reasons. Other correlates of intelligence are "measurement invariant"— meaning that the validity of the instrument is not interfered with by external changes—and these also evidence intelligence decline, as we shall now see.

Evidence for Intelligence Decline: Simple Reaction Times

Reaction times are such a reliable proxy for general intelligence that eminent intelligence researchers, such as American psychologist Arthur Jensen (1923–2012),[372] have promoted them as alternatives to pencil-and-paper IQ tests. It is possible to use so-called "simple reaction times" to measure long-term trends in general intelligence because reaction times have been measured since the 1880s and they represent an objective correlate of general intelligence. Also, going to school is assumed to raise IQ, due to greater intellectual stimulation, but not to shorten reaction times. Thus, reaction times are measurement invariant across time.

Simple reaction times (sRT) typically involve something like pressing a button as quickly as possible in response to a light being switched on, and measuring the time taken. This procedure usually takes a fraction of a second. While the negative correlation with IQ is not large, sRTs have the huge advantage of being objective and quantifiable physiological

---

[370] E. Dutton, D. Van der Linden and R. Lynn, "The Negative Flynn Effect: A Systematic Literature Review," *Intelligence,* 59 (2016): 163–169.
[371] B. Bratsberg and Ole Rogeberg, "Flynn effect and its reversal are both environmentally caused," *PNAS,* 115 (2018): 6674–6678.
[372] A. R. Jensen, *Clocking the Mind: Mental Chronometry and Individual Differences* (New York: Elsevier, 2006).

measures. It might be asked how we can measure general intelligence in Victorian England. The answer is that Galton measured simple reaction times, which is a measure of endophenotypes (such as nerve conduction velocity) that are considered by some prominent researchers to be fundamental determinants of g. A critical strength of these measures is that their *meaning* does not change over time. The low g-loading of measures like simple reaction time is therefore not relevant to their ability to reliably track the change in the underlying g over time. The crucial point is that they exhibit the property of *measurement invariance.*

A survey of historical reaction time data demonstrates something striking.[373] There was a significant slowing of sRTs from the 1880s until the late twentieth century. It should be stressed that the instruments used to measure reaction times in the 1880s are accepted as having been perfectly adequate for the job.[374] This was then replicated and confirmed.[375] This replication study furthermore found, using sRTs, that the decline in g had been around 1 IQ point per decade between 1885 and the year 2004. That is about 10 points in a century, and probably more over the past two hundred years. Bruce Charlton and I have explained that to put this in perspective, 15 points would be approximately the difference in average IQ between a low level security guard (85) and a police constable (100), or between a high school science teacher (115) and a biology professor at an elite university or an engineer (130).[376] In other words, in terms of intelligence, the average Englishman from about 1850 would be roughly at the 85th percentile of the population in the year 2000—and the difference would be even larger if we extrapolated back further towards about 1800 when the Industrial Revolution began to initiate massive demographic changes in the British population. New studies are replicating this finding. A study in Sweden, for example, based on a

---

[373] I. W. Silverman, "Simple reaction time: it is not what it used to be," *American Journal of Psychology,* 123 (2010): 39–50.

[374] M. A. Woodley, J. te Nijenhuis and R. Murphy, "Were the Victorians cleverer than us? The decline in general intelligence estimated from a meta-analysis of the slowing of simple reaction time," *Intelligence,* 41 (2013): 843–850.

[375] M. A. Woodley of Menie, J. te Nijenhuis and R. Murphy, "The Victorians were still faster than us. Commentary: Factors influencing the latency of simple reaction times," *Frontiers in Human Neuroscience,* 9 (2015): 452.

[376] Dutton and Charlton, *The Genius Famine, op. cit.,* 158–159.

sample of more than 7,000 people, found that simple audio reaction times had slowed by between 3 and 16 milliseconds between 1959 and 1985.[377]

In everyday terms, the meaning of these numbers is stark. They mean that we live in an increasingly over-promoted society, as those at the top fail to reproduce and those at the bottom substantially reproduce. Bruce Charlton and I set out the full impact of these numbers in *The Genius Famine:*

> "[...] the academics of the year 2000 were the school teachers of 1900, the school teachers of the year 2000 would have been the factory workers (the average people) of 1900, the office workers and policemen of the year 2000 were the farm labourers of 1900, those who were around 10 to 15 IQ points below average at that time. The low-level security guards and shop assistants of the year 2000 were probably in the workhouse, on the streets, or dead in 1900. The substantial long-term unemployed or unemployable, the dependent "underclass" of the year 2000, simply didn't exist in 1900. And even this estimate is ignoring the expansion of education since 1900, which expanded the middle class occupations and would, in itself, reduce the average intelligence of academics and teachers and even shop assistants in 2000 compared to what they would have been in 1900."[378]

Colour Discrimination

Colour discrimination—the ability to distinguish between ever more subtle shades of colour—is declining as well. Sensory discrimination correlates with *g* because the more acute your sensory discrimination is, the better able you are to notice subtle differences between physical quantities which can help you to solve problems more efficiently. This is why studies have found the correlation between general intelligence and general discriminative ability to be as high as 0.92 in some cases.[379] It

---

[377] G. Madison, M. A. Woodley of Menie and S. Sänger, "Secular slowing of auditory simple reaction time in Sweden, 1959–1985," *Frontiers in Human Neuroscience,* 10 (2016): 407.

[378] Dutton and Charlton, *The Genius Famine, op. cit.,* 158–159.

[379] I.J. Deary, J.P. Bell, M.J. Campbell and N.D. Fazal, "Sensory discrimination and intelligence: Testing Spearman's other hypothesis," *American Journal of Psychology,* 117 (2004): 1–18.

follows that the more intelligent people are, the better they will be able to discriminate among increasingly subtle differences in colour.

A 2015 study explored four standardization studies conducted between the 1980s and 2000 that drew upon the Farnsworth-Munsell 100-hue Colour Perception Test, which was developed in 1943. This test was found to correlate with IQ in the 1960s. The participants have to physically arrange a series of 85 caps, each of a very subtly different hue, along a spectrum defined by two clear end caps such as blue and green or pink and purple. Participants are awarded an error penalty for each cap that is in the wrong order on the spectrum, allowing a quantification of their colour discrimination abilities. It was found that, across the four studies, colour discrimination ability had significantly declined, at the equivalent rate of 3.15 IQ points per decade—even after controlling for the IQ of the countries from which the participants were drawn (Belgium, Finland, the UK and the US) and also participant age. Clearly, this is what we would expect if our hypothesis were correct.[380]

Use of High-Difficulty Words

The more intelligent people are, the larger are their vocabularies, and the more likely they are to use difficult words, as words are thinking tools. Intelligent people are more prone to using "high order," or at least unusual words. This is congruous with the association between g and colour discrimination. The more intelligent people are, the more able they are to perceive subtle differences; differences which require slightly different words in order to accurately encapsulate them. Part of the linguistic intelligence dimension of the IQ test is vocabulary and the ability to understand subtle differences in the meaning of words. Scores on vocabulary tests are *very* highly g-loaded and highly heritable.[381]

---

[380] See, M.A. Woodley of Menie and H.B.F. Fernandes, "Showing their true colours: Secular declines and a Jensen effect on colour acuity—more evidence for the weaker variant of Spearman's other hypothesis," *Personality and Individual Differences,* 88 (2015): 280–284.

[381] K. J. Kan, J. Wicherts, C. Dolan and H. Van der Maas, "On the nature and nurture of intelligence and specific cognitive abilities: the more heritable, the more culture dependent" *Psychological Science,* 24 (2013): 2420–2428.

To test what was happening with vocabulary, a study in 2015 examined historical changes in the frequency with which words from the highly g-loaded WORDSUM test were employed across 5.9 million texts published between 1850 and 2005.[382] It also examined the association between WORDSUM scores and completed fertility; how many children you have had by middle age when, typically, you don't have any more. They found that knowledge of words with higher difficulties (those that are harder to learn and use correctly) had stronger negative correlations with completed fertility, and their use declined over time. By contrast, less difficult words and less strongly selected words increased in use over time—an effect that was predicted by rising literacy.

More recently, another study has taken this further in a way that clearly illustrates the accuracy of our model. Google's Ngram Viewer (a massive text archive of scanned books, newspapers, scientific journals and other printed materials) includes texts that go all the way back to the sixteenth century. So, drawing upon this, they analysed changes in the use of the four very high difficulty WORDSUM words over time between the sixteenth century and the modern day. They found that the use of these words *increases* from the sixteenth century up until the early nineteenth century and then goes into decline. This is precisely what our model of the rise and fall of Western intelligence would predict, if indeed the usage patterns of these words among those who contribute to literature really does reflect their underlying level of g.[383]

This system also allows us to estimate roughly how intelligent we are compared to people in the past. Based on the usage frequencies of these WORDSUM words, we currently have about the same level of g as people in the early eighteenth century—a couple of generations before the Industrial Revolution. It must be remembered that WORDSUM is likely to be subject to the effects of more widespread education (recall that the

---

[382] M. A. Woodley of Menie, H. Fernandes, A. J. Figueredo and G. Meisenberg, "By their words ye shall know them: Evidence of genetic selection against general intelligence and concurrent environmental enrichment in vocabulary usage since the mid-19th century," *Frontiers in Psychology*, 6 (2015): 361.

[383] M.A. Woodley of Menie, A.J. Figueredo, M.A. Sarraf et al., *The Rhythm of the West: A Biohistory of the Modern Era, AD 1600 to the Present* (Washington, DC: Scott Townsend Press, 2017).

usage of easy words is actually increasing), which may make our vocabulary level artificially high in relation to our underlying general intelligence. So, putting these influences aside, it is likely that we have regressed considerably further, genetically, than the early eighteenth century.

Backward Digit Span

Another proxy for *g* is working memory, or the capacity to manipulate information committed to memory for the purpose of solving problems. More intelligent people tend to be better at this. This makes sense because if you have a good working memory, the amount of information that you can handle will be greater, allowing for more complex problems to be solved. This ability is reflected in measures such as "Digit Span," where the subject is presented with a list of digits and must immediately repeat them back from memory. If they can do this successfully, then they move onto a longer list. The length of a list that the subject can recall successfully is their "Digit Span." They can be asked to recall the digits in the order in which they were given ("forward"), which gives a measure of short-term memory, or they can be asked to recall them in the opposite order. The latter is known as their "Backward Digit Span" and is a measure of working memory.

Clearly, remembering numbers in reverse order is likely to be more cognitively demanding and is therefore a much better measure of *g*. In a reanalysis of previously published data, covering the period 1923 to 2008, it was found that forward digit span (short-term memory) had slightly improved over this period. However, backward digit span (working memory) had declined—equating to an IQ loss of 0.16 points per decade. In other words, we have become better at the less *g*-loaded memory task and worse at the more *g*-loaded task over a period of 85 years.[384]

---

[384] M.A. Woodley of Menie and H. Fernandes, "Do opposing secular trends on backwards and forwards digit span evidence the co-occurrence model? A comment on Gignac (2015)," *Intelligence,* 50 (2015): 125–130.

Levels of Genius as a Proxy for Intelligence

There are many other proxies for intelligence which are also declining, including spatial perception[385] and creativity.[386] But, most importantly, levels of genius, of major scientific innovation per capita, are in decline. Per capita rates of genius and the macro-innovations for which they are responsible have been declining since the early to middle nineteenth century.[387] This, of course, is the height of the Industrial Revolution.

It might be argued that this decline in "recognized important innovations" has occurred because we have already picked all of the "low-hanging fruit." But this misunderstands how problem-solving works. Problem-solving involves making connections between pieces of already available information, so that, when it comes to solving problems, there is no such thing as "low-hanging fruit." When inventions, which we are now used to, were first innovated, they were regarded as extraordinary breakthroughs; geniuses having made connections which nobody had yet been sufficiently intelligent to make. It might also be averred that though intelligence is declining, the population is rising, meaning any intelligence decline is more than offset by a rise in the absolute numbers of highly intelligent people. However, it has been shown that our intelligence decline is so rapid that this is simply not the case, not least because a decline of just 3 IQ points almost halves the percentage of people with an IQ over 130.[388] Moreover, there is substantial evidence that the average IQ of a society, as well as the percentage of it that is part of the "smart

---

[385] J. Pietschnig and G. Gittler, "A reversal of the Flynn effect for spatial perception in German-speaking countries: Evidence from a cross-temporal IRT-based meta-analysis (1977–2014)," *Intelligence,* 53 (2015): 145–153.

[386] K.H. Kim, "The creativity crisis: The decrease in creative thinking scores on the Torrance Tests of Creative Thinking" *Creativity Research Journal,* 23 (2011): 285–295.

[387] C. Murray, *Human Accomplishment: The Pursuit of Excellence in the Arts and Sciences, 800 BC to 1950* (New York: Free Press, 2006).

[388] M.A. Woodley and A.J. Figueredo, *Historical Variability in Heritable General Intelligence: Its Evolutionary Origins and Socio-Cultural Consequences* (Buckingham: University of Buckingham Press, 2013).

fraction" (who have an IQ of over 130) very strongly influences its ability to maintain all aspects of civilization.[389]

A Decline in the Frequencies of Variants in the Genome Associated with *g*

So far, we have looked at phenotypic evidence, which indicates (quite strongly) that *g* is declining and doing so for largely genetic reasons. A hugely important study, led by a Chinese researcher called Augustine Kong was published in 2017.[390] In this study, his team identified a large number of genetic variants, which collectively predicted both educational attainment and *g*. They called this set of variants POLYEDU (polygenic score for educational attainment). This team investigated the effect of this polygenic score on the reproductive histories of 109,120 Icelanders, and the impact of this history on the Icelandic gene pool over time. They demonstrated that those who had higher POLYEDU had delayed reproduction and fewer children than did Icelanders carrying lower POLYEDU. So far, this result is somewhat consistent with those of the previously discussed studies that used polygenic scores for educational attainment to predict fertility outcomes.

However, Kong and his team went one step further. Based on a sample of 129,808 Icelanders born between 1910 and 1990, they found that the average POLYEDU—the average percentage of the population with genes that predict high educational attainment—had been declining at a rate of roughly 0.010 standard units per decade, which, they noted "is substantial on an evolutionary timescale." They added that "because POLYEDU only captures a fraction of the overall underlying genetic component, the latter could be declining at a rate that is two to three times faster."

This observed decline over decades in the population's levels of POLYEDU was found to be highly consistent with the decline predicted using the negative association between POLYEDU and fertility, and the

---

[389] See H. Rindermann, *Cognitive Capitalism: Human Capital and the Well Being of Nations* (Cambridge: Cambridge University Press, 2018).
[390] A. Kong, M. Frigge, G. Thorleifsson et al., "Selection against variants in the genome associated with educational attainment," *Proceedings of the National Academy of Sciences, USA,* 114 (2017): E727-E732.

positive association between POLYEDU and age at first birth. Those with high IQ don't simply produce fewer children, they produce them later in life, meaning fewer generations. Kong and his colleagues even went so far as to estimate the IQ-loss that should result from this process—0.3 points per decade. It is important to note that in arriving at this estimate they employed a *very* low value of the heritability of IQ (0.3) in their formula. As was discussed earlier, the actual heritability of IQ (as determined using twin studies, which have the advantage of capturing *all* genetic variants that go into a given trait) is likely to be substantially higher (closer to 0.8). When Kong and his colleagues' numbers are adjusted to take this into account, the decline increases to around 0.8 points per decade—meaning that the population of Iceland may be losing IQ at a rate very close to a whole point per decade.[391] We have already seen that education level is strongly genetically correlated with *g*. So, *g* should have declined between 1910 and 1990 among the people of Iceland. The average Icelander born in 1910 was cleverer than the average Icelander born in 1990 in terms of heritable general intelligence. This decline in Iceland has furthermore occurred exclusively for genetic reasons and the key reason is the low and postponed fertility of the highly intelligent in Iceland, especially the highly intelligent women.[392]

Why is Intelligence in Decline?

In summary, then, there is nothing to criticize with regard to Watson's statements on fertility and intelligence. They are the unpalatable truth: Native Western people are becoming less intelligent for genetic reasons; intelligence is broadly negatively associated with fertility. Needless to say, in that intelligence predicts every aspect of civilization and is strongly genetic, this does not auger well.[393] Me and my colleagues have explored the likely causes and consequences of this in two books, *At Our Wits' End:*

---

[391] Woodley of Menie et al., *The Rhythm of the West, op. cit.*

[392] Kong, et al., "Selection against variants in the genome associated with educational attainment," *op. cit.*

[393] R. Lynn and T. Vanhanen, *Intelligence: A Unifying Construct for the Social Sciences* (London: ulster Institute for Social Research, 2012).

Why We're Becoming Less Intelligent and What It Means for the Future,[394] and *The Past is a Future Country: The Coming Conservative Demographic Revolution.*[395] Interested readers may wish to consult these. In summary, under harsh conditions as part of a broader fitness factor (see below) for which we were selecting, intelligence predicts using (and correctly using) contraception, intelligent women are more likely to concentrate on their education and careers and so limit their fertility and a generous welfare system encourages those of low IQ to breed.

There is also evidence that materialistic cultures are causal in people not wanting to have children, possibly because a certain level of luxury, in particular when combined with low mortality salience (immediate awareness of death) and low religiosity constitutes an evolutionary mismatch, an issue we will explore in greater detail below, meaning our evolved instincts are not induced. When people are primed with materialism, it decreases their desire to have children.[396] Thus, large families become an accidental consequence of having low IQ. An evolutionary match, it should be noted, is when an organism lives in the environment to which it is evolved. In any other environment, it is in an evolutionary mismatch to varying degrees.[397] As we will see below, intelligent people are more environmentally sensitive. Hence, this evolutionary mismatch reduces their fertility in particular.

---

[394] E. Dutton and M.A. Woodley of Menie, *At Our Wits' End: Why We're Becoming Less Intelligent and What It Means for the Future* (Exeter: Imprint Academic, 2018).
[395] E. Dutton and J.O.A. Rayner-Hilles, *The Past is a Future Country: The Coming Conservative Demographic Revolution* (Exeter: Imprint Academic, 2022).
[396] N. Li, A. Lim, M.-H. Tsai and J. O, "Too Materialistic to Get Married and Have Children?" *PLoS One* (2015), https://doi.org/10.1371/journal.pone.0126543
[397] M. Manus, "Evolutionary Mismatch," *Evolution, Medicine and Public Health,* 2018 (2018): 190-191.

Chapter Eight

Race Differences in Intelligence

IQ and the Wealth of Nations

But, of course, Watson's major controversy was with regard to race differences in intelligence. In 2002, English psychologist Richard Lynn, whom met earlier, and Finnish political scientist Tatu Vanhanen (1929-2015) together published a book called *IQ and the Wealth of Nations.*[398] The authors demonstrated that differences in gross domestic product were strongly correlated with national differences in average intelligence. They came to this conclusion by drawing on IQ test samples from 60 nations. It followed, they averred, that a nation's average IQ was a significant factor in understanding national differences in wealth and economic growth.

The book was heavily criticised for its methodology, the incompleteness of its data and its inferences. The result has been a series of follow-up books to address these criticisms such as *IQ and Global Inequality,*[399] *Intelligence: A Unifying Construct for the Social Sciences,*[400] and *The Intelligence of Nations.*[401] It seems clear that Watson either read *IQ and the Wealth of Nations* or read some of the newspaper reports about it.

---

[398] R. Lynn and T. Vanhanen, *IQ and the Wealth of Nations* (Santa Barbara, CA: Praeger, 2002).

[399] R. Lynn and T. Vanhanen, *IQ and Global Inequality* (Augusta, GA: Washington Summit, 2006).

[400] R. Lynn and T. Vanhanen, *Intelligence: A Unifying Construct for the Social Sciences* (London: Ulster Institute for Social Research, 2012).

[401] R. Lynn and D. Becker, *The Intelligence of Nations* (London: Ulster Institute for Social Research, 2019).

Watson's Comments on Race and Intelligence

Watson cited national IQs in his interview, noting that they are relatively low in Sub-Saharan Africa. "National IQs" have been heavily criticised and, thus, recalculated to take these criticisms into account. They correlate with the originals at close to 0.9.[402] National average IQ is associated with all aspects of civilization and often strongly so. National IQ is associated with educational level, literacy, low corruption, law and order, political stability, life expectancy, health and much else.[403] Moreover, there has been shown to be a correlation of 0.9 between the prevalence of alleles associated with very high intelligence – specifically associated with having very high educational qualifications, such as a PhD - and national IQ, demonstrating that these differences are strongly genetic.[404]

One noteworthy difference between blacks and whites is in specific variants of two genes relating to brain size: *ASPM* and microcephalin. *ASPM* was strongly selected for among apes, leading to humans with their larger brains. Microcephelin's selection appears to explain the evolution from proto-Simians to humans.[405] Microcephilin 1, specifically, arose in humans 37,000 years ago and spread so rapidly that it must have been under strong positive selection. It was under such selection because it allowed for bigger brains, better problem solving and, thus, a competitive advantage.[406] The variants in ASPM and microcephelin are common among Eurasians and very rare among Sub-Saharan Africans. In contrast to most of the variants on these genes, the two that are common among Eurasians actually increase brain size and, by extension, increase intelligence. It would follow that they would have spread relatively quickly in Europe's harsher, more stable and more competitive

---

[402] Lynn and Becker, *The Intelligence of Nations, op. cit.*

[403] Lynn and Vanhanen, *Intelligence, op. cit.*

[404] D. Piffer, "Correlation between PGS and environmental variables," *RPubs* (2018), https://rpubs.com/Daxide/377423.

[405] P. Evans, J. Anderson, E. Vallendar et al., "Reconstructing the evolutionary history of microcephalin, a gene controlling human brain size," *Human Molecular Genetics,* 13 (2004): 1139-1145.

[406] P. Evans, S. Gilbert, N. Mekel-Bobrov et al., "Microcephalin, a gene regulating brain size, continues to evolve adaptively in humans," *Science,* 309 (2005): 1717-1720.

environment. Indeed, the variant on *ASPM* can be dated and seems to coincide with the rise of agriculture, denser living conditions and cities. Researchers further argue that these two variants seem to control and determine human brain size and, by extension, human intelligence.[407] Accordingly, it is not unreasonable to aver that there are national differences in IQ and in that the average IQ in Sub-Saharan Africa is approximately 70, which is mildly mentally retarded by UK standards, and in that these differences are substantially genetic in nature, we can understand why Watson would be "gloomy" about the future of Sub-Saharan Africa.

It should be emphasised that a person with an IQ of 70 would be perfectly capable of engaging in basic physical labour. When a Western person has an IQ that low it is usually part of some kind of syndrome that is associated with personality problems, for example. This would not be the case in Sub-Saharan Africa. The person with such an IQ would be otherwise genetically healthy. In a relatively undeveloped economy, in which most people are simply agriculturalists and in which basic needs are met by a constantly congenial climate, it would be perfectly possible to navigate life with an IQ of 70. Moreover, a person with an IQ of 70 in Sub-Saharan Africa may well be high in certain specialised abilities that are weakly associated with general intelligence and which aid survival, such as way-finding. For example, Australian Aborigines have an average IQ of 64,[408] yet their visual and spatial memory, when they are children, appears to be considerably better than that of white children, perhaps due to localised evolutionary pressures.[409] Similarly, the Inuit have an average IQ of around 90, yet they have larger brains than whites or even than Northeast Asians, who have an average IQ of around 105.[410] This may be

---

[407] S. Richardson, "Race and IQ in the postgnomic age: The microcephaly case," *BioSocieties,* 6 (2011): 420-446.

[408] Lynn, *Race Differences in Intelligence, op. cit.*

[409] J. Kearins, "Visual memory skills of Western Desert and Queensland children of Australian Aboriginal descent: A reply to Drinkwater," *Australian Journal of Psychology,* 30 (1978): 1-5.

[410] Lynn, *Race Differences in Intelligence, op. cit.*

partly due to their scoring very high on various specialised abilities and, in particular, on spatial and visual memory.[411]

We might expect cold weather to select for intelligence, because people must solve the problems of surviving the winter. Accordingly, it has been argued that the lower than expected IQ of the Inuit may be because it was too cold to take up farming.[412] It has been argued that farming acted as a selection event for intelligence: it forced people to be future-oriented; a key aspect of intelligence.[413] Thus, it is noteworthy that the Aborigines, who never took up farming, have a significantly lower IQ than Sub-Saharan Africans, most of whom did take up agriculture. Aborigines and the Inuit remained hunter-gatherers.

Watson's Remarks on Blacks and Intelligence

Watson also made a number of remarks on race in his interview with *The Sunday Times*. "Races" refer to breeding populations that have been separated by a combination of geography and endogamy such that they are adapted to different environments, and such that correct predictions can be made when using "race" as a category. The 12 races of classical anthropology map very precisely onto distinct genetic clusters,[414] there is roughly a 0.9 correlation between "social race" and genetic ancestry cluster,[415] and these races can be identified with 80 per cent accuracy from the skeleton alone.[416] Accordingly, race is clearly a biologically useful system of categories.

---

[411] J.S. Kleinfeld, "Intellectual Strengths in Culturally Different Groups: An Eskimo Illustration," *Review of Educational Research,* 43 (1973): 341-359.

[412] Lynn, *Race Differences in Intelligence, op. cit.*

[413] G. Cochran and H. Harpending, *The 10,000 Year Explosion: How Civilization Accelerated Human Evolution* (New York: Basic Books, 2009).

[414] W. Bodmer and L. Cavalli-Sforza, *Genetics, Evolution and Man* (San Francisco: Freeman, 1976), 698.

[415] E. Kirkegaard, "Genetic ancestry and social race are nearly interchangeable," *Open Psych* (2021).

[416] D.E. Flouri, A. Alifragki, G. Garcia-Donas and F. Kranioti, "Ancestry Estimation: Advances and Limitations in Forensic Applications," *Research and Reports in Forensic and Medical Science,* 12 (2022): 13-24.

Races differ in very important areas such as disease prevalence or likelihood of accepting donor organs from other races,[417] and even superficial race differences (such as skin colour) are environmental adaptations with significant health consequences such as Vitamin D deficiency in dark winters for black people.[418] This, again, demonstrates its scientific utility; it allows correct, and important, predictions to be made. When using genetic loci that differ according to environment (rather than those that don't) 80 per cent of differences are between races and only 20 per cent are within them,[419] small differences can add up to significant overall differences if they are all in the same direction,[420] and race is little different from sub-species in non-human animals and this is "scientific," despite there being no clear line between different subspecies. Thus, there is no logical argument against the concept of race and those who reject it, or are even sceptical of it, appear to do so entirely for ideological reasons and are often inconsistent in so-doing.[421]

Race differences in intelligence are on the most genetically-influenced IQ sub-tests and, indeed, they are on general intelligence, which is strongly genetically influenced. This is known as the Jensen Effect, as we saw earlier.[422] Groups such as African-Americans perform the worst on the tests that are the most culturally fair; that is the ones the measure intelligence the best. The results are also consistent with objective measures of intelligence such as race differences in brain size, cranial capacity and in reaction times. Brain size and cranial capacity positively correlate with intelligence, as the brain is a thinking muscle, while reaction times negatively correlate with intelligence. This makes sense, as

---

[417] S. Shoker, "The health system's struggle to get more Black and Asian donors," *BBC News* (4th July 2015), https://www.bbc.com/news/uk-england-nottinghamshire-33101610

[418] S. Bejerot and M. Humble, "Inhabitants of Swedish-Somali Origin Are at Great Risk for Covid-19," *British Medical Journal*, 368 (2020): m1101.

[419] A.W.F. Edwards, "Human Genetic Diversity: Lewontin's Fallacy," *BioEssays*, 25 (2003): 798-801.

[420] Cochran and Harpending, *The 10,000 Year Explosion, op. cit.*

[421] E. Dutton, *Making Sense of Race* (Whitefish, MT: Washington Summit Publishers, 2020).

[422] J.P. Rushton, "Race Differences in *g* and the Jensen Effect," in H. Nyborg, (Ed.), *The Scientific Study of General Intelligence* (New York: Pergamon, 2003).

processing speed is an element of intelligence.[423] These differ between races in the same direction as does IQ.

In terms of the salience of environment, when black babies are adopted and raised by relatively high IQ white couples in the US then their IQ, by the time they reach adulthood, tends to be close to the black average. In addition, racial groups in the US who are far more distant from US cultural norms than blacks, such as Native Americans living on impoverished reservations, have slightly higher IQ scores than blacks, as already noted.[424] Indeed, African-Americans who are half-white tend, on average, to have an IQ score that is equidistant between the white mean of 100 and the black mean of 85, which is precisely as a mainly genetic model would predict.[425] In fact, some autopsy studies found that the higher white admixture an African-American has, based on adjudging their skin tone, then the higher is their brain weight relative to their body size.[426] Further, African-Americans in the northern states have an IQ of 90 while African-Americans in the southern states have an IQ of 80. This is paralleled by the way in which white admixture level in the northern states is about 20 per cent, while it is only 10 per cent in the southern states.[427] This is likely because migration is predicted by intelligence, the intelligent blacks migrated to the north and these blacks had higher levels of white admixture. More generally, it has been found that, based on US data, average IQ incrementally increases among blacks in parallel with their level of white admixture.[428]

How Does Average White and Black Personality Differ?

We looked earlier at Life History Strategy. There are consistent race differences in this regard, with Blacks being relatively faster Life History

---

[423] Lynn, *Race Differences in Intelligence, op. cit.*

[424] M. Levin, *Why Race Matters: Race Differences and What They Mean* (Oakton, VA: New Century Foundation, 2005).

[425] Lynn, *Race Differences in Intelligence, op. cit.*

[426] J.P. Rushton and E. Rushton, "Brain size, IQ, and racial-group differences: Evidence from musculoskeletal traits," *Intelligence,* 31 (2003): 139-155.

[427] Levin, *Why Race Matters, op. cit.*

[428] E. Kirkegaard, M.A. Woodley of Menie, R. Williams and J. Fuerst, "Biogeographic Ancestry, Cognitive Ability and Socioeconomic Outcomes," *Psych,* 1 (2019): 1-25.

Strategists, Northeast Asians being slow Life History Strategists and Europeans being intermediate but closer to Northeast Asians. Blacks are more likely to be twins, are born earlier, reach developmental milestones earlier, go through puberty earlier, become sexually active earlier, lose their virginity earlier, get pregnant earlier and go through the menopause earlier. There are also consistent personality differences with Blacks being lower in Agreeableness and Conscientiousness and higher in psychopathic personality traits in part due to higher Neuroticism, which includes traits such as anger and jealousy. Accordingly, they are less likely to marry, more likely to divorce if they do marry and are more likely to walk out on their families than Whites who are in turn more likely to pursue such behaviours than are Northeast Asians.[429] Similarly, they are more likely to commit crime, to be expelled from school and, indeed, are more likely to engage in many other forms of behaviour that evidence elevated psychopathic personality traits, such as failing to use a seatbelt when driving.[430]

On the other hand, blacks are higher in Extraversion than whites; they feel positive feelings more strongly.[431] In an unstable environment, you may as well be curious and, thus, try out new things, obtaining pleasure from risk. In a harsh yet stable ecology, breaking the established rules – when adapted to a very particular environment – could be deadly, so risk will be far less pleasurable. Cooperation and getting on with people will be crucial to survival in a harsh ecology, meaning it will pay to be socially anxious but otherwise highly emotionally controlled. Black people are adapted to a very different ecology, one which renders them low in social anxiety but high in Extraversion. In that sense, on average, they will be extremely outwardly friendly when compared to Europeans and especially when compared to Northeast Asians, who would be relatively shy and

---

[429] See, Rushton, *Race, Evolution and Behavior, op. cit.*; E. Dutton, *J. Philippe Rushton: A Life History Perspective* (Oulu: Thomas Edward Press, 2018) and Dutton, *Making Sense of Race, op. cit.*

[430] R. Lynn, "Racial and ethnic differences in psychopathic personality," *Personality and Individual Differences,* 32 (2002): 273-316.

[431] J.L. Krok-Schoen and T.A. Baker, "Race Differences in Personality and Affect Between Older White and Black Patients: An Exploratory Study," *Journal of Racial and Ethnic Health Disparities,* 1 (2014), 283–290.

reserved.[432] This will be further augmented by the fact that their IQs are verbally tilted whereas Northeast Asians are mathematically tilted, with Europeans being intermediate. For this reason, Jared Taylor (b. 1951), who is infamous for being an advocate for white interests in the US, a "notorious white supremacist" according to critics,[433] has penned an essay entitled, "What I Like About Blacks" in which he notes that they have "a kind of cheerful spontaneity that you don't find in whites . . . blacks act like whites who have had a few drinks. You see this in the easy way blacks talk to strangers . . . Blacks have a knack of turning a moment with a stranger into a friendly exchange."[434]

Watson asserted, in his interview, that there was no reason to believe different races separated by geography should have evolved identically and this is clearly true, as evidenced by the genetic psychological differences which we have already discussed and by obvious physical adaptations to different ecologies, such as dark skin being an adaptation to intense sunlight and a protection from skin cancer.[435] He further stated that while he hoped everyone was equal, "people who have to deal with black employees find this is not true." In this regard, we have seen detailed evidence that blacks are not the same as whites in various ways. In the US, they have genetically-mediated lower average IQ and, seemingly, higher Neuroticism (with the exception of social anxiety), lower Agreeableness, lower Conscientiousness and higher Extraversion. Accordingly, Watson's remarks, no matter how injudiciously expressed, appear to be empirically accurate.

Watson's Remarks on Ashkenazi Jews

In January 2007, in a kind of foreshadowing of what took place in the October, Watson gave an interview to the magazine *Esquire,* though they published it online on 19th October, perhaps to gain views due to the

---

[432] Rushton, *Race, Evolution and Behavior, op. cit.*

[433] D. Zuckenberg, *Not All Dead White Men: Classics and Misogyny in the Digital Age* (Cambridge, MA: Harvard University Press, 2018), Notes.

[434] J. Taylor, "What I Like About Blacks," in J. Taylor, (Eds.), *A Dissident's Guide to Blacks and Africa* (Oakton, VA: New Century Books, 2020), 46.

[435] See, Dutton, *Making Sense of Race, op. cit.*

furore.[436] In it, he was asked, "Should you be allowed to make an anti-Semitic remark?" to which Watson replied, "Yes, because some anti-Semitism is justified. Just like some anti-Irish feeling is justified. If you can't be criticized, that's very dangerous." This is a philosophical question, perhaps clumsily expressed due to the visceral nature of the term "anti-Semitism." Watson is merely trying to say that no group is perfect and groups should, therefore, not be above criticism. More salient to our discussion was his next remark:

> "I've wondered why people aren't more intelligent. Why isn't everyone as intelligent as Ashkenazi Jews? And it may be that societies work best when there's a mixture of abilities - the bright people would never be an army. Or has our intelligence been limited by leaders killing off any potential competitors? I suspect time is not a factor. The Ashkenazi Jews have done it in a thousand years. So these are the sorts of things we'll find out - how many mutations would you need to be more intelligent?"

For these remarks about intelligence, Watson was condemned by Ken Jacobson, the deputy director of the Anti-Defamation League. Jacobson not only objected to Watson's "disturbing" endorsement of anti-Semitism, but also objected to Watson's statement that Ashkenazi Jews are more intelligent than other people. "That also is a genetic stereotype . . . We believe that if Jews have succeeded in a certain field, it has been due to Jewish traditions, culture, and the valuing of education. We don't get into all the genetic stereotyping."[437]

These are illogical remarks. Detailed analyses have shown that stereotypes are broadly empirically accurate; that is why they arise. Thus, it makes no sense to criticise a person for employing stereotypes.[438] If anything, it would make sense to criticise people for refusing to accept the veracity of stereotypes without a clear reason. Moreover, valuing

---

[436] J.H. Richardson, "James Watson: What I've Learned," *Esquire* (January 2007).

[437] *SPME,* "Nobel Laureate James Watson, Co-Discoverer of DNA Says "Some Anti-Semitism Is Justified" in January *Esquire* Magazine" (14th January 2007), https://spme.org/spme-research/letters-from-our-readers/nobel-laureate-james-watson-co-discoverer-of-dna-says-some-anti-semitism-is-justified-in-january-esquire-magazine/2478/

[438] Jussim, *Social Perception and Social Reality, op. cit.*

education level is strongly predicted by intelligence,[439] and cultures do not fall out of the sky like thunderbolts. They differ, in part, due to group differences in intelligence: They partly reflect the genetic qualities of a people, as Jewish-American philosopher Michael Levin has noted.[440]

A systematic literature review of all of the many studies comparing the IQ of Ashkenazi Jews to Western Europeans finds it be approximately half a standard deviation higher than that of Western Europeans. This is also congruous with the average Ashkenazi score on America's National Longitudinal Study of Youth (though this was small and not necessarily representative sample) as well as with the fact that Ashkenazim are higher than Western Europeans on measures of socioeconomic status.[441] A number of genetic recessive diseases which are common among the Ashkenazim, and which express themselves if you have two copies of the mutant allele, appear to be associated with elevated intelligence if you have only one copy, explaining how they have remained common among a highly intelligent population.[442] Also, compared to various European gentile groups, Ashkenazi Jews have a higher prevalence of polymorphisms that are associated with very high educational attainment and these have been shown to have caused their intelligence advantage over these groups.[443] Moreover, the difference in IQ between European Jews and non-Jews has been found to be on g, the essence of intelligence, which is highly genetic.[444]

---

[439] Jensen, *The g Factor, op. cit.*

[440] Levin, *Why Race Matters, op. cit.*

[441] R. Lynn, *The Chosen People: A Study of Jewish Intelligence and Achievement* (Augusta, GA: Washington Summit, 2011).

[442] G. Cochran, J. Hardy and H. Harpending, "Natural history of Ashkenazi intelligence," *Journal of Biosocial Science,* 38 (2006): 659-693.

[443] C.S. Dunkel, M.A. Woodley of Menie, J. Pallesen and E. Kirkegaard, "Polygenic scores mediate the Jewish phenotypic advantage in educational attainment and cognitive ability compared with Catholics and Lutherans," *Evolutionary Behavioral Sciences,* 13 (2019): 366–375.

[444] J. te Nijenhuis, H. David, D. Metzen and E. Armstrong, "Spearman's hypothesis tested on European Jews vs non-Jewish Whites and vs Oriental Jews: Two meta-analyses," *Intelligence,* 44 (2014): 15-18.

Chapter Nine

Why Do Geniuses Tend
to be Depressed and Anxious?

Why Do Poets Write?

Now that we have explored Watson's assorted "controversies," his attraction to that which is taboo, let us return to examining the extent to which he is congruous with the scientific-genius archetype. We already observed that autism is associated with anxiety and depression and we have suggested that this may be associated with creativity. Depression, anxiety and generally experiencing the world as a frightening and difficult place is one of the key reasons why poets and novelists appear to turn to writing. It permits them to articulate precisely how they feel and why, and it is possible that this provides them with a sense of purchase on the mountain of life which they find so crumbling and unstable.

The British poet Joanne Limburg (b. 1970) recalls, in the wake of her father's premature death:

> "At the end of the month, I started writing in my notebook again. The first entry reads, 'New and horrible feelings keep nosing in like strange beasts.' Below it, I've written, 'Like the joke about cutting off your hand to cure a headache.' I know exactly what I meant by that: I'd spent most of life up till then in a fog of mild-to-moderate mental discomfort, but now it had all been blown sideways by a hurricane of grief."[445]

She is using, in a sense, prose-poetry to crisply express how she feels, and so-doing seems to have some kind of positive impact upon her. She is clear in her memoir *The Woman Who Thought Too Much* that she has struggled

---

[445] J. Limburg, *The Woman Who Thought Too Much: A Memoir of Obsession and Compulsion* (London: Atlantic Books, 2010).

with depression and anxiety since she was a child. It seems to be associated with creativity, including scientific creativity, not least because people who worry are constantly thinking; they find it hard to switch off, as we will see below.

Neuroticism, Creativity and Greatness

Felix Post's analysis has shown that as we move from famous scientists to famous writers, depression and anxiety also increase, though Post found that these were relatively high even among the world famous scientists. He estimated that 33 per cent of his sample of world famous scientists had suffered from depression or anxiety, as had 41 per cent of his politicians, 34 per cent of his composers, 36 per cent of his thinkers, 41 per cent of his artists and 72 per cent of his writers. Approximately 20 per cent of people in Western countries experience a bout of depression at some point in their lifetimes.[446] The exact age when such negative thinking begins, if it ever does, is often in adolescence due to "puberty and brain and cognitive maturation" and specifically "enhanced social understanding and self-awareness, changes in brain circuits involved in responses to reward and danger, and increased reported stress levels . . ."[447]

English psychologist Adam Perkins and colleagues have proposed that anxiety effectively means that you are always thinking and that this can elevate creativity[448] especially if you also experience feelings intensely and need to express them.[449] It may also be that experiencing the world as dangerous chaos strongly elevates your desire to make sense of it and, in that respect, to better control it. In this regard, Machiavellianism, which involves a strong desire for power and control over others, is associated

---

[446] S. Austrian, *Comprehensive Handbook of Personality and Psychopathology, Personality and Everyday Functioning* (New York: Columbia University Press, 2005).

[447] A. Thapar, S. Collinshaw, D. Pine and A. Thapar, "Depression in Adolescence," *The Lancet,* 379 (2012): 1056-1067.

[448] A. Perkins, D. Arnone, J. Smallwood and D. Mobbs, "Thinking too much: Self-generated thought as the engine of neuroticism," *Trends in Cognitive Sciences,* 19 (2015): 492-498.

[449] Nettle, *Personality, op. cit.*

with Neuroticism,[450] as we noted previously. In terms of creativity more generally, it may be that people who are high in Neuroticism feel that there is something wrong with the world, with this incentivising them to understand it better in some way. Does Watson, perhaps related to his autism, show evidence of Neuroticism?

Is Watson a Hopeless Romantic?

Watson is certainly a Romantic and, as we will see, this relates to Neuroticism. Such is Watson's Romantic passion, and fascination with beautiful women, that he penned an entire memoir on his interactions with females, *Genes, Girls and Gamow,* this being a reference to Russian physicist George Gamow (1904-1968), an academic colleague of Watson's. This memoir explores his life after the discovery of the double helix; a life that was heavily focused on the pursuit of the opposite sex. It even begins with the Jane Austen quote, from *Pride and Prejudice,* that, "It is a truth universally acknowledged, that a single man in possession of a good fortune, must be in want of a wife."[451] We are, in essence taken through all the various girls that Watson has fancied or dated. These begin, at Cambridge University in 1953, with "a good-looking English girl called Sheila Griffiths."[452] We learn that, "During the fall I kept hoping to hear from her, having given her my Clare College address when we parted because then she did not know where she would be living in Rome."[453] She is the daughter of Jim Griffiths (1890-1975), a Labour MP who had been Secretary of State for the Colonies until Labour lost the 1951 Election.

At Cold Spring Harbor, later in 1953, Watson's interest turned to the 17 year old Christa Mayr, daughter of the German ornithologist Ernst Mayr (1904-2005). He had previously been attracted to her younger sister: "Before I went to Europe three years earlier, my eyes used to turn first to Christa's year younger blonde sister, Susie, adorably pretty since birth.

---

[450] S. Jacobwitz and V. Egan, "The Dark Triad and Normal Personality Traits," *Personality and Individual Differences,* 40 (2006): 331-339.
[451] J. Austen, *Pride and Prejudice* (London: T. Egerton, 2013).
[452] Watson, *Genes, Girls and Gamow, op. cit.,* 9.
[453] Watson, *Genes, Girls and Gamow, op. cit.,* 9.

Now, however, it was the more intellectual, 17 year-old, brown-haired Christa that I found myself anticipating."[454] They spent a great deal of time together: "Increasingly I wanted to touch her but, fearing a negative reaction, avoided even holding her hand as we walked back to the Lab's center."[455] Very quickly, Watson was "in love."[456]

Nevertheless, Watson still yearned for the daughter of the Welsh cabinet minister: "Christa Mayr was much on my mind, but initially I wanted to see Sheila Griffiths again and wrote her a brief note saying that I was back from the States for a brief visit to complete work on a manuscript about *The Double Helix* . . . But now, caught up with love for the newly grown-up Christa, I prevaricated and the summer was to pass without our meeting."[457] In leaving England, he wistfully remarks: "The nights then were no longer short and innocent English girls, still in their almost shapeless light frocks, looked cold as they tried to act as if the fragile English summer was still about. The evening was still early when I went back to the immense late Victorian room that I was to have for the night. At least for the moment, my English life was over."[458]

Watson's eventual wife, Elizabeth Lewis, is twenty years younger than him, something he was clearly rather pleased about, sending a postcard to a friend, once he had married, with the words, "19 year old now mine."[459] The implication is that she is a prize for this much older man. Indeed, Watson recalls: "At the time I did not let on to Dad how my affection for Liz had increased over the past eighteen months. I knew he would worry that at nineteen she was likely to reserve her true affection for someone much closer to her own age."[460] One interpretation is that this reflects the intensity we would expect an autistic to experience. Many people might regard an age-gap of this kind as madness, certainly a significant risk, but Watson is a risk-taker and he is overwhelmed by his feelings. In fact, it has been found that both partners in large age gap

---

[454] Watson, *Genes, Girls and Gamow, op. cit.* 20.
[455] Watson, *Genes, Girls and Gamow, op. cit.,* 20.
[456] Watson, *Genes, Girls and Gamow, op. cit.,* 20.
[457] Watson, *Genes, Girls and Gamow, op. cit.,* 22.
[458] Watson, *Genes, Girls and Gamow, op. cit.,* 27.
[459] Watson, *Genes, Girls and Gamow, op. cit.,* Epilogue.
[460] Watson, *Avoid Boring People, op. cit.,* 266.

relationships tend to be risk-takers,[461] and the probability of divorce is strongly elevated when the age gap is as large as 20 years.[462] We will look at Watson's risk-taking separately. Moreover, following the highly passionate and Romantic nature of those high in autistic traits, their marriage involved the ultimate Romantic cliché: "Happily, she had no qualms, instantly accepting my proposal that we effectively elope. We decided not to let anyone know except for her parents in Providence. In the end, the only other person at Harvard in on our plan was my secretary. She found out when Liz came in saying this would be her last day of work. Susie said that Dr Watson would be much disappointed. Liz replied that, in fact, he wouldn't be disappointed at all."[463]

By the time Watson married this 19 year-old, he was 39; a significant delay which involved delaying the beginning of the nurturing process. However, he evidently selected for genetic similarity in terms of intelligence, as evidenced by his young wife's background. Her father was: "a physician, whom I discovered to be, like my father, a keen reader and skeptic. In this important way, Liz and I had similar upbringings."[464] Elizabeth's father, Robert Vickery Lewis (1917-2013), who was from Rhode Island, was educated at two Ivy League colleges, Brown and the University of Pennsylvania.[465]

As an aside, and I am not suggesting this is germane to Jim and Elizabeth, it has been found that females in relationships with much older men (a 15 year or more advantage) display many symptoms of Borderline Personality Disorder, perhaps because they yearn for a father figure who will look after them and be their "special person."[466] Another study has

---

[461] B. Oudekerk, L. Guarnera and N. Reppucci, "Older opposite-sex romantic partners, sexual risk, and victimization in adolescence," *Child Abuse and Neglect,* 38 (2014): 1238-1248.

[462] A. Francis-Tan and H. Mialon, "'A Diamond is Forever' and Other Fairy Tales: The Relationship Between Wedding Expenses and Marriage Duration," *Economic Enquiry,* 53 (2015): 1919-1930.

[463] Watson, *Avoid Boring People, op cit.,* 267

[464] Watson, *Avoid Boring People, op. cit.,* 270.

[465] Watson, *Avoid Boring People, op. cit.,* 264.

[466] K. Habibzadeh and M. Nezhad, "Comparison of primary maladaptive schemas and attachment styles of women involved in emotional relationships with an age gap of 10 years or less and an age gap of 15 years or more (with male age advantage)," *Applied Family Therapy Journal,* 40 (2023): 19.

found that males in such relationships value the "admiration" they receive from the female, which implies either Narcissistic traits or possibly neurotic insecurities, though these can overlap.[467] According to Cathy Soref, Watson is extremely close to his wife. Apparently, once, at a function, Liz went away for a while and Watson became obsessed with finding her, eschewing the opportunity to meet media personality Paris Hilton (b. 1981) in order to do so.

Watson's Reading of Tragic Novels

Seemingly obsessed with getting a girlfriend in the 1950s, the lovelorn Watson even read tragic novels on the subject: "Earlier I'd read his equally bleak, London-centred *The End of the Affair*. For [*author Graham Greene's*] protagonists, love inevitably led to more agony than pleasure, and I easily identified myself with their struggles."[468] But he met Mayr again and again. They went for forest walks and listened to the birds: "At no time during these two idyllic days did I see a Christa about to fall into my arms, and I left the next morning for New Haven knowing that I wanted her more than she needed me."[469] He found a girl called Ellen who is "not only pretty but willing."[470] However, he rejected her because he was shortly to visit the Mayrs again: "Only the alcohol in my blood kept me from immediately regretting I had rejected an immediate gem for one that might never be mine."[471] Fortunately, this gamble paid off: "After dinner back at the farm, I found Christa not anxious to sleep and after a long walk down and back the country road beside their house, we started kissing in the darkened hall outside her room . . . The next day we were quietly a couple . . ."[472] Nevertheless, "At our parting it wasn't possible for me to kiss Christa good-bye, and there was a hollow feeling in the pit of my

---

[467] E. Schoenfeld, C. Bredow and T. Huston, "Do Men and Women Show Love Differently in Marriage?" *Personality and Social Psychology Bulletin*, 38 (2012): 11.
[468] Watson, *Genes, Girls and Gamow, op. cit.*, 51.
[469] Watson, *Genes, Girls and Gamow, op. cit.*, 56.
[470] Watson, *Genes, Girls and Gamow, op. cit.*, 85.
[471] Watson, *Genes, Girls and Gamow, op. cit.*, 85.
[472] Watson, *Genes, Girls and Gamow, op. cit.*, 89.

stomach as I had my last glance of her through the car window."[473] He then told his parents how in love he was with Christa.

The intense love for Christa, with whom he developed a long-distance relationship via letter, remained.

> "Persistent anxieties about Christa, heightened by the tone and decreasing frequency of her letters, were affecting my ability to concentrate on model-building or preparing for my impending talk at Harvard. Falling asleep was becoming a nightly struggle and without medical help I feared a nervous breakdown that would not only foreclose any offer from Harvard but also give Christa the message that I was emotionally fragile."[474]

But the relationship continued, with her even visiting him at Cambridge. Though, "Whether she had become more or less in love with me, I preferred not to contemplate."[475] Watson even met up with his "Welsh almost girlfriend"[476] Sheila Griffiths, by then married, to pour out his anxieties about Christa: "With one of her brothers writing for *The Guardian* and her father a Labour Member of Parliament, Sheila's well-intentioned gossip kept our dining hours together free of Christa uncertainties."[477] An example of such uncertainty is the following: "Even more to the point, I was going on afterwards to Munich and Christa for a few days." Christa was by then studying in Munich. "Although her Munich letters to me ended "With love, Christa," uncertainty about who might then be near her was always with me." It later transpired that Watson was right to be concerned.

In Munich, in November 1955, Watson became aware of how different their interests were, even in terms of art, and they parted with just a "kiss on the cheek." This was symbolically important. She visited Watson in Cambridge and he then arranged for them to stay with the Mitchisions on the Mull of Kintyre for New Year 1956. Watson was good friends with the zoology student and later zoologist Avrion Mitchison (1928-2022) and

---

[473] Watson, *Genes, Girls and Gamow, op. cit.,* 90.
[474] Watson, *Genes, Girls and Gamow, op. cit.,* 108.
[475] Watson, *Genes, Girls and Gamow, op. cit.,* 197.
[476] Watson, *Genes, Girls and Gamow, op. cit.*
[477] Watson, *Genes, Girls and Gamow, op. cit.*

was his best man. Mitchison's father was a barrister and his mother was Naomi Mitchison (1897-1999), a left-wing novelist and poet who was the daughter of the Scottish scientist J.S. Haldane (1860-1936). Almost as soon as she arrived, Christa made a devastating announcement to Watson, obviously wrecking the entire stay for him:

> "Then, after the teapots were back in the kitchen and the main room now unoccupied with family and guests off in other places, she no longer avoided my face and blurted out what she had to say—that she was not at all in love with me and knew her mind and needs well enough to know that she would always feel this way. As hard as she tried over the past year, she found it impossible to convert her liking for me into the deep love needed to share her life completely with another person. Forcefully said, these were not off-the-cuff remarks but came as if repeated over and over in her mind ever since leaving Munich."[478]

Christa also had a long conversation with his friend and host Naomi Mitchison, which was relayed to Watson:

> "The news was not good. Christa was not going to trot, much less slide, back to me soon, if ever. She had told Nou that for more than a year she had felt trapped in an emotional box that was stifling her freedom. She wanted a bigger cage, if not wide open fields to explore. My jitters with our bodies worried her, and maybe she needed a more phlegmatic male, who would not take her so seriously and control her a little when she got out of hand. For my own good, Nou told me I should get Christa out of my mind. Almost unable to swallow, I knew that by wanting Christa so much I had never given myself a realistic chance of succeeding."[479]

They parted at Victoria Station in London:

> "The time to say good-bye was on hand. Even a slight hug, now, would be wrong, and my last memory of Christa was her sleepless face disappearing into the train compartment. Walking back along the platform, I felt like vomiting."[480]

---

[478] Watson, *Genes, Girls and Gamow, op. cit.,* 223-224.
[479] Watson, *Genes, Girls and Gamow, op. cit.,* 225.
[480] Watson, *Genes, Girls and Gamow, op. cit.,* 226.

In the wake of the break-up, Watson wrote a letter to Christa's father about what had happened, noting: "Christa's attitude toward me has always oscillated between extreme affection and almost complete indifference" and that she had previously indicated that she had wanted to marry him. It turned out that Watson had likely been lucky to be rejected by Christa. At the time when she broke up with him, she later revealed in a letter, she was pregnant by an engineering student in Munich and intended to marry him. In other words she'd been cheating on Watson; having an affair. The pregnancy was also accidental.[481] Watson, apparently, is attracted to women who are "eccentric."[482] There is evidence that witty females, such as female comedians, are elevated in Borderline Personality Traits and Bipolar Disorder.[483]

Watson, the Romantic Neurotic

We noted earlier than anxiety potentiates sexual arousal in males, partly helping to explain the relationship between autism and fetishes. For this reason, we would expect people who were higher in anxiety to experience the world in a traumatic fashion in a way that a normal person would not when given the same environmental stimuli. Accordingly, one interpretation of Watson's fascination with Romantic love is that he experiences sensations with extreme intensity and these include the sensations relating to love, causing him to fall in love quickly and passionately. That Christa regards him as too intense and as controlling would be consistent with the anxiety that is associated with autism. It has been found that extreme Romantic passion can be associated with an insecure attachment style wherein a person is generally fearful that they may be abandoned and so they attach themselves very strongly to the love object.[484]

---

[481] Watson, *Genes, Girls and Gamow, op. cit.,* 254.

[482] Cathy Soref, *op. cit.*

[483] V. Ando, G. Claridge and K. Clark, "Psychotic Traits in Comedians," *British Journal of Psychiatry,* 204 (2014): 341-345.

[484] V. Paquette, M. Rapaport, A. St Louis and R. Vallerand, "Why are you passionately in love? Attachment styles as determinants of romantic passion and conflict resolution strategies," *Motivation and Emotion,* 44 (2020): 10.

Interestingly, in a volume of essays about Watson by former colleagues, Naomi Mitchison was quoted as saying "that Jim was more or less in love with me" when he visited her home 1956. Watson even dedicated *The Double Helix* to her.[485] Watson had first stayed with the family, at their home on the Mull of Kintyre, for Christmas 1955 when Naomi tried to release Watson's potential for socialising by introducing him to Doris Lessing (1919-2013), the novelist.[486] Watson wrote most of *The Double Helix* while staying at the same house. Naomi is mentioned in *Avoid Boring People* and *Genes, Girls and Gamow,* with a photograph of her published in the latter. But Watson does not mention any feelings for this married woman who was 31 years older than him.

There is some evidence that, insomuch as they long for secure attachment, women with Borderline Personality, who fundamentally fear abandonment due to a traumatic upbringing for example or simply due to genetics and who are very high in anxiety, strongly yearn after romantic love. As one psychologist has put it:

> "Most of my clients with borderline personality disorder are very focused on finding romantic love and avoiding abandonment. Love is their Holy Grail. They are seeking as an adult what they did not get enough of during their childhood. As a result, they tend to view finding their true love as the ultimate answer to all of their life problems."[487]

Clearly, such women are unlikely to make for stable and lasting relationships as the condition is associated with relationship instability, mental instability and cycling between ardent love and burning hatred for the partner, as we saw earlier.[488] Due to their fear of abandonment, such

---

[485] Abir-Am, "Watson's World," *op. cit.*, quoting J. Inglis, J. Sambrook and J. Witkowski, (Eds.), *Inspiring Watson: Jim Watson and the Age of DNA* (Cold Spring Harbor, NY: Cold Spring Harbor Press, 2003).

[486] E. Norrby, *Nobel Prizes and Notable Discoveries* (London: World Scientific, 2016), 155-156.

[487] E. Greenberg, "Are You in Love With Someone Who Has a Personality Disorder?" *Psychology Today* (26th August 2021), https://www.psychologytoday.com/intl/blog/understanding-narcissism/202108/are-you-in-love-someone-who-has-personality-disorder

[488] K. Tan, S. Ingram, L. Lau and S. South, "Borderline Personality Traits and Romantic Relationship Dissolution," *Journal of Personality Disorders,* 36 (2021): 1–18.

people will tend to idealise those with whom they have relationships. This evidences their relatively immature way of seeing the world and their desire for someone to fill the void and emptiness and meaninglessness which they often feel. In other words, they cannot cope with their extreme negative feelings, so they create a fantasy world, which produces positive feelings; this perfect person being their rescuer.[489] But this aside, Watson's memoirs do seem to imply a kind of passionate love which has been found to be consistent with traits of Neuroticism.

Neuroticism and Sexual Fetishes

We already looked at how autism is associated with fetishes and Neurotic traits. This elevated Neuroticism, which is also related to experiencing trauma, might also help to explain the evidence of elevated levels of sexual dysfunction and other sexual aberrations among highly eminent people, especially writers, explored by Felix Post.[490] To give an extreme example, it has been found that consensual sibling incest – in which the disgust at the idea of incest is overridden – is associated with a highly unstable and somewhat traumatic upbringing in which there are family secrets, such as adultery, and forms of psychological abuse, such as distant parents who do not respect the children's sexual boundaries, examples being fondling and inappropriate discussion of sex.[491] In some cases, the closeness this can lead to among siblings can override the "Westermarck Effect," where children who are raised together become sexually repelled by each other,[492] and, anyway, trauma can lead to the maladaptive development of

---

[489] H. Jeong, M. Jin and M. Hyun, "Understanding a Mutually Destructive Relationship Between Individuals With Borderline Personality Disorder and Their Favorite Person," *Psychiatry Investigation,* 19 (2022): 1069–1077.

[490] Post, "Creativity and psychopathology," *op. cit.*

[491] C. Gilbert, "Sibling Incest: A Descriptive Study of Family Dynamics," *Journal of Child and Adolescent Psychiatric Nursing,* 5 (1992): 5-9; H. Smith and E. Israel, "Sibling Incest: A Study of the Dynamics of 25 Cases," *Child Abuse and Neglect,* 11 (1987): 101-108.

[492] D. de Smet, L. van Speybroeck and J. Verplaetse, "The Westermarck Effect Revisited: A Psychophysiological Study of Sibling Incest Aversion in Young Female Adults," *Evolution and Human Behavior,* 35 (2014): 35-42.

sexuality, such as the inability to relax during sexual situations.[493] To give an example, the poet Lord Byron (1788-1824) seemingly had a rather traumatic childhood and is supposed to have had an incestuous affair with his half-sister Augusta (1783-1851), although they were not raised together, so the Westermarck Effect may not have occurred.[494]

Tangentially related to this, it may be worth exploring something which Crick wrote to Watson in a fit of pique because he was furious about how he had been portrayed in Watson's memoir of the discovery of the structure of DNA, later entitled *The Double Helix*. The manuscript versions included remarks far stronger than the eventually accepted, "I can't ever remember seeing Francis Crick in a modest mood,"[495] these being the exact words with which Watson's memoir commenced. The final manuscript also included comments such as that "most people thought (Crick) talked too much," or that a factor in Crick not yet being a college fellow "was his laugh, against which many dons would most certainly rebel if subjected to its shattering bang more than once a week." Watson also implies that Crick is prickly in social situations: "a stray remark over sherry might bring Francis smack into your life."[496] Watson recalls part of Crick's angry letter about his manuscript as follows:

> "On the next-to-last page, Francis raised the stakes. A psychiatrist to whom he gave the manuscript reportedly said, "The book could only be made by a man who hates women." Another shrink concluded that I loved my sister to excess, "a fact much discussed by your friends while you were working in Cambridge, but so far they have refrained from writing about.""[497]

This remark jumped out at me because by this stage in *Avoid Boring People* – page 231 to be precise – I had thought a number of times: "Watson does seem oddly close to his sister." To be fair, I had already read

---

[493] A. Zoldbrod, "Sexual Issues in Treating Trauma Survivors," *Current Sexual Health Reports,* 7 (2015): 3-11.

[494] See D. Crane, *The Kindness of Sisters: Annabella Milbanke and the Destruction of the Byrons* (New York: HarperCollins, 2012).

[495] Watson, *Avoid Boring People, op. cit.,* 232.

[496] Watson, *The Double Helix, op. cit.,* Ch.1

[497] Watson, *Avoid Boring People, op. cit.,* 231.

The Double Helix in which Watson wrote, with regard to his colleague Maurice, "Neither the beauty of my sister nor my intense interest in the DNA structure had snared him."[498] Evidently, those who knew Watson well thought the same. One review of *The Double Helix* declared that Watson's sister was the, "principal object of her brother's attachment and potential for affection."[499] Perhaps I am being as indelicate as Watson was accused of being in *The Double Helix* by even mentioning this, but it was something I thought about.

Watson does mention his sister a lot in his memoir, providing us with all kinds of details we might not expect, such as that she went through puberty relatively young. He even publishes a picture of her at the Nobel Prize Ceremony; not her with him, just her, as if we are to admire his sister. To give another example, he recalls:

> "On her way back to Chicago from New Haven, my sister came to Cold Spring Harbor to see how I was living . . . She quickly sensed the tight knit of our club, where phages were at center stage and there was little sympathy for those scientists who did boring, if not stupid, experiments on other organisms. My hero worship for Max surprised Betty since his directness and self-confidence were antithetical to my parents' gentle empathy for those who could not make it to the top. She, moreover, was not at all prepared for Manny's free spirit and her obvious attraction to talented men."[500]

This anecdote adds nothing to the narrative; it is as though Watson simply enjoys reminiscing about his sister; who is also his only sibling. We have seen already that excessive sibling-love is associated with trauma in childhood. However, a person who is high in autistic traits, and who is thus hyper-sensitive, may experience a perfectly normal childhood as traumatic and develop accordingly. In addition, people who have autistic traits seem to feel romantic love to an elevated degree and, so, perhaps this is true of platonic forms of love, such as towards a sister.

---

[498] Watson, *The Double Helix, op. cit.,* Ch. 4.
[499] Quoted in McElheny, *Watson and DNA, op. cit.*
[500] Watson, *Avoid Boring People, op. cit.,* 70.

What is Religious Experience?

Returning to the relationship between Neuroticism and creativity, depression (used here to mean a chronically depressed mood) is also associated with profound religious experiences, which are adaptive because they force the person out of their depression and provide them with a sense of deep existential meaning.[501] This may increase creativity, not least in order to make sense of such experiences.

"Religious experience" can be used to describe a spectrum of experiences of varying degrees of intensity. American psychologist Lewis Rambo observes that this spectrum can extend from a very profound sense of knowing that God is real up to intense hallucinations, in which people have visions of God or hear His voice. When these more extreme experiences happen to those who are not particularly religious then they can be characterized as life-changing "conversion experiences."[502] In making sense of these kinds of experiences, American neuroscientist Andrew Newberg and colleagues argue that the mind has two systems, calming and arousal. When either of these systems is pushed to their extremes, through meditation or hyper-arousal, they argue that it is dangerous for the body. Accordingly, the other system hits in, leading to alternative states of consciousness and powerful psychological experiences.[503] Religiousness, being an adaptive instinct and having all of the dimensions of an adaptation,[504] is heightened at times of stress and there is a large body of evidence that intense religious experiences tend to be associated with times of very pronounced stress, to an even greater extent than elevated religious belief.[505]

English biologist Richard Dawkins has suggested that they may be provoked by the way in which stress makes us highly instinctive, and thus prone to religious belief anyway. However, Dawkins argues, we are also

---

[501] A. Newberg, E. D'Aquili and V. Rause, *Why God Won't Go Away: Brain Science and the Biology of Belief* (New York: Ballantine Books, 2002).
[502] L. Rambo, *Understanding Religious Conversion* (New Haven: Yale University Press, 1993).
[503] Newberg et al., *Why God Won't Go Away, op. cit.*
[504] R. Vaas, "God, gains and genes," in E. Voland and W. Schiefenhövel, (Eds.), *The Biological Evolution of Religious Mind and Behavior* (New York: Springer, 2009).
[505] Rambo, *Understanding Religious Conversion, op cit.*

evolved to over-detect agency, because if we mistake a distant rock for a wolf we have lost nothing but if we make the opposite mistake we may be killed. Accordingly, at times of very pronounced arousal, we are much more likely to mistake some unidentified sound as the voice of God and, at the same time, find that our calming system would hit in. This would lead to an intense religious experience combined with feelings of overwhelming relief and joy.[506] The propensity to undergo religious experiences can be regarded as useful in evolutionary terms on a number of levels. Most obviously, it reduces levels of stress, presumably to an even greater extent than simple religious belief. It reassures you - in an extremely potent and certainty-inducing way - that God is there for you. He is guiding your life, and everything will ultimately be well. Through meditation or prayer, in which you reach feelings of great calm, religious experience is seemingly something that can effectively be induced. This would be useful because it would reassure the believer of the absolute presence of God. Does this relate to Watson?

Profound Meaning and Flashes of Inspiration

We might also ask what it means to search for aesthetic and philosophical meaning in all experience, as geniuses do, as we saw earlier. A reasonable answer may be that they desire to know the purpose of everything which they encounter. They are strongly committed to making sense of the fundamental nature and rules of all that is around them. However, there can be said to religious dimensions to finding "meaning" in all experience; it implies, almost, a kind of implicit religion in which somebody is on a quest to find the deepest levels of life itself. A "sense of meaning in life" is often understood in a mystical sense; a profound sense of purpose and importance; an overarching mission and aim. Accordingly, the implication is that geniuses have a keen sense of existential mission; something which is associated both with religiosity and, also, with subjective happiness and self-stimulation is pursuit of goals.[507]

---

[506] R. Dawkins, *The God Delusion* (London: Bantam Books, 2006), 116.
[507] D. Krok, "The Role of Meaning in Life within the Relations of Religious Coping and Psychological Well-Being," *Journal of Religion and Health,* 54 (2015): 2292-2308.

Crucially, Watson has finally found his true calling: To understand the nature of the gene. Little else now matters; even bird-spotting becomes less intrinsically intriguing. Young Watson hardly cares about occasional B-grades in dull, poorly taught classes with typically uninspiring lecturers. He is, in his own words, on a quest.

> "The year had exceeded even my highest hopes, since I was now in the thick of the quest to understand the gene. I became more than aware of the advantages of having attended the University of Chicago, where I had learned the need to be forthright and call crap crap. It was not that I was inherently brighter than my fellow graduate students; I was just much more comfortable challenging ideas and conventional wisdom, whether it concerned politics or science."[508]

It is a quest for the truth. Watson notes, quoting his undergraduate university president, that academia "abounds in triviality" and this is to be ignored. The truth will only be reached by overcoming the vast majority of research - which is pointless, career-elevating tinkering and unnecessary, intellectually pretentious nuance – and fighting for the prize of a fundamental discovery. Vitally, "feelings" must not be a concern, nonsense must be called out as such, and the Midwit (normal range reasonably high IQ) guardians of academic vested interests must be slain; dragon-like enemies of truth every last one of them, breathing the fire of intellectual cowardice. Unsurprisingly, among creative thinkers, there is a curvilinear relationship between eminence and academic qualifications. The least eminent either have a low level of education in their field (people who think they know more than they do) or a high level of education (Midwits and Head Girls who are rule-following and, thus, unoriginal, see below).[509]

The English theologian Edward Bailey (1935-2015) proposed the concept of "Implicit Religion." This is the idea that, sometimes, if you interrogate the ideas of people who are not overtly religious, and who may even claim to be atheists, you will find that they make various religious assumptions; that the way in which they see the world ultimately implies

---

[508] Watson, *Avoid Boring People, op. cit.*, 49.
[509] Ochse, *Before the Gates of Excellence, op. cit.*, 86.

belief in a metaphysical reality. Bailey developed this model through qualitative research, sometimes simply talking to men in English pubs about their worldviews.[510] It might be argued that there is something implicitly religious about the genius. His desire to make sense of reality, and his commitment to the truth, are dogmatic and it might be averred that they can only fully make sense if truth is deified as something "ultimate," rather like God: There is an objective reality and it is our calling and duty to understand it. This begs the question of, "Too whom is it our duty? By whom are we called?" The Scholastics believed that the aim of science was to make sense of God's creation, meaning that to lie was blasphemy. The genius may not necessarily believe in God but he has retained the commitment to the truth. Indeed, ideas may occur to him in flashes of inspiration, almost akin to religious experiences, partly due to the intensity with which he experiences the world.

In this regard, it is perhaps relevant that profound religious experiences are associated with elevated Neuroticism.[511] The genius, to the extent that he is high in Neuroticism, can be predicted to feel extreme discomfort in the face of an overwhelming and uncertain world, strongly incentivising him to make sense of it. As with religious experiences, therefore, a sense of certainty may come to him almost like a feeling of divine inspiration; as something external to himself. In this regard, it is noteworthy that a feeling of "inspiration" – where subjects are primed to re-live an inspirational experience – appears to encourage belief in God.[512] One interpretation of these findings is that geniuses, and creative people more broadly, are subject to transcendental experiences that have much in common with religious experiences and which appear to imbue life with a sense of meaning. We can understand how this would lead to a sense of mission. It has been argued that these "eureka" or "light bulb" moments come from the unconscious and are, thus, experienced as flashes of

---

[510] E. Bailey, *Implicit Religion in Contemporary Society* (Leuwens: Peeters, 1997).

[511] P. Hills, L. Francis, M. Argyle and C. Jackson, "Primary personality trait correlates of religious practice and orientation," *Personality and Individual Differences,* 36 (2004): 61–73

[512] C. Critcher and C. Lee, "Feeling Is Believing: Inspiration Encourages Belief in God," *Psychological Science,* 29 (2018).

inspiration akin to transcendent experiences.[513] High Openness and hyper-arousal appear to predict having such experiences, consistent with evidence we discussed earlier that hyper-arousal, which also occurs in states of anxiety, appears to lead to religious experiences.[514]

Watson experienced his fundamental breakthrough almost like a religious experience: "But now, to my delight and amazement, the answer was turning out to be profoundly interesting. For over two hours I happily lay awake with pairs of adenine residues whirling in front of my closed eyes. Only for brief moments did the fear shoot through me that an idea this good could be wrong."[515]

The Association between
an Unhappy Childhood and Greatness

Felix Post also found that having an unhappy childhood – marked by the death of a parent or the abandonment of the family by the father, for example – was relatively high among these world famous creative people. Certainly, 56 per cent of writers, the category with the highest prevalence of psychopathy, had unhappy childhoods, as against 26 per cent of thinkers and, least often, 10 per cent of composers This would set such people up for the kind of fast Life History Strategy which is associated with relatively low General Factor of Personality. That said, he found evidence that the brilliance of these men was partly heritable: 48 per cent of thinkers and 22 per cent of writers, as well as 20 per cent of scientists, had relatives who had excelled in different disciplines, a very infrequent finding in the case of composers, artists, and politicians. This implies that environment plays a larger part in political, musical and artistic genius than it does in major literary and scientific accomplishment. That said, it should be noted that many composers do come from musical families. Post's analysis dealt only with extremely eminent composers.

---

[513] G. Klein, *Seeing What Others Don't: The Remarkable Ways We Gain Insights* (New York: Public Affairs, 2013).
[514] L. Ovington, *Who Has Insights? The Who, Where, and When of the Eureka Moment* (PhD Thesis: Charles Sturt University, Bathurst, New South Wales, Australia, 2016).
[515] Watson, *The Double Helix, op. cit.,* Ch. 25.

Regarding an unhappy childhood, Post found that, "Family histories of schizophrenia, depression, suicide, alcoholism, and various other conditions, which could only be labelled as instability, were registered in 55.5% of our 291 internationally famous subjects."[516] These unhappy childhoods were much less pronounced in scientists and Watson appears to be consistent with this.

In terms of other environmental factors, I have shown in my book *Sent Before Their Time* that people who are born severely prematurely are over-represented among accepted scientific geniuses. This is because the brain damage precipitated by prematurity elevates the likelihood of numerous traits that are associated with genius. These include skewed intelligence, psychopathy, autism, ADHD, depression and anxiety and delayed intellectual development.[517]

---

[516] Post, "Creativity and psychopathology," *op. cit.*
[517] E. Dutton, *Sent Before Their Time: Genius, Charisma and Being Born Prematurely* (Melbourne: Manticore Press, 2022).

Chapter Ten

How Vital Are Extraversion
and Narcissism to Genius?

"Je tiens l'affaire, vois!"

"Look! I've got it!" shouted the French philologist Jean-François Champollion (1790-1832) before collapsing, utterly overwhelmed with a sensation of pure joy. He had finally cracked Ancient Egyptian hieroglyphs after so much intellectual exertion.[518] We are evolved to want to solve problems and doing so fills us with positive sensations. This can act as a motivator; it can drive people forwards where others, who experience the world less intensely, would have given up long ago. Taking risks, which then pay off, induces such feelings in us as well, and often we feel "alive" while we are taking a risk, while we are racing towards "scientific gold." This seems to be the way in which the genius experiences the world.

The Importance of Taking Risks

A final dimension to the genius personality, which may seem quite surprising, is at least elements of Extraversion.[519] This is associated with taking risks due to the strong emotional high the extravert receives when the risks turn out to be worth it. Geniuses are risk-takers and they are highly competitive, as predicted by elevated androgens. Often, when a problem has needed a solution, many people have been working to solve

---

[518] P. Bailey, "How the hieroglyphic code was cracked," *The New Statesman* (15th January 2023), https://www.newstatesman.com/culture/art-design/2023/01/how-the-hieroglyphic-code-was-cracked

[519] Eysenck, *Genius: The Natural History of Creativity, op. cit.*; Feist, "A meta-analysis of personality in scientific and artistic creativity," *op. cit.*

it. The recognized genius is the one who wins the race to solve the problem, so there is a degree to which he must have a strong competitive drive. The best example of this can be seen in the way that Darwin went to print with his theory of evolution (or as he termed it *modification by descent*) in 1859 because he was under the erroneous impression that Alfred Russell Wallace (1823-1913) had, independently, come up with precisely the same theory. Darwin, however, had developed his own theory around 20 years earlier.

Indeed, it should be remembered that though the archetypal genius combines super-high intelligence with moderately high psychopathy, there will be all kinds of variations on this theme. For example, a given genius – Charles Darwin may be an example – might be quite high in Agreeableness, but extremely low in Conscientiousness. According to his son Francis, Charles Darwin's working habits were extraordinarily unsystematic and his study was always in a state of chaos.[520] As long as the overall balance between the psychological factors is optimum a genius can still be produced. As we saw earlier, scientific genius appears to be associated with genes for risk-taking and curiosity. These traits cross-over with Extraversion. Gregory Feist has summarised, based on a meta-analysis, that creative scientists tend to be: ". . . more open to new experiences, less conventional and less conscientious, more self-confident, self-accepting, driven, ambitious, dominant, hostile, and impulsive."[521] Openness, self-confidence and dominance all imply Extraversion.

Even so, as an undergraduate, we see in Watson clear evidence of high intellectual curiosity to the extent of taking risks. "Upon returning to school for the fall 1945 quarter, I decided to risk losing my scholarship aid by taking more difficult courses."[522] Despite his focus on Biology, Watson risks taking all manner of extremely difficult courses in Mathematics and Physics, and possibly receiving insufficient grades, simply because they happen to interest him, and it actually pays off in terms of the grades obtained. It also gives Watson confidence. "Extend yourself intellectually by taking courses that initially frighten you," Watson advises:

---

[520] Simonton, *Genius, Creativity and Leadership, op. cit.*
[521] Feist, "A meta-analysis of personality in scientific and artistic creativity," *op. cit.*
[522] Watson, *Avoid Boring People, op. cit.*, 26.

"Only by taking higher math courses would I develop sufficient comfort to work at the leading edge of my field, even if I never got near the leading edge of math. And so my B's in two genuinely tough math courses were worth far more in confidence capital than any 'A' I would likely have received in a biology course, no matter how demanding."[523]

At the same time, quite independent of his courses and due to his voracious outside reading, Watson becomes fascinated by the gene and the details of genetics. This appears to be an almost textbook example of the way in which the genius only genuinely excels in areas that truly inspire him and it takes time for these areas to be unearthed. As Watson summarises, "If your grades in classes you like are not largely A's, you have likely not yet found your intellectual calling."[524] Watson also observes that when writing your doctoral thesis, you should: "Keep your intellectual curiosity much broader than your thesis objective."[525] This high degree of Openness, he explains, allows you to come up with highly novel ways of interpreting your data; it permits you to make connections between superficially very different domains, something which appears to be central to genuine theoretical insights. This high Openness runs throughout Watson's life.

One of his lessons from being a postdoc in Copenhagen is, "Routinely reading the *New York Times* at breakfast will expose you to many more facts and ideas than you are ever likely to acquire during evenings with individuals who in most instances haven't had to think differently since getting tenure."[526] Watson also nearly lost his fellowship grant by transferring from Copenhagen to Cambridge to become part of a research group which the grant authorities in the US did not consider him qualified to be part of. "He was put out that I had overstepped myself in denying that I would profit from biochemistry. I wrote to Luria to save me. He and the new man were casual acquaintances, and so when my decision was set in proper perspective, he might reverse his decision."[527] Watson even left

---

[523] Watson, *Avoid Boring People, op. cit.*, 51.
[524] Watson, *Avoid Boring People, op. cit.*, 35.
[525] Watson, *Avoid Boring People, op. cit.*, 53.
[526] Watson, *Avoid Boring People, op. cit.*, 92.
[527] Watson, *The Double Helix, op. cit.*, Ch. 6.

Copenhagen for Cambridge before his grant situation was confirmed, taking an incredible risk.

This risk-taking followed him into later life. At the age of 90, when most people would have given up driving, Watson careered off a road near his home on Long Island down a 20 foot ravine. Pulled from his vehicle by emergency services, he was airlifted to hospital with a head injury.[528] In January the following year, when Watson hit the headlines due to his remarks about race, he was still recuperating in a nursing home from his injury.[529]

Sociability and Sensation-Seeking

However, it should be observed that there are two essential dimensions to Extraversion: sociability and sensation-seeking. Creative people are high in sensation-seeking. Their bodies will receive a strong "hit" of positive feelings when they solve their problem, for example, meaning that they are incentivised to absorb themselves in solving their problem. They are not high in sociability; indeed they are relatively low in it. This means that they are happy to spend a great deal of time alone. This is important because, being alone, they are able to absorb themselves in their projects without distraction and, consequently, be extremely productive.[530] In this specific sense, they are "introverts:" The stimulation of socialising is easily too much for them, something that is also true of autistics. Extraverts who are high in the sub-trait of sociability have the opposite problem. They too easily feel under-stimulated, causing them to reject the solitude of research in favour of socialising. Watson, at least with age, has become sociable, enjoying meeting new people, with one writer commenting: "He clucked and grinned like a teenager as I walked in to say hello, telling me something that made no sense about the snow and

---

[528] *News12 Long Island,* "DNA pioneer injured after driving down 20-foot ditch in Syosset" (27th October 2018), https://longisland.news12.com/sources-dna-pioneer-drove-down-20-foot-ditch-at-cold-spring-harbor-laboratory-39367255

[529] N. Yancey-Bragg, "Lab revokes honorary titles for Nobel Prize winner James Watson after repeated racist comments," *USA Today* (13th January 2019), https://eu.usatoday.com/story/news/nation/2019/01/13/dna-pioneer-james-watson-honors-racist-comments/2565503002/

[530] See, A. Storr, *Solitude* (London: Simon and Schuster, 1988).

how he liked to play tennis."[531] This almost child-like quality has been remarked upon by others and perhaps it is germane to genius; children, like many geniuses, are stereotypically excitable, enthusiastic and high in certain kinds of Openness; prone to flights of fancy. For French biologist Francois Jacob, whom we met earlier, Watson was "A surprising mixture of awkwardness and shrewdness. Of childishness in the things of life and maturity in those of science."[532] Watson's biographer notes, "Maybe he had never grown up . . ."[533]

As an aside, and consistent with Extraversion, Watson makes a number of remarks in in *The Double Helix* about his enjoyment of alcohol, such as, "Our bottle of Chablis, however, diminished my desire for hard facts, and as we walked out of Soho and across Oxford Street, Maurice spoke only of his plans to get a less gloomy apartment in a quieter area,"[534] "Instead of sherry, I let Francis buy me a whiskey"[535] and "The prospect of lunch with the alcoholic English cider more than compensated for the habit of leaving the outside doors open to the westerly winds."[536] The main reason he enjoys publicity about his discovery is because it might make it easier to pull girls: "They planned to devote several pages to young celebrities who were making it big in the States, and I was to be included for the discovery of the double helix. The resultant publicity, I thought, should make "with it" American girls more eager to know me."[537]

As we have discussed, the genius combines extremely high intelligence with an optimum placing on a number of personality traits in relation to that level of intelligence. This is because intelligence is associated with the ability to delay gratification via time preference (which acts like aspects of impulse control),[538] and with elements of cognitive

---

[531] D.E. Duncan, *The Geneticist Who Played Hoops With My DNA: Genius and the Quest to Rewrite Life* (London: Fourth Estate, 2005), 175.
[532] Hargittai, *The DNA Doctor, op. cit.,* 195. Quoting, F. Jacob, *The Statue Within: An Autobiography* (London: Unwin, 1988), 264.
[533] McElheny, *Watson and DNA, op. cit.,* Prologue.
[534] Watson, *The Double Helix, op. cit.,* Ch. 23,
[535] Watson, *The Double Helix, op. cit.,* Ch. 22
[536] Watson, *The Double Helix, op. cit.,* Ch. 15.
[537] Watson, *Genes, Girls and Gamow, op, cit.,* 66.
[538] Jensen, *The g Factor, op. cit.*

empathy (specifically the ability to solve social problems).[539] If a person is too low in Agreeableness and Conscientiousness in relation to their intelligence then they may end up in prison for violence or addicted to drugs to a degree that their productivity is impaired. If they were too high in sensation seeking (with the same caveat) they may also end up addicted to drugs or alcohol. If they were too high in Openness-Intellect in relation to their intelligence then they would be dreamers, obsessed with bizarre, paranoid and otherwise empirically inaccurate theories. If they were too high in Neuroticism in relation to their intelligence they might end up in prison due to serious violence or become absorbed in periods of religious fervour or in very high extrinsic religiousness – and thus "the Current Thing"- as a way of allaying social anxiety.[540] If this were combined with low Agreeableness and Extraversion, then a Grandiose Narcissist might emerge – as Narcissism is a coping mechanism for negative feelings especially among those low in Agreeableness and high in Extraversion – resulting in a status-obsessed individual who, therefore, does not challenge convention or only does so within certain boundaries that are useful to achieving status.[541]

Genius as a Matter of Balance

Consistent with this it has been found that hyper-Wokeness is associated with Narcissism and Machiavellianism. In a society in which left-wing dogma is dominant, you will achieve Narcissistic supply and status by competitively signalling your Wokeness, so this is to be expected. However, there is some evidence being on the extreme right in such as a society is associated with psychopathy. This also follows because such people enjoy risk and even enjoy upsetting people.[542] An optimum

---

[539] Kaufman et al., "General intelligence predicts reasoning ability for evolutionarily familiar content," *op. cit.*

[540] Hills et al, "Primary personality trait correlates of religious practice and orientation," *op. cit.*

[541] C. Montoro, P. de la Coba, M. Moreno-Padilla and C. Galvez-Sanchez, "Narcissistic Personality and Its Relationship with Post-Traumatic Symptoms and Emotional Factors: Results of a Mediational Analysis Aimed at Palersonalizing Mental Health Treatment," *Behavioral Sciences*, 12 (2022): 91.

[542] J. Moss and P. O'Connor, "The Dark Triad traits predict authoritarian political correctness and Alt-Right attitudes," *Heliyon*, 6 (2020): e04453.

relationship between these traits, which all inter-correlate, could produce a relatively Narcissistic individual who concomitantly challenges social convention and, indeed, in a leftist society might find himself branded "far right."

Similarly, it should be remembered that each of these personality disorders are composed of a shopping list of traits. Thus, you might find an individual who is rated as sub-clinically Narcissistic, or Psychopathic, because he is extremely high in some of the traits, though only moderate or even low in others. For example, he could be extremely high in grandiosity and lack of empathy but, nevertheless, be low in "lack of realistic long-term goals," "impulsivity" or "parasitic lifestyle." Indeed, very high intelligence (depending on the strength of these traits) would mediate in favour of ameliorating these traits because it will make him future-oriented and, possibly, sufficiently socioeconomically successful not to need to be parasitic.

The Relationship between Genius and Narcissism

Perhaps it can be said that an optimum level of Narcissism is necessary for some forms of genius to emerge, insomuch as there is a clear crossover between Grandiose Narcissism and Psychopathy via the Dark Triad wherein Narcissism is correlated with Psychopathy and Machiavellianism.[543] As we have seen, to be truly successfully creative you must be able to cope with knock-backs and there is an extent to which you must have intense self-belief. In addition, creative achievement will provide people with Narcissistic supply. As such, we would expect there to be an association between trait Narcissism and creativity and even, though such people would be far less mentally stable, between creativity and Narcissistic Personality Disorder.

There is some evidence that this is the case, though part of this appears to be mediated by the way in which Narcissists are better at persuading others than they are highly creative; they are better at promoting and

---

[543] See, S. Jakobwitz and V. Egan, "The 'Dark Triad' and normal personality traits," *Personality and Individual Differences*, 40 (2006): 331–339.

marketing their creativity.[544] However, other research argues that there is simply a weak positive correlation between the ability to think in a creative way and Narcissism, perhaps because the latter gives people the confidence to engage in the former.[545] Narcissists are, for example, highly enthusiastic about their creativity, which is likely to aid creative accomplishment.[546] Another study has found that "creative deviance" (new ideas which strongly question accepted ways of doing things) and "creative self-efficacy" are predicted by Narcissistic traits.[547] It is also been averred that there is a feedback loop involved. Narcissism leads to creative achievement, but creative achievement further heightens the Narcissism as the world is telling us how special we are.[548]

But, evidently, the key point is that there appears to be a kind of "Goldilocks Zone" of personality strength in relation to intelligence – an optimum relationship, in which there may be subtle variations, resulting in subtle differences – which permits the emergence of genius or of extremely high levels of creative achievement. An example of such differences would be that an eminent poet would be expected to be far higher in Neuroticism, and lower in intelligence, than an eminent Physicist but we might expect both to be more intelligent and more Neurotic (in optimum balance) than less creative and less successful people within their own fields.

It might also be argued that there is something Narcissistic about a feeling of religious calling, despite the fact that those who claim to have it will tend to signal their humility. As we discussed earlier, Grandiose Narcissism is associated with high Neuroticism and develops as a defence

---

[544] L. Chang and Z. Gong, "The relationship between narcissism and creativity: A chain/serial mediation model," *Personality and Individual Differences,* 205 (2023): 112070.
[545] R. Raskin, "Narcissism and Creativity: Are They Related?" *Psychological Reports,* 46 (1980): 55-60.
[546] J. Goncalo, F. Flynn and S. Kim, "Are two narcissists better than one? The link between narcissism, perceived creativity, and creative performance," *Personality and Social Psychology Bulletin,* 36 (2010): 1484-1495.
[547] K. Zhang and Z. Cui, "Are narcissists always bad apples? The relationship between employee narcissism and creative deviance," *Frontiers in Psychology,* 13 (2022).
[548] E. Jauk and N. Sordia, "On Risks and Side Effects: Does Creative Accomplishment Make us Narcissistic?" *Creativity,* 5 (2018): 182-187.

mechanism against extreme negative feelings, sometimes induced by a traumatic environment. Dramatic religious experiences are also associated with Neuroticism and a stressful environment. An element of many of these experiences involves the feeling that you are chosen by God; you are have special knowledge and are "saved" in a way that others are not. According to Calvinist Theology, you are part of the Elect that has been chosen by God to be saved. In this sense, to the extent that God talks to you and appears to you during the conversion experience, it might be averred that we are dealing with a psychotic episode, as such dramatic experiences appear to be,[549] via which the Narcissistic coping mechanism is adopted by a relatively mentally unstable or traumatised person. Thereafter, they have a sense of being called by God; of their life having eternal purpose.

Consistent with this, it has been found that religious leaders, who supposedly have a feeling of divine calling, tend to display elevated levels of Narcissism, often as a response to Post-Traumatic Stress.[550] We would expect geniuses to have elevated Narcissistic traits and this would, therefore, make sense of the possibility that they might feel a sense of calling, by God or by the universe, to pursue the truth and do so, sometimes, no matter what the cost. Newton would potentially exemplify this trend and perhaps also the feedback loop wherein original Narcissism is elevated by the world telling you what a genius you are.

Does Watson Have Narcissistic Traits?

Certainly, some critics have suggested that Watson has traits of Narcissism (sub-clinical Narcissism rather than Narcissistic Personality Disorder), and this should not be a surprise in light of our above discussion of its relationship with creativity and even its indirect relationship with autism. Critics have described him as "insulting and arrogant," as a professor at Harvard University termed Watson. Edward O. Wilson referred to him as

---

[549] E. Murray, M. Cunningham and B. Price, "The Role of Psychotic Disorders in Religious History Considered," *Journal of Neuropsychiatry and Clinical Neurosciences,* 24 (2012): 410-426.
[550] E. Ruffing, C. Bell and S. Sandage, "PTSD symptoms in religious leaders: Prevalence, stressors, and associations with narcissism," *Archive for the Psychology of Religion,* 43 (2020): 1.

the "Caligula of Biology" due to his "contempt" for scientists who studied anything other than molecules.[551] Specifically, Wilson writes:

> "At department meetings Watson radiated contempt in all directions. He shunned ordinary courtesy and polite conversation, evidently in the belief that they would only encourage the traditionalists to stay around. His bad manners were tolerated because of the greatness of the discovery he had made, and because of its gathering aftermath. In the 1950s and 1960s the molecular revolution had begun to run through biology like a flash flood. Watson, having risen to historic fame at an early age, became the Caligula of biology. He was given license to say anything that came to his mind and expect to be taken seriously. And unfortunately, he did so, with a casual and brutal off-handedness."[552]

Indeed, Wilson goes much further, proclaiming Watson to be the most dreadful man he had ever met:

> "James Dewey Watson, the co-discoverer of the structure of DNA, served as one such adverse hero for me. When he was a young man, in the 1950s and 1960s, I found him the most unpleasant human being I had ever met. He came to Harvard as an assistant professor in 1956, also my first year at the same rank. At twenty-eight, he was only a year older. He arrived with a conviction that biology must be transformed into a science directed at molecules and cells and rewritten in the language of physics and chemistry. What had gone before, "traditional" biology—my biology—was infested by stamp collectors who lacked the wit to transform their subject into a modern science. He treated most of the other twenty-four members of the Department of Biology with a revolutionary's fervent disrespect."[553]

A writer for a British newspaper opined: "Watson, as arrogant as he was obscure, found himself working with an equally self-possessed but somewhat overlooked older man at the Cavendish, Francis Crick . . ."[554]

---

[551] *Chicago Tribune,* "Elementary, Watson. You're Wrong on Race," (1st December 2014).

[552] Wilson, *Naturalist, op. cit.*

[553] Wilson, *Naturalist, op. cit.*

[554] R. McCrum, "The 100 best nonfiction books: No 15 – The Double Helix by James D Watson (1968)," *The Guardian* (9th May 2016), https://www.theguardian.com/books/2016/may/09/the-double-helix-james-d-watson-100-best-nonfiction-books

The description as "arrogant" seems to come up in discussion of Watson many times.[555] Apparently, he once visited South African Nobel biologist Sydney Brenner (1927-2019), whose children were having a birthday party, and ate all the cake that had been prepared for the children. Even so, as one biographer notes:

> "He may have been inconsiderate in more serious things than birthday cakes, yet people kept seeking his company and returning to him, so he must have charmed them at the same time in addition to being world-famous and increasingly influential. His intelligence combined with external shyness and shabby clothing — even if it was affected — may have made him an anti-hero, who elicited sympathy and support."[556]

He fired someone at Cold Spring Harbor for blocking his parking space and he engaged in personal attacks on a journalist who gave one of his books a poor review.[557]

Watson once stood up in a boring lecture and shouted, "Shut up! We're fed up with this."[558] For Austro-Hungarian biochemist Erwin Chargaff (1905-2002), "It was clear to me that I was faced with a novelty: enormous ambition and aggressiveness, coupled with an almost complete ignorance of, and a contempt for, chemistry, that most real of exact sciences."[559] Austrian Nobel chemist Max Perutz (1914-2002) commented of Watson and Crick, "They shared the sublime arrogance of men who had rarely met their intellectual equals."[560] Cathy Soref observes that: "He is a provocateur. He is iconoclastic to a greater degree than any one I have ever encountered. He is fiercely dedicated to finding the truth as he is able to see it, to the best of his ability, regardless of consequence, obviously; he

---

[555] J. Kastor, *The National Institutes of Health, 1991-2008* (Oxford: Oxford University Press, 1963), 99.

[556] I. Hargittai, *The DNA Doctor, op. cit.*, 160.

[557] Hargittai, *The DNA Doctor, op. cit.*, 161. Quoting, E. Chargaff, *Heraclitean Fire: Sketches from a Life Before Nature* (New York: The Rockerfeller University Press, 1978), 102.

[558] T. Lazar, "The Making of a Great Scientist," *Nature Medicine,* 10 (2004): 15.

[559] Hargittai, *The DNA Doctor, op. cit.*, 193. Quoting, M. Perutz, *I Wish I'd Made You Angry Earlier: Essays on Science, Scientists and Humanity* (Oxford: Oxford University Press, 1998), 188.

[560] Hargittai, *The DNA Doctor, op. cit.*, 193.

therefore lacks tact, more than most. He is able to hurt the feelings of others with his blunt and unedited opinions and I have not been exempt from this experience."

By the 1980s, Watson was upsetting people by his determination that the human genome should be sequenced, with some scientists believing his approach was "reductionist" and somehow "anti-human." Of course, it might be countered that the positive consequences of this sequencing have been enormous, in terms of the extension and preservation of life and simply in understanding the nature of humanity. Watson may have felt, having been right before about the double helix, that these were Midwits standing in the way of something crucial and they had to be despatched. As Edward O. Wilson put it, "Watson evidently felt, at one level, that he was working for the good of science, and a blunt tool was needed."[561] Newton famously said, "If I have seen further, it is by standing on the shoulders of giants." Nobel Prize-winning American Nobel physicist Murray Gell-Mann (1929-2019) retorted, "If I have seen further than others, it is because I am surrounded by dwarfs."[562] American biologist Robert Sinsheimer (1920-2017) summarises, of Watson, "Brilliant, arrogant, verbally crude, with a skewed, off-center personality, fond of publicity, he sees the world in black and white with little gray in between. In his career, he has consistently demonstrated excellent scientific judgment and has been a superb director of the Cold Spring Harbor Laboratory."[563]

Watson is also sufficiently self-obsessed to write books about how he solved the structure of DNA (*The Double Helix*), about his own journey through a life of science (*Avoid Boring People*), about his own love life (*Genes, Girls and Gamow*), and even about his own family history (*Father to Son: Truth, Reason, and Decency*). But perhaps a personality of this kind is necessary: the importance of mapping the human genome speaks

---

[561] Wilson, *Naturalist, op. cit.*
[562] A. Gefter, Wilson vs Watson: The blessing of great enemies, *New Scientist* (10th September 2009), https://www.newscientist.com/article/dn17771-wilson-vs-watson-the-blessing-of-great-enemies/
[563] Hargittai, *The DNA Doctor, op. cit.*, 198. Quoting, R.L. Sinsheimer, *The Strands of Life: The Science of DNA and the Art of Education* (Berkley: University of California Press, 1994) 90.

for itself. It should be added that Watson and Wilson eventually reconciled. "I became close to Ed because I hated Ed's enemies," Watson says. "I'm trying to be polite tonight so I won't describe how awful they are."[564] These enemies are the enemies of science who attacked Wilson – literally, a bucket of iced water was poured over him by "Science for the People" protestors in 1978[565] – for developing "sociobiology" which made sense of humans as an advanced form of ape and argued that most key psychological differences, including between races and sexes, were partly genetic.[566]

Indeed, Wilson himself conceded that Watson's behaviour ultimately had useful results: "When Watson became director of the Cold Spring Harbor Laboratory in 1968 (he kept his Harvard professorship by joint appointment until 1976) I commented sourly to friends that I wouldn't put him in charge of a lemonade stand. He proved me wrong. In ten years he raised that noted institution to even greater heights by inspiration, fund-raising skills, and the ability to choose and attract the most gifted researchers . . . I had never been able to suppress my admiration for the man. He had pulled off his achievement with courage and panache."[567]

Comments by Watson's Colleagues and Former Students

It is noteworthy that, during Watson's various controversies, his supporters, though not inclined to be so forthright themselves, were not especially surprised. His scientist detractors referred to his comments, on race for example, as "infuriating," "unfounded" and as "racist bullshit" that "does harm to our science."[568] By contrast, image-conscious friends expressed a kind of weary resignation, even in November 2000 when

---

[564] Gefter, "Wilson vs Watson," *op. cit.*

[565] R. Pearson, *Race, Intelligence and Bias in Academe* (Washington, DC: Scott-Townsend Publishers, 1991), 266.

[566] See, U. Segerstråle, *Defenders of the Truth: The Sociobiology Debate* (Oxford: Oxford University Press, 2000); E.O. Wilson, *Sociobiology: The New Synthesis* (Cambridge, MA: Harvard University Press, 1975).

[567] Wilson, *Naturalist, op. cit.*

[568] S. Begley, "'I really don't know what happened to Jim': Friends ask where James Watson's odious attitudes about race came from," *Stat* (3rd January 2019), https://www.statnews.com/2019/01/03/where-james-watsons-racial-attitudes-came-from/

Watson's first proto-Woke "controversy" took place. The major report on this commented that some people "chalked up Watson's remarks to his penchant for deliberately stirring things up . . ." "Doesn't a guy like Jim Watson have the responsibility to make this not ugly?" rhetorically enquired UC Berkeley biologist Michael Botchan, who was referred to as a "Watson protégé." Botchan answered his own question with: "Yes. But I cannot tell Jim Watson to change his ways." The obvious implication of such remarks is that Watson has long enjoyed making controversial comments, though, for various reasons, they did not create a public furore until November 2000. Indeed, Botchan added, "Jim says startling things. He is a person who tends to shock people."[569]

Watson's "friends," or, at least, sometime colleagues, also made a series of very telling remarks about him. Specifically, these were that he is highly intuitive in his thinking, that he enjoys the limelight and, in effect, stirring up controversy ("He loved getting a rise out of people"), that he has concluded that one must oppose "establishment consensus," that he views himself "as the greatest scientist since Newton or Darwin" to the extent that he refused to appear on a camera with a critic because the critic's "not good enough" to be on camera with Watson, and that he was in favour of female equality when the establishment wasn't ("At a time when almost no men supported women, he insisted I get a Ph.D. and made it possible for me to do so . . ."). Perhaps most significant is a remark by Australian biologist Jerry Adams (b. 1940), another former student of Watson's:

> "When he joined Francis Crick at England's Cavendish Laboratory, Watson knew virtually nothing about molecular structures or "the basic fundamentals of the field," Jerry Adams, also one of Watson's graduate students, told a Cold Spring Harbor oral history project; Watson was "self-taught." He saw his double-helix discovery as proof that outsiders, unburdened by establishment thinking, could see and achieve what insiders couldn't." That belief became cemented in the 1960s, when Watson dragged Harvard's biology department kicking and screaming

---

[569] Abate, "Nobel Winner's Theories Raise Uproar in Berkeley / Geneticist's views strike many as racist, sexist," *op. cit.*

into the molecular era. Disdaining the establishment, he seemed to conclude, pays off."[570]

This does rather seem in line with the modal genius psychological profile and with aspects of trait Narcissism. When Watson was asked if he wanted to meet the American biologist Leroy Hood (b. 1938), he retorted, "Why would I want to listen to him to talk about himself!"[571] In particular, this analysis implies that a certain degree of Narcissism aided the creativity necessary for Watson to discover the structure of DNA and win the Nobel Prize with these very traits then being elevated via a feedback loop wherein the world told Watson how brilliant he was. This, however, appears to have had positive consequences, because Watson's next major step was to lead the vitally important Human Genome Project.

---

[570] S. Begley, "'I really don't know what happened to Jim': Friends ask where James Watson's odious attitudes about race came from," *Stat* (3rd January 2019), https://www.statnews.com/2019/01/03/where-james-watsons-racial-attitudes-came-from/

[571] L. Timmerman, *Hood: Trailblazer of the Genomics Age* (Grand Rapids, MI: Bandera Press, 2016), 385.

Chapter Eleven

How Did Geniuses Evolve?

William Hamilton and Group Selection

Now that we are clear on the nature of genius, with reference to Watson, and the fact that it is a package that includes many anti-social traits, we may be left wondering why geniuses even exist. Shouldn't anti-social traits have been selected out? There is no evidence that geniuses have lots of children. Indeed, quite the opposite seems to be true. They are anti-social and often don't reproduce at all.[572] Why, then, do they exist? Shouldn't they be shunned by the prehistoric tribe – as dangerously uncooperative - and removed from the gene pool?

There are different means by which you can pass on your genes. Firstly, there is doing so directly. If you have a child it will carry 50 per cent of your genes and so it makes sense, genetically, for you to look after this child and help it to pass on its own genes. However, there are indirect ways of passing on your genes as well. This "indirect breeding" model was articulated by the English biologist William Hamilton (1936-2000).[573] The idea of "group selection" – that there is a battle between groups and certain groups, with certain traits triumphs – was examined by Darwin in his 1871 book *The Descent of Man*: "A tribe including many members who, from possessing in a high degree the spirit of patriotism, fidelity, obedience, courage and sympathy, were always ready to aid each other, and to sacrifice themselves for the common good would be victorious over most

---

[572] D.K. Simonton, "Exceptional creativity across the life span: The emergence and manifestation of creative genius," in L.V. Shavinina (Ed.), *The International Handbook of Innovation* (New York: Pergamon Press, 2003).

[573] W. Hamilton, *The Narrow Roads of Gene Land* (Oxford: Oxford University Press, 1996); W. Hamilton, "The genetical evolution of social behavior. I and II," *Journal of Theoretical Biology*, 7 (1964): 1–52.

other tribes."[574] Scottish anthropologist Sir Arthur Keith (1866-1955) nuanced Darwin's idea by arguing that the process would select for a "dual code" in humans: loyalty to the in-group and hostility to the out-group. "Conscience has a two-fold role in the soldier: it is his duty to save and protect his own people and equally his duty to destroy their enemies . . . Thus, conscience serves both codes of group behaviour: it gives sanction to practices of the code of enmity as well as of the code of amity."[575]

Hamilton developed these ideas with the concept of "inclusive fitness" – that you can pass on your genes through means other than having direct descendants. You can follow a process of "kin selection" where you invest in nephews and nieces (25 per cent of your genes), cousins (12.5 per cent of your genes) and so on. This is why many a spinster auntie will be inclined to spoil rotten her sibling's children. She is aiding her kin and so indirectly perpetuating her own genes. For this reason, in some circumstances, it would make sense, in terms of inclusive fitness, to lay down your life if a large number of your cousins were under mortal threat, especially if you had already had children yourself. According to Hamilton, people will act altruistically if the benefit to their inclusive fitness is greater than the fitness cost of the act. Thus, it would make sense for a menopausal mother to lay down her life to save her only child. This would not make so much sense if the mother, aged 21, was told to make a choice between her child's life and her own, because she could go on to have many more children.

The idea of kin selection can be logically extended to group selection. It has been established that ethnic groups are genetic clusters. The average Englishman is highly genetically similar to the next average Englishman *relative* to the average Dane, based on genetic assay data. The Australian political psychologist Frank Salter has calculated that if the world were divided between only English and Danes, then the relationship between two average English people would have a kinship coefficient of 0.0021, whereas it would be zero for an Englishman and a Dane. This coefficient would be the equivalent of sharing a set of 6 time great grandparents; that is being 7th cousins. So, from a genetic perspective, it would be adaptive

---

[574] C. Darwin, *The Descent of Man* (London: John Murray, 1871), Ch. 5
[575] A. Keith, *A New Theory of Human Evolution* (London: Watts and Co., 1948), 120.

for an Englishman to fight to protect his ethnic group from Danes, even if it risked him having no children at all. If his actions saved enough of his people, this would more than compensate for the lack of direct breeding.[576] The soldier, who laid down his life in this way, would be operating at the level of group selection. Computer models have shown that the more ethnocentric group – the group whose members are more inclined to repel outsiders and make sacrifices for the good of the group – always eventually dominates in between-group competition, all else being equal.[577] Thus, the successful group will produce more people – though not too many – who are prepared to shun individual and even kin selection in favour of a group selection strategy.

"Group selection," meaning "New Group Selection," has been criticized in depth by Canadian psychologist Steven Pinker.[578] His key criticisms are that: (1) "Group Selection" deviates from the "random mutation" model inherent in evolution. (2) We are clearly not going to be selected to damage our individual interests, as group selection implies. (3) Human altruism is self-interested and does not involve the kind of self-sacrifice engaged in by sterile worker bees. Each of these points can be answered. Firstly, if the group selection model is building on the individual selection model, then it is bound to present a slightly different metaphor. To dismiss it on these grounds seems to betoken nothing more than a fervent attachment to the original metaphor. Secondly, the group selection model merely suggests that a group will be more successful if there is genetic diversity, meaning that an optimum percentage of its members are inclined to sacrifice themselves for their group. Thirdly, it is clearly the case that a small percentage, in many groups, is indeed prepared to sacrifice itself for the group, sometimes damaging their individual genetic interests. So, it seems to me that it is reasonable to accept multi-level selection.

---

[576] F. Salter, *On Genetic Interests: Family, Ethnicity and Humanity in an Age of Mass Migration* (New Brunswick, NJ: Transaction Publishers, 2007).

[577] R. Hammond and R. Axelrod, "The evolution of ethnocentric behaviour," *Journal of Conflict Resolution,* 50 (2006): 1-11.

[578] S. Pinker, "The false allure of group selection," *The Edge* (18th June 2012), www.edge.org/conversation/the-false-allure-of-group-selection

Furthermore, computer-modelling has shown that groups that are internally cooperative but harsh to members of other groups—those that are high in positive and negative ethnocentrism—tend to eventually win in the battle of group selection. They always dominate the computer grid after many generations when they battle with those who cooperate with nobody, cooperate with everybody, or only cooperate with members of another group.[579] Of course, this is not necessarily the only means by which one group can dominate another. A group could be lower in ethnocentrism than another group but much higher in average intelligence, resulting in superior warfare tactics and a genius caste with outlier high IQ that innovated brilliant weapons. However, all else being equal, it is the most ethnocentric group which triumphs.

It is also worth noting the language that Pinker employs in criticising group selection. He refers to it as having a "false allure," terms it a "dust bunny" and a "hairy blob" that apparently "bleeds outwards to a motley collection of other, long-discredited versions." It has, claims Pinker, "placed blinkers on psychological understanding by seducing many people." This is extremely emotionally manipulative language that attempts to compel the reader to associate "group selection" with being sexually manipulated, with stupidity, with beasts of burden, and with the word "discredited." It is the "poisoning of the well" fallacy, and the fact that Pinker engages in this would tend to imply cognitive dissonance; that he rejects group selection for his own personal reasons, realizes that the model is likely reasonable, and is thus triggered to react in an emotional fashion.

"Group selection" has also been criticized by American physicist Gregory Cochran, who claims it is vanishingly unlikely to ever manifest; "almost impossible."[580] However, it can be responded that given the millions of different species on Earth it would have come about eventually, and if it is the simplest explanation for available data on how humans behave, then it very probably has done. Group selection is real and

---

[579] Hammond and Axelrod, "The evolution of ethnocentric behaviour," *op cit.*
[580] G. Cochran, "Group Selection (and homosexuality)," *West Hunter* (13th January 2013),   https://westhunt.wordpress.com/2013/01/10/group-selection-and-homosexuality/.

necessary to explain evolution, but its mechanisms are not yet fully understood.[581] Even so, how could positive and negative ethnocentrism ever evolve without group selection? It wouldn't make sense.

Finally, it has been argued that early human groups were too small and sparse for group selection, but this has been comprehensively refuted by abundant evidence of genocide among such groups, with genocide levels increasing with adoption of agriculture, and separated clans seeming to form large groups in order to repel invaders from different tribes.[582] Moreover, detailed modelling has found that group selection is a reality, with researchers concluding that: "If culturally transmitted systems of rules (institutions) that limit individual deviance organize cooperation in human societies, then it is not clear that any extant alternative to cultural group selection can be a complete explanation."[583] Clearly, there are no logical criticisms of group selection.

Group Selection for Genius

Building on an idea first proposed by William Hamilton,[584] it has been proposed that geniuses can be understood to operate precisely this kind of strategy.[585] Their inventions do not benefit themselves or even their families. However, they benefit the group to which the genius belongs. The inventions which kicked-off the Industrial Revolution, for example, allowed the British population to soar in size and wealth and to expand around much of the globe. Clearly, then, a successful society needs to maintain an optimum but relatively low number of geniuses. The number

---

[581] For further exploration see: B. G. Charlton, "Reconceptualizing the metaphysical basis of biology: a new definition based on deistic teleology and a hierarchy of organizing entities," *The Winnower*, 6 (2016): e145830.07350

[582] See B. Kiernan, *Blood and Soil: A World History of Genocide and Extermination from Sparta to Darfur* (New Haven, CT: Yale University Press, 2007).

[583] P. Richerson, R. Baldini, A. Bell and K. Demps, "Cultural group selection plays an essential role in explaining human cooperation: A sketch of the evidence," *Brain and Behavioural Sciences,* 39 (2016): e30.

[584] W. Hamilton, "A review of *Dysgenics: Genetic Deterioration in Modern Populations,*" *Annals of Human Genetics,* 64 (2000): 363-374.

[585] M.A. Woodley and A.J. Figueredo, *Historical Variability in Heritable General Intelligence: Its Evolutionary Origins and Sociocultural Consequences* (Buckingham: University of Buckingham Press, 2013).

cannot be too many, because a society full of uncooperative, impractical dreamers will be dominated by a more internally cooperative and practical one. And it cannot be too few, or the society will be dominated by one which has the appropriate number of geniuses to allow the necessary level of innovation.

Geniuses will be formed – to the extent that genius is genetic – by chance but possible combinations of genes which will stay in the population precisely because they occasionally produce genius and this is outweighed by the negative which those genes in slightly different combinations can produce. This negative is people of low intelligence and high anti-social traits – in other words, those who may be criminally-prone. Although the bulk of the genetics of intelligence involves genes with additive, or small and incremental effects, there is also a role played by rarer genes with large effects and also epistasis, or gene-gene interactions, not just among those responsible for intelligence, but involving personality and other traits as well. It is these rare genetic factors that play the biggest role in the genetics of extreme talent and genius.[586] It has been noted that both geniuses and criminals are anti-social risk-takers, though geniuses are more intelligent.[587]

The Ancestors of Geniuses

For geniuses to happen, the available gene pool cannot be too small – otherwise geniuses will be too unlikely to be produced; the odds of getting precisely the right interactions among genes are very small. Thus, the genius is likely to be born to parents who are within the normal range of intelligence and who have normal personalities and this genius is likely to have siblings who are much more like his or her parents. It seems very clear that Watson's background is indeed one of normal range high intelligence. Our expectation would be that Watson would be from a family who were highly intelligent, but only so within the normal range.

---

[586] A.R. Jensen, "The puzzle of nongenetic variance," in R. Sternberg and E. Grigorenko, (Eds.), *Heredity, Intelligence, and Environment* (Cambridge: Cambridge University Press, 1997).

[587] S. Kanazawa, "Why productivity fades with age: The crime–genius connection," *Journal of Personality,* 37 (2003): 257-272.

Following Post's analysis, in which only 29 per cent of scientists had close relatives who had excelled in their field, we would not necessarily expect Watson's close relatives to be especially eminent. Due to the relatively low levels of psychopathy in creative scientists, creative in other fields, we would not expect to find pronounced evidence of an unhappy childhood in Watson's case as already noted.

An exploration of Watson's background, however, does imply normal range high intelligence. His father, James Dewey Watson, Senior, was evidently intelligent, a businessman who had studied at Oberlin College during a time in which higher education was a relative rarity.[588] His father's brother, William Weldon Watson (1899-1992), was a physicist, and Professor of Physics at Yale, so likely highly intellectually able.[589] James Watson's mother, Margaret "Jean" Mitchell (1899-1957) "attended the University of Chicago for two years until there was no more family tuition money."[590] Watson's sister, Betty (b. 1930), also studied at the University of Chicago.[591] This is consistent with broader evidence that geniuses are overwhelmingly drawn from the professional and business classes and very rarely from the working class. Indeed, 82 per cent of science Nobel Prize winners as of 1977 were from professional or business backgrounds.[592]

However, the genius will be very different from his normal range intelligence relatives. As discussed, the genius will be an outlier not just in terms of intelligence, but also in terms of creativity and personality. In general, intelligence and personality are strongly genetic and, in addition, parents tend to be relatively genetically similar to each other, more similar than two random members of the same ethnic group. We are attracted to people who are relatively genetically similar to ourselves – though not too similar, as this causes inbreeding depression – because this allows us to

---

[588] J.D. Watson, *Father to Son: Truth, Reason, Decency* (Cold Spring Harbor, NY: Cold Spring Harbor Laboratory Press, 2014), 41.
[589] Watson, *Avoid Boring People, op. cit.*, 24.
[590] Watson, *Father to Son, op. cit.*, 89.
[591] Watson, *Father to Son, op. cit.*, 139.
[592] R. Ochse, *Before the Gates of Excellence: The Determinants of Creative Genius* (Cambridge: Cambridge University Press, 1990), 58-60.

maximize the number of our genes that are passed on.[593] Consequently, children tend to have relatively similar IQs and personalities to their parents, with the heritability of personality being at least 0.5 and the heritability of IQ being approximately 0.8 as we have already noted. However, sometimes, albeit rarely, things don't work out like this. Both intelligence and personality are massively *polygenic.* They are not products of single genes – such as resistance to malaria might be – but, rather, the products of thousands of genes working together to produce the desired trait. This means that sometimes, by random genetic chance, unlikely combinations of genes can occur which result in children being markedly different from their parents.

This is widely documented in terms of physical appearance. There have been many cases in multiracial societies – such as the US – of two legally "black" parents having a child who could pass for white. African-Americans are on average 25 per cent white,[594] and about 40 per cent of them are descended, in the direct male line, from a white slave master.[595] As a result, sometimes, though very rarely, all of these "European genes" can combine in a child whose parents are African-Americans, resulting in a child who looks "white." In much the same way, genes for intelligence can sometimes, though exceedingly rarely, combine in such a way that a child has either much lower or much higher intelligence than his parents. The same thing can happen with genes for personality. In the vanishingly unlikely event that both of these combinations occur when two parents of reasonably high intelligence have a child, the result may be a genius.

With Watson, we find evidence of the genius personality traits within his family, but only in him have they optimally combined. His paternal grandfather, Thomas Tolman Watson (1876-1930), was a stockbroker, implying that he was a relatively intelligent person who was comfortable

---

[593] J.P. Rushton, "Ethnic Nationalism, Evolutionary Psychology and Genetic Similarity Theory," *Nations and Nationalism,* 11 (2005): 489-507.

[594] K. Bryc, E. Durand, J. MacPherson et al., "The Genetic Ancestry of African Americans, Latinos, and European Americans across the United States," *American Journal of Human Genetics*, 96 (2015): 37-53.

[595] J. Torres, M. Doura, S. Keita and R. Kittles, "Y Chromosome Lineages in Men of West African Descent," *PLoS One* (2012), https://doi.org/10.1371/journal.pone.0029687

with taking considerable risks for considerable rewards; a mind-set which a genius must inherit to some extent. His risk-taking had disastrous consequences for his previously wealthy family's finances. "In early 1916 Tolman put virtually all of his money at risk through betting on highly speculative penny stocks. By the summer's start they lost most of their value. Then insufficient family monies existed to pay Dad's tuition and board charges if he had been allowed, as was likely, to be readmitted to Oberlin." The family would have been "destitute" if his wife hadn't kept her inheritance under her control.[596]

Taking risks was evidently inherited by Watson's father, who, as a young man, enthusiastically joined the Illinois National Guard and went off to fight in France during World War I. In terms of being unconventional, it is noteworthy that Watson's father was an "atheist" in the 1930s, at time when atheism was relatively rare in the US and was, indeed, socially unacceptable.[597] He was also a "socialist-leaning Democrat"[598] This was in a social context in which socialism was itself relatively socially unacceptable.[599] Consistent with risk-taking, Watson's father was a very heavy smoker who died of cancer as a result.[600] In addition, the eminent director and writer Orson Welles (1915-1985) was a Watson on his mother's side (his maternal grandmother was a Watson) and was raised by Watson's great uncle, the Chicago artist Dudley Crafts Watson (1885-1972), after Welles' mother died.[601] So, clearly there is creativity in the family. In terms of earlier ancestors, Watson's great-great-great-grandfather, William Weldon Watson (1794-1874), originally from New Jersey, was a wealthy silversmith, a skilled profession, and also a Baptist minister in Kentucky. He then opened a successful confectionary business in Illinois.[602] This man's son, Benjamin Watson (1818-1901), was a wealthy gold prospector and businessman who ran a successful

---

[596] Watson, *Father to Son, op. cit.*, 46

[597] See, E. Dutton, *Religion and Intelligence: An Evolutionary Analysis* (London: Ulster Institute for Social Research, 2014).

[598] Watson, *Avoid Boring People, op. cit.*, 10.

[599] S. Lipset and G. Marks, *It Didn't Happen Here: Why Socialism Failed in the United States* (New York: W.W. Norton, 2000).

[600] *Avoid Boring People, op. cit.*, 264.

[601] *Avoid Boring People, op. cit.*, 19.

[602] J.D. Watson, *Father to Son, op. cit.*

health spa. In turn, his son, William Weldon Watson (1847-1913), was a successful businessman, focussing on real estate. He also owned a hotel.[603]

Not Breeding True

Consistent with this theory that genius involves unlikely but possible genetic combinations, when geniuses, such as Charles Darwin, have children then the children, though likely highly intelligent, will not generally be geniuses themselves. Darwin's children were evidently highly intelligent. Sir Francis Darwin (1848-1925) was an eminent naturalist, Major Leonard Darwin (1850-1943) was a Member of Parliament as well as an academic and Sir George Darwin (1845-1912) was a barrister and eminent astronomer, but they were not of the significance of their father.[604] As English writer Andrew Robinson has summarised: ". . . children of geniuses have typically seemed insubstantial or totally forgotten figures in the eyes of posterity. In encyclopaedias and reference books, they are often relegated to a mere sentence or phrase, if that, even in the case of Darwin . . ."[605]

In much the same way, Watson's son, Duncan (b. 1972) has achieved nothing comparable to that of his father, though he is obviously highly intelligent. According to his *LinkedIn* page, he is a data analyst, living in Oakland in California. He studied Russian at Brown University, an Ivy League institution, before moving into editorial work for a news group and then moving into data analysis. Duncan has also done courses in water colour painting and Italian at the City College of San Francisco.[606] He is married to Heather and they have a son called Angus.[607] Watson's oldest son, Rufus (b. 1970), simply lives at home with his parents in Cold Spring

---

[603] J.D. Watson, *Father to Son, op. cit.*

[604] T. Berra, *Darwin and His Children: His Other Legacy* (Oxford: Oxford University Press, 2013).

[605] A. Robinson, *Genius: A Very Short Introduction* (Oxford: Oxford University Press, 2011).

[606] "Duncan Watson," *LinkedIn.*

[607] *Chapel of the Chimes Oakland,* "Anne Veronica (Rochette) Hay" (2015), https://oakland.chapelofthechimes.com/obituaries/Anne-Rochette-32955/#!/Obituary

Harbor "unable to cope with the outside world . . . bright but troubled."[608] On his *LinkedIn* page, Rufus Watson tells us that his profession is "Angel at Purgatory." He adds that he's been an apprentice angel "Somewhere" since October 2023.[609]

Making Sense of Rufus Watson

Watson fathered his two sons when he was in his 40s, with a much younger wife, and the eldest of those two sons, Rufus has schizophrenia. This is important because a key predictor of schizophrenia is paternal age.

Mutations are more likely to stem from the father and there may manifest as many as 200 new mutations per generation, though perhaps as few as 40.[610] Having an older father raises the risk of new mutations because the spermatogonia, the stem cells from which the sperm cells are formed, undergo many rounds of cell division in a man's life, with a risk of new mutations every time the genome replicates and is distributed to the daughter cells.[611] This reflects a broader process whereby we all acquire so called "somatic mutations" as we get older, due to our cells copying with decreasing accuracy. In addition, as we age, reduced effectiveness of DNA repair makes us more vulnerable to the low-level background radiation to which we are continuously exposed.[612] Some chemical elements are unstable, which means that their nuclei decay, releasing energy in the form of radiation. The immune system doesn't fight ionizing radiation, but we have DNA repair systems that repair the damage that the radiation does to the DNA. Also, the older you are the more oxidizing "free radicals"—atoms with unpaired electrons that increase

---

[608] P. Sherwell, "DNA father James Watson's 'holy grail' request," *Daily Telegraph* (10th May 2009), https://www.telegraph.co.uk/news/worldnews/northamerica/ usa/53 00883/DNA-father-James-Watsons-holy-grail-request.html

[609] "Rufus Watson," *LinkedIn*.

[610] Y. Xue, Q. Wang, Q. Long et al., "Human Y Chromosome Base-Substitution Mutation Rate Measured by Direct Sequencing in a Deep-Rooting Pedigree," *Current Biology,* 19 (2009): 1453–1457.

[611] S. Wu, F. Wu, Y. Ding et al., "Advanced parental age and autism risk in children: a systematic review and meta-analysis," *Acta Psychiatrica Scandinavica,* 135 (2016): 29–41.

[612] J. Tong and T. Hei, "Aging and age-related health effects of ionizing radiation," *Radiation Medicine and Protection,* 1 (2020): 15–23.

your exposure to radiation—you have in your body, which damage the DNA and thereby cause mutations.[613]

All of this causes our bodies to age, and so function less well.[614] Somatic mutations will not affect your offspring, of course, but mutations in the spermatogonia will, and these, like the somatic mutations, will accumulate with age. It is likely no coincidence, in this regard, that Queen Victoria's father was past the age of 50 when she was conceived, significantly elevating the probability of *de novo* mutations, including haemophilia. We also inherit *de novo* mutations from our mothers, though to a much lesser extent, and the likelihood of inheriting them also increases with maternal age. One study found that with two parents in their late teens or early twenties, a child would inherit 9 new mutations from their mother, but 39 *de novo* mutations from their father. By the time the parents were aged 40, the child would, on average, inherit 15 new mutations from the mother but 91 from the father.[615] The odds of autism are 3 times higher when you are born to a father aged 45 than they are when you are born to a father in his twenties. The likelihood of schizophrenia is doubled, while intelligence is slightly decreased.[616]

The potential implication is that we might expect geniuses to have older fathers, mediated by the elevated autism and a study has implied that this may be so. Specifically, male offspring of older fathers were higher in a "geek index" that included "strong focus on the subject of interest and little concern about 'fitting in,'" something which may be partly reducible to autism.[617] Another study found that the likelihood of schizophrenia is 0.7 per cent if your father is under 25, 1 per cent if your father is 30 to 35

---

[613] V. Lobo, A. Patil, A. Phatak, and N. Chandra, "Free radicals, antioxidants and functional foods: Impact on human health," *Pharmacognosy Review,* 4 (2010): 118–126.

[614] R.A. Risques and S.R. Kennedy, "Aging and the rise of somatic cancer-associated mutations in normal tissues," *PLOS Genetics,* 14 (2018): e1007108.

[615] Kong et al., "Rate of de novo mutations and the importance of father's age to disease risk," *op .cit.*

[616] B. D'Onofrio, M. Rickert, E. Frans et al., "Paternal age at childbearing and offspring psychiatric and academic morbidity," *JAMA Psychiatry,* 71 (2014): 432-438.

[617] M. Janecka, F. Rijsdijk, A. Modabbernia and A. Reichenberg, "Advantageous developmental outcomes of advancing paternal age," *Transactional Psychiatry,* 7 (2017): e1156.

and 2 per cent if your father is 50 or older.[618] This overlap may occur, in part, due to copying errors. Hence, people who have autism are more likely than are controls to have schizophrenic or bipolar relatives.[619] This is partly because these conditions, though genetically distinct, have a number of alleles in common.[620]

By the time Watson's son Rufus was 3 his parents noticed that he had trouble interacting with other children. When he was 10, a child psychologist was consulted about his social problems at school. Rufus Watson's schizophrenia is sufficiently severe that he has spent time in psychiatric institutions. In early 1986, Rufus had a psychotic episode and was sent home from school. A few days later, he tried to break a window at the top of the World Trade Centre in New York in order to jump out of the building. He was diagnosed with schizophrenia and placed in a psychiatric institution.[621] James Watson wanted him cured or, at least, wanted to understand why schizophrenia developed so that it could be combatted. This meant understanding the human genome. He later told an interviewer: "Of course we should use germ line therapy to fix things like schizophrenia that nature got horribly wrong." He averred that nobody would want to inflict schizophrenia on a person or on the family who have to cope with the schizophrenic.[622]

Watson called a symposium at Cold Spring Harbor to discuss this possibility. However, the night before the symposium, on 27th May 1986, Rufus escaped from the psychiatric facility, in White Plains, New York, as he had threatened to do. He was later found wandering around the woods, near some railway tracks. His parents had been so desperate to find

---

[618] D. Malaspina, S. Harlap, S. Fennig et al., "Advancing Paternal Age and the Risk of Schizophrenia," *Archives of General Psychiatry,* 58 (2001): 361-367.

[619] P. Sullivan, C. Magnusson, A. Reichenberg et al., "Family history of schizophrenia and bipolar disorder as risk factors for autism," *Archives of General Psychiatry,* 69 (2012): 1099-1103.

[620] L. Carroll and M. Owen, "Genetic overlap between autism, schizophrenia and bipolar disorder," *Genome Medicine,* 1 (2009): 102.

[621] D. Nickell, *Scientific Indiana* (Charleston, SC: History Press, 2021), 132-133.

[622] W. Isaacson, *The Code Breaker: Jennifer Doudna, Gene Editing, and the Future of the Human Race* (New York: Simon and Schuster, 2021), 352.

Rufus that they had appealed to the nation newspapers for assistance.[623] Rufus Watson's schizophrenia would seem to make sense as a result of mutation due to his father's relatively advanced age when he was conceived. In 2005, Watson gave a blood sample and permitted his genome to be released to the public. It was released two years later. He carried no gene for schizophrenia, which would be consistent with this explanation.[624]

The genius traits do not "breed true," because the extremely improbable genetic combinations involved do not happen a second time. Geniuses tend, however, not to father children, as predicted by their autism and psychopathy, where you have little desire to nurture others. Felix Post's study of 291 great men found that 9 per cent of scientists never married, which rose is 29 per cent of artists.[625] Post's study further found that geniuses appear to have greater physical health, though worse mental health, than the general population. Usually, physical and mental health are correlated producing a so-called "general fitness factor" that reflects a low mutational load, as we saw earlier.[626] With geniuses, it appears that the opposite is true, further evidencing how difficult they are to produce. We have seen that geniuses may be "group selected;" passing on their genes indirectly by benefitting the group of which they are a part.

The result is that certain negative traits – which are generally associated with mutation and developmental instability – such as optimally low levels of psychopathy must stay in the population. It would further follow that, under harsh conditions, we would expect a small minority to combine physical health – low mutational load – with these antisocial traits that would generally be selected out. Geniuses may well be this sub-group; hence somebody like Isaac Newton was so genetically

---

[623] S. Mukherjee, *The Gene: An Intimate History* (New York: Simon and Schuster, 2016), 303.

[624] K. Davies, *The $1000 Genome: The Revolution in DNA Sequencing and the New Era of Personalised Medicine* (New York: Free Press, 2010), 21.

[625] Post, "Creativity and psychopathology," *op. cit.*

[626] D. Houle, "Is there a g factor for fitness?" in G.R. Bock, J.A. Goode and K. Webb (Eds.), *The Nature of Intelligence* (Hoboken, NJ: John Wiley and Sons, 2000); G. Miller, "Mental traits as fitness indicators," in D. LeCrosy and P. Moller, (Eds.), *Evolutionary Perspectives on Human Reproductive Behavior* (New York: New York Academy of Sciences, 2000).

healthy that he was able to survive the huge environmental insult of being born about two months prematurely as were a number of other historical geniuses such as Johannes Kepler (1571-1630).[627] In essence, genius combines a fast Life History Strategy, at least on many measures, with very high intelligence, but intelligence appears to be associated with a slow Life History Strategy even at the individual level, with intelligent children learning to walk later.[628]

The Growth of Genius Across Time

The genius, then, is one of the most significant people society has to offer at any given time, as they combine super-high intelligence with the optimum level of moderately high anti-social traits which, within the context of a particular society, allows scientific and technological breakthroughs to be made. We can imagine that the inventor of the wheel, or the boat – people whose names are lost to history – would have been this kind of person, in comparison to the rest of his society. As the intelligence of the society increases, so the scarcity of genius would decrease, and as the society becomes more complex – coming into conflict with other groups – so, the need for genius would increase.

A number of researchers have shown that rates of innovation do indeed climb as we reach the eighteenth century. Jonathan Huebner, an American physicist, published a paper in 2005 in the journal *Technological Forecasting and Social Change,* in which he demonstrated precisely this.[629] He drew upon a list of 8,583 important events in the history of science and technology, agreed to be highly significant by scientists, from the Stone Age up until 2004. Huebner limited this to the most recent 7,198 events, those since 1450. He noted down the year in which each event happened. Huebner then worked out what the world population was in each year, meaning he could track the per capita level of innovation. He found that scientific innovation rates per capita

---

[627] Dutton, *Sent Before Their Time, op. cit.*
[628] A. Gui, A. Hollowell, E. Wigdor et al., "Genome-wide association meta-analysis of age at onset of walking" (2024), doi: https://doi.org/10.1101/2024.05.07.24306845
[629] J. Huebner, "A possible declining trend for worldwide innovation. *Technological Forecasting and Social Change,* 72 (2005): 980–986.

increased 4-fold between 1450 and 1870. This can be seen in Figure 1 below.

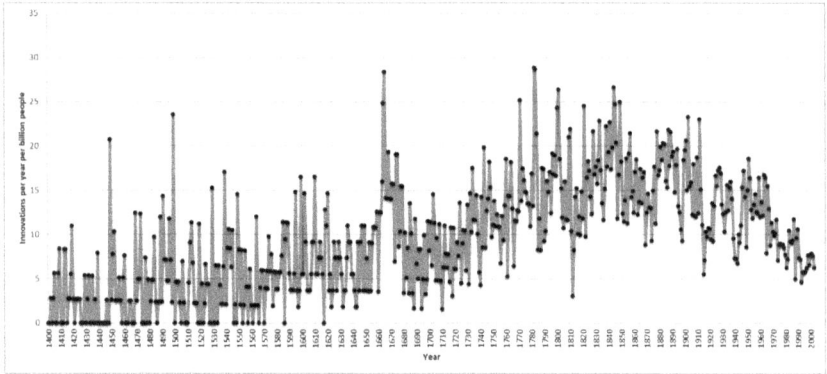

Figure 1: Per capita rates of significant innovation from 1450 to 2004 (Adapted from Huebner, 2005, p.982).

The American political scientist Charles Murray, in his 2003 book *Human Accomplishment,* showed that it was not only significant innovations that were increasing between the Middle Ages and the mid-19th century, but (unsurprisingly) the eminent individuals responsible for them (i.e. geniuses) were increasing too.[630] There were humps and bumps, of course. Innovation was reduced during periods of war and famine for example. But we can see there is a dramatic rise and then, as of about 1873, a fall.

Michael Woodley of Menie, whom we met earlier, has developed Huebner's model.[631] Huebner drew upon a particular inventory compiled by two scientists so, to avoid subjective bias, Woodley of Menie tested to see how well it correlated with other, similar, inventories. For example, he compared it to an index of significant scientific breakthroughs between 1400 and 1950 compiled by Murray.[632] In each case, the correlation was over 0.8, showing that the inventory was not merely subjective. Woodley of Menie used a number of sources to calculate the average intelligence of the population in each year charted by Huebner. He showed that the simplest explanation for Huebner's findings was that intelligence was

---

[630] Murray, *Human Accomplishment, op. cit.*
[631] M.A. Woodley, "The social and scientific temporal correlates of genotypic intelligence and the Flynn effect," *Intelligence*, 40 (2012): 189-204.
[632] C. Murray, *Human Accomplishment, op. cit.*

increasing between 1455 and about 1850 and then decreasing after that. The consequences for the future of innovation are obvious; there will be less of it and, if they trend continues, we won't be able to do things which we used to be able to do. This, and its consequences, I have explored in depth elsewhere.[633]

The Year Two Thousand and Seven Again . . .

Now that we are clear on the nature of genius and why it manifests, we will return to the significance of the year 2007, and Watson's cancellation, once again. Why was 2007 a true turning point in the history of Western Civilization?

---

[633] See, Dutton and Woodley of Menie, *At Our Wits' End, op. cit.* and Dutton and J.O.A. Rayner-Hilles, *The Past is a Future Country, op. cit.* Huebner's methodology has been criticised in depth. L. Low, "Debunking Huebner's 'A Possible Declining Trend for Worldwide Innovation," *Uncorrelated* (7th January 2025), https://www.uncorrelated.xyz/p/debunking-huebners-a-possible-declining However, as Woodley has shown, Huebner's findings replicate in many other datasets.

Chapter Twelve

Why Did Watson Live
in the Ideal Time for Genius?

How Are Woke Activists Like Hoverflies?

Wasps practice aposematism. They have bright colours to warn attackers, "I am poisonous. Stay away." Hover flies, which are completely harmless, have evolved to mimic wasps. They look extraordinarily similar to wasps and predators avoid them for this reason, but they cannot sting you. They are physically harmless.

The stereotypical Woke person - one who has radical left-wing views especially in relation to the equality of minorities and in relation to environmental activism, the kind of person that spearheaded calls to cancel James Watson in 2007 - appears to have evolved a similar tactic: blue hair, tattoos and dark clothes. They imitate punks but, unlike the stereotypical punk, they are, as we will see in more detail below, physically and mentally weak. Like the hoverfly, this is why they want people to stay away from them. Dying your hair an unnatural colour is specifically associated with depression, presumably because such people fear others, and so wish to be feared, and because they are plagued by doubt about who they are and what they should do, due to general anxiety, so over-compensate by asserting a strong sense of identity. In addition, inducing disgust and fear in other people is a way of feeling a sense of power and control over them.[634]

---

[634] E. Dutton and E. Kirkegaard, "Blue Hair and the Blues: Dying Your Hair Unnatural Colours is Associated with Depression," *Psychreg: Journal of Psychology*, 6 (2022):2.

"Not as Bad as Vegans"

This is directly relevant to Watson due to remarks he made about leftists. In an interview in Dublin in 2012 at the Open Euro Forum, Watson referred to environmentalists as "whacko" but added that they are "not as bad as vegans."[635] Again, this is congruous with the available evidence. Supporting left-wing causes is associated with mental instability and especially with depression, with those on the far left being particularly mentally unstable.[636] In addition, being conservative is associated with Agreeableness, Conscientiousness and mental stability where liberalism is associated with the opposite.[637] Compared to conservatives, liberals are selfish,[638] criminal,[639] hateful of those who dare disagree with them,[640] authoritarian,[641] and dishonest people.[642] Environmental activism, in a liberal society, involves believing you are morally superior, at least via

---

[635] F. Macrae, "Possible cure for cancer in decade - DNA pioneer," *IOL* (13th July 2012), https://www.iol.co.za/news/possible-cure-for-cancer-in-decade-dna-pioneer-1340965

[636] E. Kirkegaard, "Mental Illness and the Left," *Mankind Quarterly*, 60 (2020): 487-510.

[637] B. Verhulst, P. Hatemi and N. Martin, "Corrigendum to 'The nature of the relationship between personality traits and political attitudes' [Personal. Individ. Differ. 49 (2010): 306–316]," *Personality and Individual Differences*, 99 (2016): 378–379.

[638] Y. Yang and P. Liu, "Are conservatives more charitable than liberals in the U.S.? A meta-analysis of political ideology and charitable giving," *Social Science Research,* 99 (2021): 102598.

[639] J. Wright, K. Beaver, M. Morgan and E. Connolly, "Political Ideology Predicts Involvement in Crime," *Personality and Individual Differences,* 106 (2017): 236-241.

[640] Liberals are far more likely to distrust and dislike conservatives than *vice versa*. This would make sense in terms of high liberal Neuroticism and liberal Narcissism, in the sense that conservatives are puncturing the worldview which the liberal adopts in order to convince himself of his own moral superiority. See, P.H. Ditto, B.S. Liu, C.J. Clark et al., "At Least Bias Is Bipartisan: A Meta-Analytic Comparison of Partisan Bias in Liberals and Conservatives," *Perspectives on Psychological Science*, 14 (2019): 273–291.

[641] L. Conway, A. Zubrod, L. Chan et al., "Is the myth of left-wing authoritarianism itself a myth?" *Frontiers in Psychology,* 13 (2023).

[642] C. Lin and T. Bates, "Each is to count for one and none for more than one: Predictors of support for economic redistribution" (2021), https://doi.org/10.31234/osf.io/3jq4c. For example, they are strong on the belief that "the ends justify the means" and are prepared to engage in instrumental harm and lying in pursuit of their goals.

your environmentalist actions, and may elicit praise. It is associated with Narcissistic Personality Disorder,[643] as is leftism more generally.[644] This is a serious personality disorder which involves delusions of grandeur and even of omnipotence, meaning sufferers can be colloquially termed "whacko."

There is some evidence that veganism is associated with suffering from depression,[645] and that both vegetarianism and veganism are associated with it.[646] An analysis of the UK Biobank, with a sample of 181,990, has found that unusual dietary preferences (including vegetarianism) are related to alleles that cause poor mental health.[647] Such dietary choices have also been found, among females, to be very weakly associated with Agreeableness, presumably due to high levels of empathy for animals. The main predictor of them was high Openness.[648] Even those who eat organic food have been found to be partly motivated by Narcissism and Machiavellianism.[649] So, in colloquial terms, these people are indeed "whacko." Why is leftism associated with mental instability? In order to understand why leftism is associated with anti-social personality traits and also with depression we must explore what we were selecting for prior to the breakthrough of the Industrial Revolution. In doing so, we will see that Watson lived in the ideal period in which to do genius work.

---

[643] H. Zacher, "The dark side of environmental activism," *Personality and Individual Differences,* 219 (2024): 112506.

[644] J. Moss and P. O'Connor, "The Dark Triad traits predict authoritarian political correctness and Alt-Right attitudes," *Heliyon,* 6 (2020): e04453.

[645] I. Iguacel, L. Huybrechts, L. Moreno and N. Michels, "Vegetarianism and veganism compared with mental health and cognitive outcomes: a systematic review and meta-analysis," *Nutrition Reviews,* 79 (2021): 361–381.

[646] Dutton and Kirkegaard, "Blue Hair and the Blues," *op. cit.*

[647] R. Zhang, B. Zhang, C. Shen et al., "Associations of dietary patterns with brain health from behavioral, neuroimaging, biochemical and genetic analyses," *Nature Mental Health,* 2 (2024): 535-552.

[648] W. Reist, W. Bleidorn, T. Milfont and C. Hopwood, "Meta-analysis of personality trait differences between omnivores, vegetarians, and vegans," *Appetite,* 191 (2023): 107085.

[649] H. Zacher, "The dark side of environmental activism," *Personality and Individual Differences,* 219 (2024): 112506.

Life before the Industrial Revolution

Until about 1800, the key "Crucible of Evolution" was child mortality, which may have been as much as 50 per cent in much of Europe.[650] Every generation, high child mortality purged the European gene pool of mutant genes. If you did not have a strong immune system—if you could not fight off the numerous pathogens from which you were under attack—then, harsh at it sounds, you would be "selected out." Height, strength and a symmetrical face all imply low mutational load. A person with high mutational load would be using disproportionately more of his bio-energetic resources to fight off disease, leaving fewer resources left over to produce muscle, to grow tall or to produce a symmetrical face. Thus, all of these traits can be understood to be honesty signals of genetic quality, rather like a peacock's tail. An unhealthy peacock will only be able to produce a small, asymmetrical or gaudy tail. The peahens will reject him accordingly. Also, we would expect a body that was high in mutational load to be connected to a brain that is likewise. About 84 per cent of our genes relate to brain functioning, rendering it a massive target for mutation.[651] It follows that if the body is high in mutational load, the brain will be even more so. Traits which are selected for, or selected against, tend to become bundled together in a process known as pleiotropy, as we noted earlier. With this in mind we must ask, "What were we selecting for up until 1800?" As we have seen, computer modelling has shown that under harsh Darwinian conditions, the group which tends to dominate all others is the one which is high in positive (in-group cooperation) and negative ethnocentrism (out-group-hostility).[652] In other words, computer modelling demonstrates the veracity of group selection.

Humans have five key moral foundations, reflecting the fact that they are a pack animal but they must also survive within the pack, and preferably rise to the top of it, in order to accrue resources and pass on

---

[650] T. Volk and J. Atkinson, "Is Child Death the Crucible of Human Evolution?" *Journal of Social, Evolutionary, and Cultural Psychology,* 2 (2008): 103–116.

[651] M. Sarraf, M.A. Woodley of Menie and C. Feltham, *Modernity and Cultural Decline: A Biobehavioral Perspective* (Basingstoke: Palgrave Macmillan, 2019).

[652] R. Hammond and R. Axelrod, "The Evolution of Ethnocentric Behavior," *Journal of Conflict Resolution,* 50 (2006): 1–11.

their genes. There are the group-oriented foundations of obedience to authority, in-group loyalty and sanctity (we tend to sanctify that which is good for the group and taboo that which is bad for it) and the individually-oriented foundations of equality (getting your fair share) and harm avoidance (which avoids harm to you). Conservatives are roughly equal in all five moral foundations, whereas leftists are only concerned with the individually-oriented foundations; they are concerned with individual power over the success of their ethnic in-group.[653] This does not mean, for example, that liberals care about the homeless; as we have seen they are low in empathy compared to conservatives. It means that, when it may aid their empowerment to do so, they will identify with the homeless and become agitated on their behalf. In this sense, for them, equality and harm avoidance are important. But they are also important for conservatives, who genuinely do care, although this may not be true of radical conservatives, who would strongly focus on group-oriented foundations.[654] The political divisions are rather nuanced, however. Liberals recognize sanctity, for example, but they place less value on it as an independent moral justification than do conservatives. Thus, they will feel disgusted by the mere presence of a conservative, but this disgust is not their main motivation for action. Likewise, liberals will reject "obedience to authority" in general but endorse it if the authority is perceived as liberal; as part of their in-group.[655]

---

[653] J. Graham, J. Haidt and B. Nosek, "Liberals and Conservatives Rely on Different Sets of Moral Foundations," *Personality Processes and Individual Differences,* 96 (2009): 1029–1046.

[654] The relationships between individual moral foundations and personality traits are, however, very weak indeed in Western samples. See J. Hirsch, C. DeYoung, X. Xu & J. Peterson, "Compassionate Liberals and Polite Conservatives: Associations of Agreeableness with Political Ideology and Moral Values," *Personality and Social Psychology Bulletin,* 36 (2019): 655-664. This is likely because, for example, Agreeable people will claim to value equality and harm avoidance, as will Narcissists, who persuade themselves they care about these things, weakening the relationship. Low Agreeableness people will not care about sanctity and Agreeable people will often persuade themselves they don't, again weakening the relationship.

[655] A. Fasoli, A, Saunders and I. Andrade, "What is moral sanctity? Sanctity in the moral worldviews of U.S. political liberals," *The Social Science Journal,* 55 (2018): 473-486.

In other words, until the Industrial Revolution and the consequent relaxation of harsh conditions via abundant food and better medicine, we were selecting for conservatism, because it was conservative groups that survived that battle of group selection. On average conservatives are higher in Agreeableness, Conscientiousness and mental stability than liberals; they are more pro-social,[656] something that is also true of the traditional religious in contrast to the irreligious.[657] There is a strong cross-over between traditional religiosity and conservatism.[658] Based on twin studies, conservative religiosity is up to 70 per cent genetic (depending on which measure is employed),[659] conservatism is roughly 60 per cent genetic,[660] and Life History Strategy[661] and personality traits are approximately 50 per cent genetic.[662]

We were selecting for religiousness insomuch as it tends to sanctify conservatism or aspects of it. Religiousness has all of the dimensions of an adaptation, as noted above: it is significantly genetic, it is associated with health and fertility, it is an instinct that is elevated at times of stress and mortality salience, and it is found in all cultures.[663] If God is sitting on your shoulder telling you to be pro-social you are less likely to be cast out

---

[656] B. Verhulst, P. Hatemi and N. Martin, "Corrigendum to 'The nature of the relationship between personality traits and political attitudes' [Personal. Individ. Differ. 49 (2010): 306–316]," *Personality and Individual Differences,* 99 (2016): 378–379.

[657] P. Hills, L. Francis, M. Argyle and C. Jackson, "Primary personality trait correlates of religious practice and orientation," *Personality and Individual Differences,* 36 (2004): 61–73.

[658] A. Malka, Y. Lelkes, S. Srivastava and A. Cohen, "The Association of Religiosity and Political Conservatism: The Role of Political Engagement," *Political Psychology,* 33 (2012): 275-299.

[659] M. Bradshaw and C. Ellison, "Do Genetic Factors Influence Religious Life? Findings from a Behavior Genetic Analysis of Twin Siblings," *Journal for the Scientific Study of Religion,* 47 (2008): 529–544.

[660] I. Schwabe, W. Jonker, S. van den Berg, "Genes, Culture and Conservatism: A Psychometric-Genetic Approach," *Behavior Genetics,* 46 (2016): 516-528.

[661] A.J. Figueredo, "The heritability of life history strategy: The *K*-factor, covitality, and personality," *Social Biology,* 5 (2004): 121–143.

[662] Nettle, *Personality, op. cit.*

[663] R. Vaas, "God, gains and genes," in E. Voland and W. Schiefenhövel, (Eds.), *The Biological Evolution of Religious Mind and Behavior* (New York: Springer, 2009); A. Norenzayan and A. Shariff, "The origin and evolution of religious pro-sociality," *Science,* 322 (2008): 58–62.

by the band. If God is there telling you that your life has eternal meaning, your anxiety levels will be heavily reduced, which will help you to survive.[664] Religiousness is associated with a pro-social personality and we would be selecting for this insomuch as pro-social people would be less likely to be cast out by the band and pro-social people would be more positively ethnocentric; more co-operative.[665] Indeed, religiousness is genetically associated with pro-social traits,[666] and stimulating the anterior frontal cortex makes people both more religious and more ethnocentric.[667] So we were selecting for religiousness as well. And, of course, related to this we were selecting for mental and physical health, which themselves correlate, seemingly genetically, with religiousness,[668] and with conservatism.[669] In other words, we were selecting for a "General Fitness Factor."[670] Since around 1800, child mortality has collapsed from 50 per cent down to less than 1 per cent in developed countries.[671] This is obviously going to lead to a massive rise in mutation and, thus, far more people who are mentally and physically ill, traits which are associated with liberalism and atheism.

On many measures people who are religious, or conservative, are simply healthier than those who are liberal or atheistic.[672] Not only do they

---

[664] A. Norenzayan and A. Shariff, "The origin and evolution of religious pro-sociality," *Science*, 322 (2008): 58–62.

[665] Hills et al., "Primary personality trait correlates of religious practice and orientation," *op. cit.*

[666] L. Koenig, M. McGue, R. Krueger and T. Bouchard, "Religiousness, antisocial behavior, and altruism: genetic and environmental mediation," *Journal of Personality,* 75 (2007): 265-290.

[667] C. Holbrook, K. Izuma, C. Deblieck et al., "Neuromodulation of group prejudice and religious belief," *Social Cognitive and Affective Neuroscience,* 11 (2016): 387-394.

[668] H. Koenig, "Religion, Spirituality and Health: The Research and Clinical Implications," *ISRN Psychiatry* (2012), http://dx.doi.org/10.5402/2012/278730

[669] Kirkegaard, "Mental Illness and the Left," *op. cit.*; V. Kannan, J. Pacheco, K. Peters, S. Lapham and B. Chapman, "The relationship between health and political ideology begins in childhood," *SSM – Population Health,* 19 (2022): 1012014.

[670] Sarraf et al., *Modernity and Cultural Decline, op. cit.*

[671] Volk and Atkinson, "Is Child Death the Crucible of Human Evolution?" *op. cit.*

[672] Vaas, "God, gains and genes," *op. cit.*

have lower levels of depression,[673] but their faces are more good-looking and symmetrical,[674] as are their bodies,[675] and they are both physically stronger,[676] and physically taller.[677] It has further been found that the sicklier a child is then the more likely he or she is to be liberal rather than conservative as an adult,[678] consistent with liberals having poorer immune systems than conservatives due to higher mutational load. It follows that we would expect leftism to be, at least in part, an expression of elevated mutational load. We were strongly selecting for religiosity, conservatism, genetic health and pro-social traits, so any deviation from this should be associated with the mutations that have been able to accrue since the Industrial Revolution weakened harsh Darwinian conditions with improved medicine, inoculations and easier living conditions. Liberalism, with its focus on individually-oriented foundations, and atheism, are clearly deviations from this, so they should be associated with markers of mutational load, and this is precisely what we find. In effect, up until the Industrial Revolution, we were selecting for a slow Life History strategy: pro-social, intelligent, mentally stable, adapted to a specific harsh ecology and its pathogens, religious and group-oriented.[679]

With the breakdown of these conditions, we would expect a rise in the survival of fast Life History Strategists, and there is some direct evidence that conservatives are slower Life History strategists than non-

---

[673] O. Lahtinen, "Construction and validation of a scale for assessing critical social justice attitudes," *Scandinavian Journal of Psychology* (2024), https://doi.org/10. 1111/sjop.13018

[674] R. Peterson and C. Palmer, "Effects of physical attractiveness on political beliefs," *Politics and Life Sciences*, 36 (2017): 3–16.

[675] M. Price, S. Brown, A. Dukes and J. Kang, "Bodily Attractiveness and Egalitarianism are Negatively Related in Males," *Evolutionary Psychology*, 9 (2015): 140-166.

[676] M. Peterson and L. Laustsen, "Upper-Body Strength and Political Egalitarianism: Twelve Conceptual Replications," *Political Psychology*, 40 (2019): 375–394.

[677] R. Arunachalam and S. Watson, "Height, Income and Voting," *British Journal of Political Science*, 48 (2018): 1027-1048.

[678] Kannan et al., "The relationship between health and political ideology begins in childhood," *op. cit.*

[679] A.J. Figueredo, P. Wolf, S. Olderbak et al., "The Psychometric Assessment of Human Life History Strategy: A Meta-Analytic Construct Validation," *Evolutionary Behavioral Sciences*, 8 (2014): 148-185.

conservatives.[680] We would thus expect a rise in people who espoused individually-oriented moral foundations. Eventually, even if a conservative culture held this back, a tipping-point would be reached—as experiments have shown occurs when about 20 per cent of a group dissent from the old way of thinking[681]—and we would flip over into a liberal culture characterised, in the absence of external threats, by runaway individualism. It has been calculated that the rise in leftism in Western countries over the last 70 years is likely substantially due to rising mutational load, as I have explored in greater depth elsewhere.[682] However, it should be emphasised that there will always be variance in such an ecology, because there are many specific niches to fill. Hence, there will always be some fast Life History strategists who are genetically healthy in such an ecology; they will just be relatively unusual.

Indeed, as we noted above, liberalism is an expression of selfishness and mental and physical weakness. Liberals, like females, are physically weak and they are high in mental instability, including in anxiety. It follows that they will fear a fair fight so will play for status covertly, by signalling concern about equality and harm avoidance; virtue-signalling. Engaging in this has been shown to be associated with Machiavellianism.[683] This will help them to accrue status due to asymmetrical empathy between the conservative, who is concerned about all 5 moral foundations, and the liberal, who is only concerned about the individually-oriented foundations. In many ways, in fact, the liberal can be understood as a born traitor. These people would be expected to have maladaptive drives, including a drive not to have children and even to actively hinder their own families and their own ethnic group, favouring other ethnic groups over their own. In this regard, it has been shown that the moral circle of leftists—those with whom they identify—is more

---

[680] S. Koljevic, "Life History Strategy in Poland: Population Displacement as a Life History Accelerating Event," *Evolutionary Psychological Science,* 10 (2024): 100-109.

[681] D. Centola, J. Becker, D. Brackbill and A. Baronchelli, "Experimental evidence for tipping points in social convention," *Science,* 360 (2018): 1116-1119.

[682] Dutton and Rayner-Hilles, *Woke Eugenics, op. cit.*

[683] E. Ok, Y. Qian, B. Strejcek and K. Aquino, "Signaling Virtuous Victimhood as Indicators of Dark Triad Personalities," *Journal of Personality and Social Psychology,* 120 (2021): 1634-1661.

genetically distant from self than is the case with conservatives. In other words, they might identify with a different ethnic group over their own, whereas conservatives will identify with their own ethnic group. This may be adaptive: collaborate with outsiders to gain individual power within your own group.[684] But the key point is that we would expect liberals to be "whacko" on the basis of this model and this precisely what we find.

How Was Intelligence Selected For?

We were also selecting, under harsh conditions, for intelligence; something which is genetically correlated with physical and mental health[685] and is, therefore, a component of the "General Fitness Factor." Congruous with this, it has been found that couples who have trouble conceiving actually tend to die younger, implying elevated mutational load.[686]

There are a number of lines of evidence for our selecting for this fitness factor: in the seventeenth century the richer half of European populations had double the completed fertility of the poorer half; head size, literacy, numeracy, per capita major innovations and even the prevalence of alleles associated indirectly with intelligence increased up until about 1850. In essence, the ecology was at its carrying capacity, it became increasingly cold between about 1300 and 1700, and, consequently, there was strong selection for intelligence – as it allowed you to accrue resources – and a general fitness factor of which intelligence was a component.[687] Consistent with this, intelligence correlates with having a symmetrical face,[688] it negatively correlates with left-handedness (left-handedness is associated with a strongly asymmetrical brain, with

---

[684] A. Waytz, R. Iyer, L. Young, J. Haidt and J. Graham, "Ideological differences in the expanse of the moral circle," *Nature Communications*, 10 (2019): 1–12.

[685] Sarraf et al, *Modernity and Cultural Decline, op. cit.*

[686] R. Lindhahl-Jacobsen, M. Petersson, L. Priskorn et al., "Time to pregnancy and life expectancy: a cohort study of 18 796 pregnant couples," *Human Reproduction,* 39 (2024): 595-603.

[687] Dutton and Woodley of Menie, *At Our Wits' End, op. cit.*

[688] G. Banks, J. Batchelor and M. Mcdaniel, "Smarter people are (a bit) more symmetrical: A meta-analysis of the relationship between intelligence and fluctuating asymmetry," *Intelligence,* 34 (2010): 393–401.

developmental instability),[689] and it genetically correlates with height. In the latter case, this is partly because females sexually select for status (and so intelligence) and also for height. Being tall is evidence of the ability to win fights and also of low mutational load; since if you have a poor immune system then you will invest more of your bio-energetic resources in fighting off disease and so you will be less able to grow tall. Consequently, they have become pleiotropically related, something rendered more pronounced by assortative mating between tall and intelligent people.[690]

The reduction in selection pressure since approximately 1800 is reflected in our becoming more left-handed,[691] less intelligent (as we discussed earlier), and our faces becoming less symmetrical.[692] White Americans reached a peak height in the generation born around 1980 and have been shrinking since. This would be congruous with their reaching their phenotypic maximum height, so allowing an underlying decline in height, predicted by falling intelligence, to reveal itself. However, there may be other possible causes, such as worsening diet, and childhood obesity shrinking the growth period during puberty.[693] A period of declining height among late Victorians was seemingly explicable partly in terms of a poorer diet occasioned by the rise of tinned food and the

---

[689] M.A. Woodley of Menie, H. Fernandes, S. Kanazawa and E. Dutton, "Sinistrality is associated with (slightly) lower general intelligence: A data synthesis and consideration of secular trend data in handedness," *HOMO: Journal of Comparative Human Biology,* 69 (2018): 118–126.

[690] M. Keller, C. Garver-Apgar, M. Wright et al., "The Genetic Correlation between Height and IQ: Shared Genes or Assortative Mating?" *PLoS One Genetics,* 9 (2013): e1003451.

[691] Woodley of Menie et al., "Sinistrality is associated with (slightly) lower general intelligence," *op. cit.*

[692] M.A. Woodley of Menie and H. Fernandes, "The secular decline in general intelligence from decreasing developmental stability: Theoretical and empirical considerations," *Personality and Individual Differences,* 92 (2016): 194–199.

[693] L. Andrews, "Americans are SHRINKING: Data shows men and women are up to half an inch shorter now than they were in the 1980s," *Mail Online* (15th December 2023), https://www.dailymail.co.uk/health/article-12868421/americans-shorter-professions-tallest-workers.html

increasing migration into urban living conditions which meant less access to fruit and vegetables.[694]

Many studies have found intelligence to be weakly negatively associated with religious belief, with the association being with general intelligence, which is strongly genetic.[695] However, this association has become weaker across time and no longer exists in the most up-to-date samples. A feasible explanation for this change is that atheism or atheistic ideologies have spread so far down the societal, and thus intelligence, hierarchy in younger cohorts that the correlation has ceased to exist.[696] A possible reason for the broader anomaly – religiousness and intelligence are both part of the General Fitness Factor - may be that intelligence is associated with both social conformity and with a high ability to overcome cognitive biases or instincts, with being highly environmentally sensitive and low in instinct. This would make sense because solving problems—intelligence—involves rising above your instinctive cognitive biases, so people who were less instinctive, and so more environmentally sensitive, would be better at solving problems. This is termed the Intelligence-Mismatch Association Model.[697] In this regard, "individuals with high IQ show high environmental influence on IQ into adolescence (resembling younger children), whereas individuals with low IQ show high heritability of IQ in adolescence (resembling adults), a pattern consistent with an extended sensitive period for intellectual development in more-intelligent individuals."[698] In an evolutionary mismatch, in which mortality salience was low, we would, therefore, potentially expect high intelligence to predict low religiousness.

---

[694] P. Clayton and J. Rowbotham, "How the Mid-Victorians Worked, Ate and Died," *International Journal of Environmental Research and Public Health*, 6 (2009): 1235–1253.

[695] E. Dutton and E. Kirkegaard, "The Negative Religiousness-IQ Nexus is a Jensen Effect on Individual Level Data: A Refutation of Dutton et al.'s 'The Myth of the Stupid Believer,'" *Journal of Religion and Health*, 61 (2023): 3253–3275.

[696] E. Dutton and D. van der Linden, "Why is Intelligence Negatively Associated with Religiousness?" *Evolutionary Psychological Science*, 3 (2017): 392–403.

[697] Dutton and van der Linden, "Why is Intelligence Negatively Associated with Religiousness?" *op. cit.*

[698] A. Brant, Y. Munakata, D. Boomsma, "The nature and nurture of high IQ: An extended sensitive period for intellectual development," *Psychological Science*, 24 (2013): 1487–1495.

The relationship between intelligence and social conformity would also explain the paradox that intelligence is a marker of low mutational load, yet it is associated, in left-wing societies, with leftism, which is a marker of high mutational load. Leftism is even associated with alleles that predict intelligence.[699] Intelligence predicts social conformity and, in a society that is focused on the leftist values of equality and harm avoidance, this means conforming to leftism. In right-wing societies, by contrast, intelligence – at least when using the proxy of education - is associated with being right-wing, again because intelligence predicts social conformity.[700]

Why Was Watson's Time So Special?

So bringing all of this together, what does it mean in terms of the promotion of genius; in terms of having a safe-space in which geniuses can do their genius work? It means that there is likely to have been an optimum period in which scientific creativity can take place. As we saw earlier, the peak for per capita genius was about 1870, where the English people were at peak intelligence. But the problem, from the perspective of the genius, was that the society was still strongly religious and there were still many religious taboos in place. As we will see in more detail in the next chapter, the English universities were dominated by the Anglican Church until 1871, so they were not conducive to a questioning disposition. They were, perhaps, built on the religious idea, known as Thomism, that the purpose of scholarship was to seek truth by making sense of God's creation, but, nevertheless, certain dogmas were not to be questioned. Darwin, an independent scholar, heavily delayed publishing his research on evolution, fearing the massive offence it would cause to Christian sensibilities, to the group-oriented religion. At the time of writing, scholars must fear offending against the dogmas of Wokeness, which, again, limits creativity. There is an oppressive environment which

---

[699] N. Carl and B. Winegard, "Can mutation load explain the rise of leftism?" *Aporia Magazine* (26th April 2024), https://www.aporiamagazine.com/p/can-mutation-load-explain-the-rise
[700] H. Rindermann, H., C. Flores-Mendoza and M.A. Woodley, "Political orientations, intelligence and education," *Intelligence*, 40 (2012); 217-225.

discourages people from having a questioning attitude, as that attitude may lead to their questioning Woke dogmas.

It would follow that there would be an optimum period in which the group-oriented religion was in decline and the individually-oriented replacement was at a very low level of influence. It is difficult to say precisely when this was but perhaps it was the time between about 1900 and the year 2000, and perhaps there was a specific decade, such as the 1970s, which was optimum. In scientific terms, belief in God, or at least in religious dogmas, would be lost but belief in the importance of the truth would be maintained. Eventually, this would give way to individually-oriented moral foundations being more important than the truth, just as group-oriented foundations had once been more important than the truth.

There would be a number of factors behind this optimum period. Victorian England was highly intelligent, but mortality salience was relatively high. This made people traditionally religious and group-oriented. Mutational load was accruing but a tipping point had not been reached, so the culture still pushed people in a group-oriented direction. Life was more perilous than today and geniuses could be appreciated insomuch as they improved living standards, meaning they had to be tolerated, but there were certain lines that the creative could not cross. By 2007, mortality salience had collapsed, living standards were extremely high, society had tipped over to individually-oriented foundations and these substantially trumped empirical truth. There would have been an optimum between the two extremes; a generation that was born in the traditional society, meaning an inculcation with the importance of truth, but which came of age as the society collapsed into a relative free-for-all. This was Watson's generation.

A related issue, which only compounds the influence of individually-oriented foundations on society, as well as reflecting the decline of traditional values, is the rise of females to positions of power. It is to this that we will now turn. The consequences of this rise are something we have already looked at implicitly. In the year 2000, it was very specifically female students and academics who became enraged by Watson's remarks.

Chapter Thirteen

Upsetting the Sisterhood

Girl Power

Does the presence of females help males (and most geniuses are males due to the need for outlier high intelligence, autism and psychopathy) to think profoundly? The English anthropologist J. D. Unwin (1895-1936) argued in his book *Sex and Culture* that the answer was "No."[701] He demonstrated, drawing on analyses of a large number of cultures, that as societies become more developed, they tend to become more sexually repressed. On the one hand, control of sexuality means fewer adulterous affairs, less intra-group conflict, more internal cooperation, and thus higher ethnocentrism. Congruous with this model, experiments have found that Protestants are more creative when they are forced to suppress their anger, when they are primed with feelings of damnation and primed with the idea that sexual desires are unacceptable.[702] Certainly, geniuses are more likely to never marry and never have children based on a biographical analysis of 291 "Great Men."[703]

On the other hand, it means people directing their repressed sexual impulses into group-selected activities such as inspiring art or invention; giving the group a further advantage in the group-selection battle. When civilizations go into decline, it has been noticed – whether in Greece, Rome, Baghdad or even in the West – that people stop believing in the civilization's religion, a religion which promotes sexual repression, ethnocentrism, and the idea that they are God's chosen people. They cease

---

[701] J.D. Unwin, *Sex and Culture* (Oxford: Oxford University Press, 1934).
[702] E. Kim, V. Zeppenfeld and D. Cohen, "Sublimation, Culture and Creativity," *Journal of Personal and Social Psychology*, 105 (2013): 639-666.
[703] F. Post, "Creativity and psychopathology: A Study of 291 World Famous Men," *British Journal of Psychiatry,* 165 (1994): 22-34.

to be as sexually repressed and they become less creative. As such, it follows that the presence of females at university might make a certain kind of male – the genius-type – less creative. But, obviously, you're not allowed to say something like that in public. It might be considered "sexist;" it might "hurt people's feelings," even if it's true. But the problem is that Watson has a tendency to tell the truth with regard to scientific matters. This includes with regard to women.

Watson's Remarks on Women

At the Euro Open Forum in Dublin, in 2012, Watson remarked, of his discovery, that: "I was just lucky there were no women there – I might have been thinking about them instead of DNA. I think having all these women around makes it more fun for the men but they're probably less effective."[704] This statement may be regarded as provocative, even as outrageous to certain sensibilities, but is it empirically reasonable?

It is a simple fact that boys achieve better grades if they go to all-boys schools. Boys who attend all-male schools modestly out-perform females as a whole on school leaving certificates such as GCSEs (General Certificates of Secondary Education) which are sat by English pupils at 16, whereas, more generally, girls outperform boys in their GCSEs. Thus, from an academic perspective, co-educational institutions are bad for males.[705] The key reason why males seem to perform less well academically than females relates to male differences in modal personality, as their average intelligence is little different from that of females at this stage. Male pupils are "more prone to inattentive, restless and distractible behaviours and aggressive, antisocial and oppositional behaviours than females."[706] This is important, because it has been found that the mere presence of women – a mere 5 minutes in the presence of an attractive woman – increases testosterone levels in men, and especially in

---

[704] F. Macrae, "Possible cure for cancer in decade - DNA pioneer," *IOL* (13th July 2012), https://www.iol.co.za/news/possible-cure-for-cancer-in-decade-dna-pioneer-1340965

[705] S. Gibb, D. Fergusson and L.J. Horwood, "Effects of single-sex and coeducational schooling on the gender gap in educational achievement," *Australian Journal of Education*, 52 (2008): 3.

[706] Gibb et al., "Gender differences in educational achievement to age 25," *op. cit.*

men who are more aggressive and socially dominant. Testosterone would be the mediating factor in the kind of behaviours that appear to reduce male academic achievement.[707] It is seemingly for this reason that when females were permitted to start attending lectures at English universities they were sometimes not allowed to be in the lecture theatre with the males, as it was felt that this would distract the males and the males might even try to seduce the females.[708] The females would be chaperoned in groups and could not enter the lecture theatre until all of the males were seated. Sometimes, they had to listen-in from the corridor. There was concern that females would be unable to cope with indelicate subjects or that males would fear asking questions of lecturers because they wouldn't want to look ignorant in front of the ladies.[709]

Females, Empathy and the Culture of Universities

In addition, a high female presence is likely to alter the culture of the university; to, in effect, render it more focussed on emotion and social conformity. This will also reduce male effectiveness and, indeed, creativity.

There are fundamental average differences between the male and female brain, as we have already discussed. The extreme male brain is strongly focused on systematizing but it is empathy blind; in other words, it is autistic; it is high in systematizing but low in empathy, meaning it is hyper-focused on problem solving. The extreme female brain is the opposite; it is very high in empathy but it is system-blind.[710] The female average IQ differs little from the male IQ. Males, in adulthood, appear to have approximately a 4 point advantage, but, more importantly, the male

---

[707] L. van der Meij, A. Buunk, J. van de Saande and A. Salvador, "The presence of a woman increases testosterone in aggressive dominant men," *Hormones and Behavior,* 54 (2008): 640-644.

[708] S. Wollenberg and M. van Goldbeck, "Music in Oxford Women's Colleges, 1879-1939" in R. Darwell-Smith and S. Goldberg, (Eds.), Music in Twentieth-century Oxford: New Directions (Woodbridge: The Boydell Press, 2023), 96.

[709] S. Sheffield, *Women and Science: Social Impact and Interaction* (Santa Barbara, CA: ABC-Clio, 2004), 106.

[710] S. Baron-Cohen, "The extreme male brain theory of autism," *Trends in Cognitive Sciences,* 6 (2002): 248-254.

range is wider.[711] This makes sense in terms of the "Male Variability Hypothesis: you get more men with outlier low IQ – becoming tramps and criminals – but also more men with outlier high IQ. This is why almost all scientific geniuses are male. Males are more variable because they are under higher levels of sexual selection. This requires an aside.

What is Sexual Selection?

Males operate different sexual selection strategies from females. The male has little to lose from the sexual encounter. Consequently, it pays for him to have sex with as many women as he can and, to the extent that he is selective, he will select for youth and beauty. This is because youth is a clear sign of fertility while beauty – a symmetrical face and feminine features – is a sign of low mutational load and, consequently of genetic health and, thus, of fertility.

Females, though they are interested in genetic health, are more evolved to be attracted to high status males because, under harsh conditions, high status males can invest more in the offspring and in them, making it more likely that both will survive. In addition, the offspring will carry whatever genes have permitted the male to attain status, with status being associated with fertility under pre-industrial conditions. Females also tend to sexually select for age, because age tends to be an indirect marker of social status. Accordingly, females will tend to select *hypergamously* (upwards) for socioeconomic status while males will marry hypergamously for looks; tending to be less good-looking than their female partner.[712] Females, of course, also select for physical traits, but they are simply less interested in them than are males. For example, as we discussed earlier, females sexually select for height – because taller males will be better able to win fights and protect them – with the consequence that, in males, intelligence, which they select for via selecting for social status, is genetically correlated with height.[713]

---

[711] R. Lynn, *Sex Differences in Intelligence: The Developmental Theory* (London: Arktos, 2021).

[712] D. Buss, *The Evolution of Desire: Strategies of Human Mating* (New York: Basic Books, 1989).

[713] M. Keller. C. Apgar, M. Wright et al., "The Genetic Correlation between Height and IQ: Shared Genes or Assortative Mating?" *PLoS Genetics,* 9 (2013): e1003451.

We can understand, following this system, why patriarchy – the male control of female sexuality - developed. The male desires sex and the female desires investment. The male wants to be sure that the investment is actually in *his* children. Therefore, he demands to be able to control the female, such that her sexual behaviour can be controlled.[714] If a male is inclined to invest in his offspring, he may be more interested in the female's personality traits, and less interested in youth and beauty, and may make trade-offs accordingly. Similarly, if the female desires a nurturing male then she may trade this for social status or height.

There is some evidence that women will trade male age for other factors, such as socioeconomic status.[715] It may follow that relationships with an extreme age-gap, where the male is much older than the female, would reflect two people that were relatively fast Life History strategists. Consistent with this prediction, these relationships have very high levels of divorce,[716] and the younger partner is likely to ultimately be dissatisfied in the relationship.[717] Moreover, there is some evidence that approval of them, in males and females, is weakly associated with psychopathic traits,[718] and such relationships have elevated levels of domestic violence.[719] People high in psychopathic and related traits, such as Narcissism, tend to sexually select for each other, as it elevates the extent to which they pass on their genes.[720] Such relationships are taboo, it has

---

[714] R. Grant and V.T. Montrose, "It's a Man's World: Mate Guarding and the Evolution of Patriarchy," *Mankind Quarterly,* 58 (2018): 384–418.

[715] C. Shehan, F. Berardo, H. Vera and S. Carley, "Women in age-discrepant marriages," *Journal of Family Issues,* 12 (1991): 3.

[716] A Francis-Tan and H. Mialon, "'A Diamond is Forever' and Other Fairy Tales," *op cit.*

[717] A. Bender, *Predictors and Consequences of Involvement in Age-Discrepant Romantic Relationships* (PhD Thesis: Hanover College, IN, 2007).

[718] Alexander, "Age Gaps & Hierarchical Relationships," *Date Psych* (26th March 2023), https://datepsychology.com/age-gaps-hierarchical-relationships/

[719] L. Tarzia, "Toward an Ecological Understanding of Intimate Partner Sexual Violence," *Journal of Interpersonal Violence,* 36 (2021): 23-24.

[720] Grandiose Narcissists tend to date women who have some grandiose traits: J. Lamkin, W.K. Campbell, M vanDellen and J. Miller, "An exploration of the correlates of grandiose and vulnerable narcissism in romantic relationships: Homophily, partner characteristics, and dyadic adjustment," *Personality and Individual Differences,* 79 (2015): 166-171. Women with Narcissistic traits are attracted to Narcissistic men: M. Lyons and A. Blanchard, "'I could see, in the depth of his eyes, my own beauty

been found, because the two-way exploitation dimension – the sex for resources trade off – is so blatant.[721] Perhaps it confronts us with something unpalatable that we all know that we have done. There is also some evidence that the beauty-status exchange is more pronounced in highly age-discrepant relationships.[722] Indeed, women who endorse such relationships are also more likely to endorse prostitution.[723] People involved in such relationships tend to have had insecure attachments to care-givers as children.[724]

Selecting for Alpha Males

But returning to the reasons for male variability, humans are a polygynous species in which the females, historically, gathered around the most dominant male, as he seemingly had the best genes. Traits that are sexually selected for tend to have high variability because a high mutation rate increases the probability of a beneficial mutation. In general, as we are so finely adapted to our ecology, mutations will damage us; they will make us less well-adapted. However, the more variation there is – the more mutations there are – the more likely any given mutation is to be adaptive; to provide an advantage. Females, in pre-History, selected for the top males, meaning that the majority of males did not pass on their genes at all. In such a context, the "risk" of mutation may as well be taken, because any random male will almost certainly lose in the game of evolution. It follows, therefore, that there should be greater male variability. The carrier of the beneficial mutation will come to dominate the gene pool.[725]

---

reflected": Women's assortative preference for narcissistic, but not for Machiavellian or psychopathic male faces. *Personality and Individual Differences*, 97 (2016): 40-44.
[721] Y. Sela, M. Pham, J. Mogilski et al., "Why do people disparage May–December romances? Condemnation of age-discrepant romantic relationships as strategic moralization," *Personality and Individual Differences*, 130 (2018): 6-10.
[722] K. Marsh, *My Spouse is Amazing Like Me: The Association Between Homogamy for Narcissism and Relationship Satisfaction* (PhD Thesis: Liberty University, Lynchburg, VA, 2020), 34.
[723] Y. Saela, M. Pham, J. Mogliski et al., "Why do people disparage May–December romances? Condemnation of age-discrepant romantic relationships as strategic moralization," *Personality and Individual Differences*, 130 (2018): 6-10.
[724] K.J. Prager, *The Psychology of Intimacy* (New York: The Guilford Press, 1995).
[725] D. Geary, *Male, Female: The Evolution of Human Sex Differences* (Washington, DC: American Psychological Association, 1998).

So males are operating a very risky strategy, but this makes sense because, to risk labouring the point, among hunter-gatherers only about 40 per cent of males father any children at all.[726] As stated, this means that there are more males with outlier high intelligence and there is some evidence that outlier high intelligence is associated with autistic traits because, all else being equal, autistic traits render you hyper-focused on systematizing and so better able to solve problems.[727]

The Priestly Cycle of Universities

With the rise of females, then, university will inherently become less autistic. This, of course, is what is set-off by the collapse of the group-oriented religion. This religion promotes that which is adaptive at the group-level as the will of God, and this includes patriarchy, as it reduces inter-male conflict meaning that the group is more cooperative in the face of outsiders. Patriarchy also encourages males to nurture their offspring in a harsh ecology as it reduces paternity anxiety.

As people become less religious, due to decreased mortality salience or even due to rising mutational load, this system begins to fall apart. In addition, in the absence of harsh selection, we would expect females to become masculinised, meaning they would desire power, and for males to become feminized. There is a large body of evidence that feminist females are physically more masculinised, with this tending to be correlated with being mentally more masculinised.[728] They are more socially dominant than women who don't identify as feminists.[729] It has been shown that the more socially dominant a female is, and in that sense the more masculine she is, the more likely she is to fantasise about being raped. It has been suggested that this is adaptive because it allows dominant females to be

---

[726] See, R. Lynn, *Dysgenics, op. cit.*

[727] B. Crespi, "Autism As a Disorder of High Intelligence," *Frontiers in Neuroscience,* 10 (2016): 300.

[728] See, G. Madison, U. Aasa, J. Wallert and M.A. Woodley, "Feminist activist women are masculinized in terms of digit-ratio and social dominance: a possible explanation for the feminist paradox" *Frontiers in Psychology,* 5 (2014): 1011.

[729] A. Zucker and L. Bay-Cheng, "Minding the Gap Between Feminist Identity and Attitudes: The Behavioral and Ideological Divide Between Feminists and Non-Labelers," *Journal of Personality,* 78 (2010): 1895-1924.

attracted to dominant males, who would, it might be argued, be evolved to the same unstable, fast Life History ecology. In other words, in an unstable ecology, in which the man will abandon you meaning you must become masculinized, the only way you can be sure that he is a truly dominant male, whose offspring will therefore survive and flourish, is if he can dominate you. It would follow that you would fantasise about him raping you; this would ultimately be arousing as you would be having sex with a clearly dominant male.[730] One study has found a weak but significant correlation between strength of "Feminist" identification and having fantasies about being raped.[731] Such females, high in Neuroticism and thus power-hungry, open up the possibility for greater influence for all females, not just masculinized females such as themselves. But they, or their increase in prominence, are likely a result of weakened selection pressures brought about by the fruits of the Industrial Revolution.

Females may be highly intelligent but within the normal range. This kind of intelligence is associated with social conformity - it is associated with norm-mapping and the effortful control necessary to force yourself to believe that which it is socially useful to believe; that is, the dominant world-view. You then competitively signal your adherence to this worldview in ever more intelligent-seeming and creative ways.[732] Females are also lower in the non-conformist personality traits that are associated with genius: they are low in psychopathy and low in autism. Even in the absence of females, a university founded by intelligent autistics will shift as it gains prestige due to its genius innovations. It will attract ambitious normal range high IQ people, who are socially conformist both due to their intelligence and Machiavellianism, so it will move away from being focused on the unfettered exploration of ideas to being, in a sense, a branch of a society's literal or *de facto* church. Females are higher in Neuroticism, partly due to their high social anxiety, which predicts extrinsic

---

[730] P. Hawley and W. Hensley, "Social Dominance and Forceful Submission Fantasies: Feminine Pathology or Power?" *Journal of Sex Research,* 46 (2009): 568-585.

[731] J. Schulman and S. Horne, "Guilty or Not? A Path Model of Women's Sexual Force Fantasies," *Journal of Sex Research,* 43 (2006): 368-377.

[732] M.A. Woodley of Menie and C. Dunkel, "Beyond the Cultural Mediation Hypothesis: A reply to Dutton (2013)," *Intelligence,* 49 (2015): 186–191.

religiousness and thus social conformity,[733] with the difference being strongest at about the age that people are students. Likewise, the male female difference in Intellect is highest at the age of about 20.[734] In other words, while females may represent a problem for maintaining a university system which values genius, females in their late-teens and early-twenties constitute a particularly pronounced problem. This is rendered even worse by the fact that Neurotic females, but not Neurotic males, tend to respond very negatively and punitively to socially dominant males who have transgressed in some way; with autistics tending to be masculinised and being more likely to break the social rules.[735]

Indeed, Norwegian psychiatrist Hannah Spier has argued that left-wing activist groups tend to be largely female and tend to reflect Borderline Personality Disorder and Narcissism, more subtle than male Narcissism due to the female concern with safety. Such women cloak their aggression in virtue-signalling, grandiosely regard themselves as unique moral authorities, feel entitled to be obeyed, employ manipulative and Histrionic techniques to garner attention, including symbolically self-harming, such as by gluing themselves to roads. They are also highly vindictive to their opponents, indicating low empathy. Speer explains, of the areas women have come to dominate: "Infantilization in these spaces is often driven by childless women projecting unmet maternal instincts onto students, patients, and co-workers. What follows is maternal-style censure: punishment for disobedience and failing to align with the 'right' causes, such as objecting to displaying the rainbow flag." More women at universities inherently means more people of this kind; people who are antithetical to logic and reason.[736]

---

[733] Hills et al, "Primary personality trait correlates of religious practice and orientation," *op. cit.*

[734] Y. Weisberg, C. DeYoung and Jacob Hirsch, "Gender Differences in Personality across the Ten Aspects of the Big Five," *Frontiers in Psychology,* 2 (2011): 178.

[735] B. O'Neil and M. Brown, "Women's Dangerous World Beliefs Predict Biases Against Formidable Men in Legal Domains," *Evolutionary Psychological Science,* 10 (2024), 388–396.

[736] H. Spier, "Borders or Borderliners: The Psychopathology Behind the Angry Female Protestors," *Psychobabble* (15th June 2025), https://substack.com/home/post/p-165991946

So the presence of females will make this shift even more pronounced, leading to the university gradually becoming dominated by social conformists who will kick out the genius types, or not appoint them, resulting in the universities decreasingly generating cutting edge knowledge and discoveries. Congruous with this model, a study of American psychology departments has found that female academics, and especially young female academics, are more opposed to controversial scholarship; they put feelings above truth.[737] To some extent, they turn the university into a kind of nursery school; into what young females are adapted to run. In our evolutionary history, after all, this is the precise age at which women would be part of harems in which they were alloparenting each other's children. They would, therefore, be particularly concerned about feelings and everyone getting along and they would be very averse to risk.

In other words, we would expect there to be an optimum period in terms of the influence of females on society and, indeed, on the universities. When they have no influence on society, then the struggling highly intelligent autistic child may have a miserable childhood which, in some cases, may crush his spirit such that he does not reach his potential. When they have too much influence, the autistic adult is ostracised because he is unable to avoid hurting people's feelings. Similarly, in relation to university, if you keep women out completely then there are no Rosalind Franklins, a woman who Watson himself claimed was "partially autistic"[738] and so masculinised in her thinking processes, but if you admit too many then the culture of the university becomes insufficiently autistic.

The Previous Decline of English Universities

This decline of the universities, it should be noted, has happened before. The universities, in England, in the Middle Ages, began at the cutting edge of philosophy: Scholasticism. Leading heresies emerged from the

---

[737] C. Clark, M. Fjeldmark, L. Lou et al., "Taboos and Self-Censorship Among U.S. Psychology Professors," *Perspectives of Psychological Science* (2024).
[738] A. Boyle, "DNA pioneer James Watson's genetic prescription: Have kids early," *NBC News* (27th September 2012), https://www.nbcnews.com/sciencemain/dna-pioneer-james-watsons-genetic-prescription-have-kids-early-8c11273666

universities both in the late Middle Ages and during the Reformation. These universities also followed the philosophy of Italian friar St Thomas Aquinas: the purpose of scholars was to make sense of the world, which was God's revelation, and, therefore, to lie was blasphemous. Science was a kind of "Natural Theology" with a fundamental focus on objective truth.[739] However, the English universities gradually became branches of the Established Church; you had to be a confessing Anglican to matriculate or graduate and an ordained Anglican minister in order to be a don. Fortunately, King Charles II (1630-1685) exempted Newton from this requirement.[740] They went into decline, considered to be little more than expensive finishing schools that were dominated by the Church. Their curriculums were out-of-date, teaching little of use or interest to intelligent middle class people, let alone teaching science, meaning that they became dominated by the aristocracy.[741] Teaching standards, in fact, were so poor that undergraduates were forced to hire private tutors if they hoped to obtain an honours degree.[742]

In other words, such universities ceased to be an indicator of intelligence and useful knowledge. They merely indicated that your parents were wealthy and they were regarded as a rite of passage for upper class men. Science was taught at Dutch and German universities, with many intellectual Englishmen in the eighteenth and early nineteenth centuries preferring to attend these,[743] especially Leiden University.[744] British Prime Minister the Earl of Bute (1713-1792), who was regarded as strongly academic, was exclusively educated at Dutch universities,

---

[739] N. Monteiro and P. Cardim, *Political Thought in Portugal and Its Empire, C.1500-1800* (Cambridge: Cambridge University Press, 2018), 16.

[740] E. Dutton, *Churchill's Headmaster: The 'Sadist' Who Nearly Saved the British Empire* (Melbourne: Manticore Press, 2019).

[741] L. Stone, "The Size and Composition of the Oxford Student Body, 1580-1909," in L. Stone, (Ed.). *The University in Society, Volume I: Oxford and Cambridge from the 14th to the Early 19th Century* (Princeton, NJ: Princeton University Press, 2019).

[742] D. Leader, V. Morgan and P. Searby, *A History of the University of Cambridge: Volume 3, 1750-1870* (Cambridge: Cambridge University Press, 1988), 62.

[743] W. Brickman, *Introduction to the History of International Relations in Higher Education* (New York: New York University, 1960), 100.

[744] K. Davids, "The Scholarly Atlantic: Circuits of Knowledge Between Britain, the Dutch Republic and the Americas in the Eighteenth Century," in G. Oostindie and J. Roitman, (Eds.), *Dutch Atlantic Connections, 1680-180* (Leiden: Brill, 2014), 245.

specifically Groningen and Leiden.[745] They signalled not just wealth but intelligence and useful knowledge.

Well into the nineteenth century, the Scottish universities also had a superior academic reputation to those in England. They – specifically Glasgow, Aberdeen and Edinburgh - were centres of the Enlightenment and taught the latest science, while Oxford and Cambridge, and later Durham, were finishing schools for "the idle and the rich" offering "little that was new for the well-prepared student" in contrast to the Scottish universities which thus attracted the "serious student."[746] The exception was St Andrews University which made little impact on the Scottish Enlightenment where the other three contributed about equally, with Aberdeen University being the most important in the early stages.[747] St Andrews University was not a centre of science. It only began teaching medicine in 1881 when it established a medical faculty in Dundee, now the, separate, Dundee University.[748] Scottish economist Adam Smith commented that, "In the university of Oxford, the greater part of the public professors have, for these many years, given up altogether even the pretence of teaching."[749] Due to such problems, Lord John Russell (1792-1878), another Prime Minister regarded as highly intellectual, attended Edinburgh University,[750] while Viscount Palmerston (1784-1865) credited his time at Edinburgh University for "whatever useful knowledge and habits of mind I possess."[751]

Sometimes, during this period, wealthy young men simply eschewed university altogether, completing their education with the "Grand Tour"

[745] F. Russell, *John, 3rd Earl of Bute: Patron and Collector* (London: Merrion Press, 2004).

[746] W. Horner, *Nineteenth-century Scottish Rhetoric: The American Connection* (Carbondale, IL: Southern Illinois University Press, 1993), 171.

[747] A. Broadie, *The Scottish Enlightenment* (Edinburgh: Birlinn, 2001).

[748] R. Lamont-Brown: *St Andrews: City by the North Sea* (San Rafael, CA: Origin, 2022).

[749] A. Smith, *The Wealth of Nations* (New York: Random House, 1937), 780.

[750] M. Davidson, *Downing Street Blues: A History of Depression and Other Mental Afflictions in British Prime Ministers* (Jefferson, NC: MacFarland Publishing, 2014), 68-69.

[751] D. Steele, "Temple, Henry John, Third Viscount Palmerston (1784-1865)," *Dictionary of National Biography* (Oxford: Oxford University Press, 2009).

of Europe, often accompanied by a personal tutor,[752] though this might sometimes involve spending a little time at, for example, a German university.[753] The British Prime Minister the Duke of Devonshire (1720-1764), for example, who was Prime Minister from November 1756 to June 1757, never attended an English university but simply went on the Grand Tour with a private tutor.[754] They were able to attend foreign universities because in the eighteenth century and to a lesser extent even at the beginning of the nineteenth century, teaching at universities was conducted in Latin, which they had learned at school.[755] Famous examples of Englishmen who attended Continental universities include the poet Samuel Taylor Coleridge (1772-1834) who studied at the University of Göttingen,[756] and the Prime Minister who lost America, Lord North (1732-1792), who spent time at Leipzig University.[757] It was German universities that popularised the academic doctorate, where a scholar presented extremely detailed research on a particular narrow subject, thus contributing to knowledge.[758]

Within England, there were many "Dissenting Academies" that operated as alternative universities. Some of these were considered of such a high academic standard that even some Anglicans sent their sons to them. The scientist Joseph Priestly (1733-1804), who discovered oxygen, taught at Warrington Academy,[759] while the demographer and Anglican priest Thomas Malthus (1766-1834) was educated at this so-called "Athens of

---

[752] N. Fyson, *Growing Up in the Eighteenth Century* (London: Batsford, 1977), 22.

[753] D. Le Faye, *Jane Austen* (London: British Library, 1998), 29.

[754] K. Schweizer, "Cavendish, William, 4th Duke of Devonshire (1720-1764), *Dictionary of National Biography* (2008).

[755] C.A. Eggert, "The problem of higher education" *Popular Science Monthly*, 28 (1885): 84-94.

[756] A. Brandl, *Samuel Taylor Coleridge and the English Romantic School* (London: John Murray, 1887), 239.

[757] C. Smith, *The Early Career of Lord North, the Prime Minister* (Madison, NJ: Fairleigh Dickinson University Press, 1979), 58.

[758] C. Park, "Refining the Doctorate," *The Higher Education Academy. Discussion Paper* (York: The Higher Education Academy, 2007).

[759] M. Mercer, "Dissenting academies and the education of the laity, 1750-1850," *History of Education*, 30 (2001): 35–58.

the North."[760] In addition, due to the religious nature of English universities, the nineteenth century was marked by many independent researchers: scholar rectors such as Edmund Cartwright (1743-1823) who invented the power loom, a vital contribution to the Industrial Revolution,[761] gentleman scientists such as Charles Darwin,[762] and enthusiastic amateurs such as the Aberdeenshire shoe-maker Thomas Edward (1814-1886) who was a noted expert on molluscs.[763] Indeed, it has been argued that genius can only truly flourish if the genius-type, once identified, is permitted freedom from normal labours such that he can focus on his quest; meaning that a society focused on production and conformity must value innovation enough to allow someone to be non-conformist and superficially unproductive for a lengthy period.[764] Assisting such people was American businessman Oliver R. Grace's (1909-1992) purpose in endowing the professorship that was held by James Watson. Oxford and Cambridge only became eminent academic institutions, gradually, from reforms in the 1870s onwards, by imitating German universities, dropping religious entry requirements and, in a sense, providing a safe space for genius.[765]

Prior to this, geniuses were driven out to these alternative institutions or into becoming independent scholars. Thus, the universities dropped the religious entry requirements, in 1871, and the "Priestly Cycle of Universities" began all over again.[766] At the time of writing, "Wokeness" is clearly in charge of British universities, assenting to Anglican dogma has been replaced by statements assenting to "diversity, equity and inclusion," and dissident academics, and students, are sent down, fired or

---

[760] J. Toman, *Kilvert's World of Wonders: Growing Up in Mid-Victorian England* (Cambridge: Lutterworth Press, 2013).

[761] B. Bryson, *At Home: A Short History of Private Life* (London: Transworld, 2010), 54.

[762] E. Peterson, *Understand Charles Darwin* (Cambridge: Cambridge University Press, 2023), 174.

[763] S. Smiles, *Life of a Scotch Naturalist: Thomas Edward* (London: John Murray, 1879).

[764] C. McCreery, *The Abolition of Genius* (Cuddesdon: Oxford Forum, 2012), 26.

[765] J. Williams, *Academic Freedom in an Age of Conformity* (Basingstoke, Hants: Palgrave Macmillan, 2016).

[766] See, Dutton and Rayner-Hilles, *The Past is a Future Country, op. cit.*

driven out either to specific dissident institutions or into the burgeoning world of independent scholarship. Canadian political scientist Eric Kaufmann (b. 1970), has explored this development in depth. He was driven out of Birkbeck College, London, in 2023 by constant Woke investigations into him and he joined the (private) University of Buckingham.[767]

The Evolution of the Female Mind: The Rise of the Head Girl

In addition, the average female personality is different from that of the male, as already noted. Females are higher in Conscientiousness, which is a crucial predictor of educational attainment, and also in Agreeableness, which weakly predicts it.[768] However, females are also higher in social anxiety and, consequently, in social conformity.[769] As psychologist Joyce Benenson has explored, females are adapted to live in harems in polygamous mating systems. In this context, they require "alloparents;" other members of the harem that will assist them in raising their children. To achieve this, they must be able to absolutely trust these alloparents.

Accordingly, they foster a small number of extremely close, one-to-one friendships in which there is complete equality and in which they share their vulnerabilities in order to create a strong bond. They also tend to evaluate each other in terms of "niceness;" that is lack of competitiveness, because you cannot truly trust a person who is competitive. She might steal a woman's long-cultivated friends or obtain more resources from the male.[770] Thus, girls who act "superior" must be socially shunned as must those who hurt people's feelings. This is likely because females are higher

---

[767] Kaufmann, *The Third Great Awokening, op. cit.*

[768] Nettle, *Personality, op cit.*; M. Almlund, A. Duckworth, J. Heckman and T. Kautz, "Personality, psychology and economics," in S. Hanushek, S. Machin and L. Woesmann, (Eds.), *Handbook of the Economics of Education* (Amsterdam: Elsevier, 2011).

[769] V. Caballo, I. Salazar, M. Irurtia et al., "Differences in social anxiety between men and women across 18 countries," *Personality and Individual Differences,* 64 (2014): 35-40; A. Eagly and C. Chrvala, "Sex Differences in Conformity: Status and Gender Role Interpretations," *Psychology of Women Quarterly,* 10 (1986): 3.

[770] Benenson, *Warriors and Worriers, op. cit.*

in empathy than males,[771] because they must compete to appear "kind," because they are higher in social and more general anxiety, because hurting people's feelings may cause community discord (with females desiring a safe environment in which to raise their offspring) and because they are evolved, as mothers and maintainers of intimate friendships, to attend to hurt feelings and to soothe them.[772]

In terms of the moral foundations discussed earlier, cross-culturally, women score higher on Harm Avoidance, Equality and Purity[773] than do men and lower on Authority and In-group Loyalty. We would also expect females to be more likely to play for status using these foundations, in other words, to some extent, play for status in the way that the Left do. Females, compared to males, are physically weaker and they are higher in anxiety, which means they fear a fair fight. Losing a physical fight is also more damaging for them as they may have children who are reliant upon them. Consequently, they can be expected to play for status covertly, by signalling their concern with, for example, Equality and Harm Avoidance.[774] Women are also more likely to be highly empathetic and blind to systematising;[775] more likely to put "feelings" above "truth."

The result is the rise of what Bruce Charlton has called "Head Girls" in academia. The "Head Girl" – the chief prefect at British girls' schools - combines normal range high intelligence with high Conscientiousness, high Agreeableness and the higher social conformity, and concern with empathy over systematizing that, on average, distinguishes stereotypical females from stereotypical males. Anxiety decreases with age from late adolescence onwards, so the Head Girl will be relatively high in this by female standards, further leading to social conformity.[776] Clearly, the Head Girl, charming and ambitious towards socially approved goals, will be

---

[771] J. Benenson, E. Gauthier and H. Markovits, "Girls exhibit greater empathy than boys following a minor accident," *Scientific Reports,* 11 (2021): 7965.

[772] Benenson, *Warriors and Worriers, op. cit.*

[773] M. Atari, C. Lai and M. Dehghani, "Sex differences in moral judgements across 67 countries," *Biological Sciences,* 287 (2020): 137.

[774] Benenson, *Warriors and Worriers, op. cit.*

[775] Baron-Cohen, "The extreme male brain theory of autism," *op. cit.*

[776] C. Soto, O. John, S. Gosling and J. Potter, "Age Differences in Personality Traits From 10 to 65: Big Five Domains and Facets in a Large Cross-Sectional Sample," *Journal of Personality and Social Psychology,* 100 (2010): 330–348

appointed ahead of the autistic, socially inept, obsessive, laughably dressed, potential genius, removing him from the one "safe space" for his genius work which society previously permitted. Eventually, therefore, "feelings" would be put above the pursuit of truth at the university and even in society more broadly. When this is permitted to continue, "equality" will be put above academic standards, with people being let into university, or promoted within it, because of their place on the grievance hierarchy, not due to ability, because to do otherwise might hurt people's feelings. Eventually, you have the insanity of Claudine Gay (b. 1971) being put in charge of Harvard because she's black and a woman and her, of course, being forced to resign due to incompetence and corruption.[777] Confidence is lost in the university and the entire atmosphere shifts to reflect the thinking of increasingly intellectually average people, even below average people as student numbers grow and people are decreasingly admitted on merit: Diversity Equity and Inclusion students and hires, such as Claudine Gay.

It seems obvious that this process would make highly intelligent men less effective. They would be less able to logically and vigorously criticise ideas in case it offended the females, who would be more likely to react in an emotional way. Potential geniuses might force themselves not to criticise a presentation that a female had worked on because they were attracted to her and did not want to upset her. As female ways of thinking took over, these men would have to grapple with concepts such as speech codes and criticism of "micro-aggressions." The entire atmosphere of the university would become less about reasoned discourse and more about everybody "getting along" and "feeling validated." This would reduce the degree to which the university was an intellectually stimulating environment and, thus, reduce the degree to which people's intelligence was pushed to its phenotypic maximum; reducing the ability of intelligent men to have original ideas. Even if they did have original ideas, there would be a chilling effect on voicing them in case they "caused offence" to the people who had worked on the ideas under attack. In fact, some people might feel "literally unsafe" if something central to their worldview

---

[777] *BBC News,* "Claudine Gay resigns as Harvard University president" (3rd January 2024), https://www.bbc.com/news/world-us-canada-67868280

was subject to withering critique. Original ideas can only develop if we can toy with all kinds of possibilities without fear of reaction, but this new female-run university would render this atmosphere very difficult to achieve.

In this regard, it is worth remembering that female students, indeed one specific student, are the reason why Watson, who had been delivering amusing and outspoken lectures for many years, ended-up being part of a public furore in November 2000. As the local newspaper reported at the time:

> "The controversial talk was profoundly disturbing to some graduate students in Berkeley's molecular biology department, who ultimately brought Watson's comments into the public spotlight. "I found it really offensive," said Sarah Tegen, one of several graduate students who recounted Watson's remarks."[778]

Manifestly, some female scientists are just as analytically-focused as male scientists. But the nature of the female bell curve will be different, with a higher percentage of feeling-focussed individuals who permit feelings to over-ride other, more academic, considerations. It only takes one of these "Head Girls" to go and "tell the teacher" for there to be a potentially career-ruining "controversy" and a consequent chilling effect on freedom of expression and, thus, the ability to generate new and original ideas. As George Orwell (1903-1950) put it in *Nineteen Eighty Four:* "It was always the women, and above all the young ones, who were the most bigoted adherents of the Party, the swallowers of slogans, the amateur spies and nosers-out of unorthodoxy."[779]

---

[778] Abate, "Nobel Winner's Theories Raise Uproar in Berkeley / Geneticist's views strike many as racist, sexist," *op. cit.*

[779] G. Orwell, *Nineteen Eighty Four* (London: Secker and Warburg, 1949).

Chapter Fourteen

Returning to the 1950s

A Man of the Left

In his January 2007 interview in *Esquire,* James Watson explained that, "I turned against the left wing because they don't like genetics, because genetics implies that sometimes in life we fail because we have bad genes. They want all failure in life to be due to the evil system."[780] But he opposed them only in that specific way. Watson is a man of the left. He was raised in a household that not only voted Democrat but who were active members of the party. Watson himself donated the maximum amount he could to American President Barack Obama's election campaign.[781] But Watson is not a man of the New Left. The Old Left was concerned with equality and harm avoidance when it came to individuals. It was focussed on redistributing wealth to avoid abject poverty for a segment of the population, to give people what they needed, and it wished to create equality of opportunity for the most able people born into the working class.

The Old Left even favoured eugenics as a means of reducing suffering, in a context in which little could be done to assist epileptics, for example. Eugenics was something many conservatives, before World War II, were actually opposed to on the religious grounds that it interfered with the sanctity of life.[782] By contrast, many leftists were very enthusiastic about it. J.B.S. Haldane (1892–1964), who was Galton Professor of Eugenics at University College London and was the brother of Naomi Mitchison,

---

[780] Richardson, "James Watson: What I've Learned," *op. cit.*
[781] Sherwell, "DNA father James Watson's 'holy grail' request," *op. cit.*
[782] See, G. K. Chesterton, *Eugenics and Other Evils* (London: Cassell and Company, 1922), 7–8.

whom we met earlier, argued that a sperm bank should be set up for the genetic elite in order to improve the quality of the national stock.[783] Haldane was also a convinced Marxist who espoused eugenics in the pages of the *Daily Worker* in 1949, writing: "The dogma of human equality is no part of Communism [...] 'from each according to his ability, to each according to his needs' would be nonsense if abilities were equal."[784] In 1959, Sir Peter Medawar (1915–1992), Professor of Zoology at University College London, who was a member of the socialist Labour Party in the 1930s,[785] argued in *The Future of Man,* a BBC Reith Lecture, that British intelligence was clearly declining for genetic reasons and that there needed to be a "humane solution" to the problem.[786] Medawar received the Nobel Prize for Science the following year.[787] Indeed, Francis Crick (1916–2004), averred, at a conference in 1963, that there should be a tax on children such that the poor—who would tend to be of low intelligence on average—might be discouraged from having any.[788]

Wokeness, which developed out of the New Left of the 1960s, radically differs from this. It does not appear to be particularly concerned with economic issues, but rather with identity issues; perhaps implicitly because once everyone agrees you should help the native working class via some form of socialism then you can only competitively virtue-signal by moving on from them to something you perceive as even more marginalised. You justify this by asserting that you inherently possess "privilege" if you are white.[789] Those in positions of power before World War II and even for some time after it believed in biological determinism (or rather that biology was more important than environment), but leftists,

---

[783] R. Lynn, *Eugenics: A Reassessment* (Westport, CT: Praeger, 2001), 21.

[784] D. Paul, "Eugenics and the Left," *Journal of the History of Ideas,* 45 (1984): 567–590.

[785] Anon, "Lady Jean Medawar," *British Medical Journal,* 330 (2005): 1392.

[786] P. Medawar, *The Future of Man: The BBC Reith Lectures, 1959* (London: Basic Books, 1959).

[787] A. Silverstein, "The curious case of the 1960 Nobel Prize to Burnet and Medawar," *Immunology,* 147 (2016): 269–274.

[788] Lynn, *Eugenics, op cit.,* 22.

[789] See, R. DiAngelo, *White Fragility: Why It's So Hard for White People to Talk About Racism* (London: Penguin, 2019).

being motivated by malicious envy[790] and anti-hierarchical hostility as studies have shown they are,[791] decided to challenge this, despite the sound evidence upon which it was based, to assert environmental determinism, even producing fraudulent research to substantiate this. Anthropologist Margaret Mead (1901-1978), a student of the leading cultural determinist anthropologist Franz Boas, literally falsified, or selectively and very poorly carried out, her fieldwork with the Samoans in order to prove that they were a negative instance in terms of teenage angst, meaning that this phenomenon, and perhaps most others, were a matter of environment not genetic hardwiring. She went to Samoa with the intention of proving something and proved it. At the very best, it turned out to be incredibly poor fieldwork, with her tiny number of (young and female) informants admitting that they lied to her about their supposedly promiscuous sex lives. At worst, she just falsified the scientific record.[792]

From this basis, they could claim that they would reorder society to make it better for all, with dissenters being immoral liars who wished to uphold privilege. The desire to challenge power is strong in leftists, as noted above, and the biological perspective was associated with the Old Order. In addition, as we have seen, the leftist moral circle is genetically further from self, meaning they have moved from lauding working class people from their own society to lauding foreigners and ethnic minorities. Anti-hierarchical aggression would predict creating disorder by promoting to power anything that was previously marginalised: women, ethnic minorities, homosexuals, transsexuals, religious minorities and even

---

[790] C. Lin and T. Bates, "Each is to count for one and none for more than one: Predictors of support for economic redistribution," (2022), https://doi.org/10.31234/osf.io/3jq4c

[791] See, H. Zacher, "The Dark Side of Environmental Activism," *Personality and Individual Differences,* 219 (2024): 112506.

[792] See, P. Schankman, *The Trashing of Margaret Mead: Anatomy of an Anthropological Controversy* (Madison, WI, University of Wisconsin Press, 2009). See also, D. Freeman, *The Fateful Hoaxing of Margaret Mead: An Historical Analysis of Her Samoan Research* (New York: Basic Books, 1998).

potential and actual child abusers, who are being rebranded as "Minor Attracted Persons."[793]

A significant component of leftism is simply self-interest,[794] especially among Machiavellian and Narcissistic people. Perhaps, by the 1960s, sufficient meritocracy meant that a process of cognitive stratification had occurred,[795] such that there were fewer people of working class backgrounds who were involved in left-wing politics, pushing for this particular "marginalised" group. It might even be argued that leftist agitators, by this stage, were educated and well-off, with genuine economic socialism being a threat to their interests, meaning that division should be sown among the working class; division based around assorted "identities."

Another possible explanation for the Woke displacement of economic leftism is that the mass immigration into the US caused people's identity-nexus to change from social class to ethnicity, with recent immigrants being supposedly marginalised and discriminated against. Hence, the left became more interested in them and, thence, a series of other "marginalised" social groups who developed a group consciousness, due to discrimination, and became part of the left to agitate in their interests.[796] Leftists then competitively signalled their leftism by agitating for more and more obscure marginalised groups, such as transsexuals. Thus, an economic movement was turned into a social one. Moreover, the next virtue-signalling step, once everyone agrees with equality of opportunity, is to fight for equality of outcome, rejecting the evidence that, in a fair system, genetic racial and sexual differences mean there will not be equality of outcome. As runaway virtue-signalling continues, you naturally reach a point of fervour in which those who disagree with you are evil and must be utterly destroyed; totally cancelled.

---

[793] See, S. Jahnke, N. Blagden and L. Hill, "Pedophile, Child Lover, or Minor-Attracted Person? Attitudes Toward Labels Among People Who are Sexually Attracted to Children," *Archives of Sexual Research,* 51 (2022): 4125-4139.

[794] Lin and Bates, "Each is to count for one and none for more than one," *op. cit.*

[795] See, C. Murray, *Coming Apart, op. cit.*

[796] E. Hobsbawm, "Identity Politics and the Left," *New Left Review,* (May-June 1996).

"Do You Remember How Stupid We Were?"

In 2007, this happened to James Watson and, in 2019, out of pure spite, he was even stripped of the little with which he had been left, the ultimate example of kicking a man when he's down. That such a genius, whose breakthrough is so important to so many aspects of modern life, could be treated in this way tells us just how fanatical the Woke are, and the extent to which we have sat and watched as they have gradually taken away our freedom even to think. As I discussed earlier, Galileo was placed under house arrest for his heresy, where he remained for the rest of his life, unable to publically discuss his ideas.[797] There is a sense in which this is true of Watson.

In about 2020, Watson was interviewed as part of a book entitled *The Code Breaker*. The author went to Watson's house with Watson already being banned from the laboratory due to his views on race.

> "When the conversation sails dangerously close to the race issue, someone shouts from the kitchen: "If you are going to let him say these things, then I am going to have to ask you to leave." The 91-year-old Watson shrugs and changes tack. The voice from the kitchen belonged to Rufus, Watson's middle-aged son who suffers from schizophrenia."[798]

Rufus may have had good reason to be concerned. Watson lives in a house that is owned by Cold Spring Harbor Laboratory. Bruce Stillman, the head of the laboratory whom we met earlier, told me: "Dr Watson can stay in the house on the CSHL campus for his entire life, with support from CSHL . . . most people who have contacted me about Dr Watson did not know any of the details about his employment at CSHL and the support provide to him and his family by CSHL. We have not made these details public and will not do so because of the Watson family privacy issues." This appears to imply that the laboratory are housing and supporting Watson, meaning that it's probably in his interests to stay on the right side of them.

---

[797] See, M. Livio, *Galileo and the Science Deniers* (New York: Simon and Schuster, 2021).
[798] W. Isaacson, *The Code Breaker: Jennifer Doudna, Gene Editing, and the Future of the Human Race* (New York: Simon and Schuster, 2021), 352.

In that, as we have seen, Watson's autistic traits and obsession with the truth and his relatively poor impulse control mean that he can't anticipate the reaction to his remarks or can't stop himself from making them, this was essentially a way of completely silencing him; of forcing him to make no public speeches, no scientific presentations and to give no interviews. In a sense, it was a kind of intellectual house arrest for the remainder of his life. In researching this, I have found the fear of speaking about what has happened to Watson to be frightening. A few people spoke to me on condition of anonymity about it, but most would not even do that. As Soref explained to me: "No one at the lab wants to go on record; even anonymously. Sadly it is a potent and disastrous comment on the power of cancel culture and the effective methods that are being used to create censorship."

Watson is testimony to the fact that the genius comes as a package. You cannot have one side of genius – the astoundingly original breakthrough – without the other: a person who is socially clumsy, causes offence and doesn't really care, speaks his mind, takes the logical view no matter how upsetting it is, and is fascinated by that which is taboo because that is where truth lies. A topic is only "taboo" because there are some issues that those in power do not want discussed or even thought about because it will undermine the current moral system and part of their power comes from being seen as highly moral within that system.

Accordingly, our current situation creates an atmosphere of fear and conformity and suppresses genius. Only the most autistic and psychopathic are likely to question this system; hence being "Alt Right" is associated with psychopathy at present, as such people enjoy risk and they relish upsetting the NPCs.[799] If such a system had been in place in 1953, it is perfectly possible that someone like Watson would never even have been hired to work at Cambridge University. The atmosphere certainly wouldn't have been conducive to unfettered logical thinking.

Until we revert back to an academia more like that experienced by Watson in the early-1950s, highly creative scientists will have to self-censor, live in fear of losing their livelihoods or move into alternative

---

[799] J. Moss and P. O'Connor, "The Dark Triad traits predict authoritarian political correctness and Alt-Right attitudes," *Heliyon*, 6 (2020): e04453.

funding models, such as secretive patrons or crowd-sourcing and even these will come under attack. Where Watson should be living out his final years basking in public acclaim, as did the elderly Newton, he is closeted away in his home, rather like the frightened younger Newton who wrote-up his findings in code or like Galileo, who lived out his final years under house arrest. Rather that delivering scintillating lectures with contagious, child-like enthusiasm, mainstream academia daren't invite Watson anywhere.

The Graham Greene novel which the lovelorn young Watson read, *The End of the Affair,* contains the line, "Do you remember how stupid we were?"[800] It is to be hoped that in years to come, looking back on how Watson has been treated, the majority of scientists ask of themselves this exact question. But it will be too late for Watson. Like Galileo, he will have lived out his final days, in effect, under house arrest with so many fascinating ideas in his head that he dare not publically express.

---

[800] G. Greene, *The End of the Affair* (London: Heinemann, 1951).

Index

www.ingramcontent.com/pod-product-compliance
Lightning Source LLC
Chambersburg PA
CBHW061725270326
41928CB00011B/2119